Nina's Story

Surviving the German Occupation

Nina's Story
Surviving the German Occupation

Nina Markos

Thunderbird Press
P.O. Box 524
Rancho Mirage, CA 92270

Nina's Story
Surviving the German Occupation
Nina Markos

Copyright ©2014 by Nina Markos

Published by
Thunderbird Press
P.O. Box 524
Rancho Mirage, CA 92270
www.thunderbirdpress.net

Cover Design by Karoline Butler
Book Design by Jean Denning

Library of Congress Control Number: 2013950865

Markos, Nina
  Nina's Story
  Surviving the German Occupation
  ISBN: 978-0-9860149-2-5 (paperback)
  ISBN: 978-0-9860149-3-2 (ebook)

Printed in the United States of America

In loving memory of
my grandmother Anastasia
and her two daughters, Raisa, my mother,
and Valentina, my aunt

Acknowledgments

I would like to thank Jean Denning, Frances Noble, and the late Dr. Joyce Wade Maltais for their guidance and editorial help, and the following people for their suggestions and comments: Pamela Farr-Collaro, Elia Vasquez Gentry, Dr. A. J. Harris, Yetta Harris, Lou Ann Henkens, Rita Lamb, Brad Oliver, Sylvia Selfman and Richard Vasquez. I would also like to thank Karoline Butler for the InDesign layout, for scanning and enhancing all photographs, and for designing the cover.

Contents

1. The Fateful Sunday of June 22, 1941 / 1
2. An Intermediate Stop at Gavrilov Posad / 7
3. At Grandparents' Place / 11
4. The End of the Summer of 1941 / 21
5. Life under German Occupation / 25
6. Everyday Activities for Survival / 32
7. Our Moonshine Adventure / 38
8. Soap-Boiling / 41
9. Uncle Mitya's Ingenuity / 47
10. The Farmers' Market / 57
11. Meat and Fish Trade Row / 65
12. Schoolless, Shoeless, Toyless, Joyless and Photoless / 70
13. Uninvited House Guests / 81
14. August and Otto / 86
15. The Military Art of Marauding / 90
16. Misbehavior is Contagious / 94
17. The Perpetual Cycle / 102
18. Acquaintance With a Newcomer / 111
19. Post-Occupation Challenges / 117
20. At the Communal Grave / 120
21. A Short Visit to Grandma's Place / 126
22. Post-Occupation Revival / 130
23. Back to School! / 135
24. School Workday Routine / 143
25. After-School Activities / 146
26. My First Trip to Summer Pioneer Camp / 151
27. Pioneer Camp Routine / 155
28. Farewell Pioneer Camp! / 164
29. Surprise! Surprise! / 173

30.   The Chocolate Treat / 177
31.   Boys and Girls Socializing / 183
32.   Hitler Kaputt! / 192
33.   American Gifts / 195
34.   Reburial Ceremony in the Town Park / 201
35.   Surviving the Aftermath of the War / 206
36.   A Glimmer of Hope for a Better Future / 213
37.   Post-War Worries and Expectations / 219
38.   My Pre-War Childhood Memories in Minsk,
        Byelorussia / 226
39.   My Pre-War Childhood Memories in Shauliai,
        Lithuania / 230
40.   Leaving Lithuania for Estonia / 237
41.   Tallinn—Trip Down Memory Lane / 243
42.   The Long-Awaited Apartment / 248
43.   Plucking Feathers for a New Life / 253
44.   Grandma's Suitcase / 260
45.   In Anticipation of Father's Arrival / 265
46.   Father's Visit / 268
47.   Departure / 275
48.   The Return Trip to a Promising Future / 277
49.   Soviet Veterans of World War II / 280
50.   Another Trip Down Memory Lane / 285
51.   Good Morning, Lvov! / 292
52.   The Streetcar Ride to a New Home / 296

Epilogue / 303

Photo Gallery / 305

1. The Fateful Sunday of June 22, 1941

I remember the beginning of World War II, called *The Great Patriotic War II* in the Soviet Union, as if it happened yesterday. We lived in Tallinn, Estonia, where my father's military unit was stationed at that time.

June 22, 1941 started out as a very pleasant Sunday morning. The day before had been wonderful! Mother took my little sister Louisa and me to Kadriorg Park where we fed the squirrels. So cute and charming, they were not afraid of people. One just had to extend the palm with some treats — a cube of sugar, a candy, some cookies or some nuts — and several squirrels would come down from the branches to treat themselves to those delicacies. All over the park, one could hear the voices of children and the adults calling the squirrels, *"Mikki, mikki, mikki."* They quickly descended from the trees and sat fearlessly on the shoulders or arms of the visitors. We expected Sunday to be good, as well. Father had to return soon from night duty in his unit, and we all planned to go to the beach.

My sister Luisa was seven years old; I was nine and a half, and had just finished the second grade. I made excellent final marks and received two gifts — all new school materials for the third grade and a fluffy, grey kitten that Louisa and I named "Murzik." I lovingly admired my new things, feasting my eyes upon the pictures in the newly-printed textbooks. More than once I repacked them in my new school portfolio. And how I enjoyed my silly, playful Murzik.

My sister was nearby playing with her toys and with the kitten. Unexpectedly, we heard powerful peals of thunder from far away. The sky was blue, and the sun was shining brightly, but the din continued. Soon Father called from his military unit. "Don't panic, Raisa, the war has begun. The Germans have attacked us!" he told my mother.

"What Germans?" she asked. She thought he was talking about the maneuvers which were to begin the following week.

Father quickly replied, "The real German troops have crossed the Soviet-Polish border. These are not maneuvers, Raisa. This is War!"

My mother started to cry; my sister and I followed her. Very soon, the three of us were in floods of tears, even without knowing what the war meant for us, or what was waiting for us in the near future. But it was clear that something had definitely changed, and probably not for the better.

One week later, on June 29, we were forced to evacuate our home in Tallinn. There were no choices: the three of us had to leave, but Father had to stay with his unit. He was a captain in the Soviet Air Force. We left all our belongings behind, including our little Murzik. Father didn't allow us to take him, but he promised to look after him, since he had to stay in Talinn. I decided to give him away to the Estonian family who were the caretakers of our apartment building. The children of the family, our playmates, gladly agreed to shelter our kitten. Because their family was Estonian, they did not have to evacuate. My mother had decided we would go to her parents' home in Southern Ukraine.

We received only two letters from our father while he was still in Tallinn. In both letters he wrote that when he visited our apartment, Murzik was sleeping comfortably on the outside window-sill, enjoying the pleasant summer sun. He probably missed us too.

The previous November, before the war started, when my father had been transferred to the Baltic Republic of Estonia, we started our trip from Shauliai, a small city near Vilnius, the capital of Lithuania. We drove from home to the railroad terminal in a horse sleigh through the charming snow-covered streets, because there were no taxis back then. The rails of the street cars were covered with thick layers of snow. Heavy equipment was needed to plow the streets and roads after the abundant snowfall, but the city didn't have any.

The main surprise, however, was waiting for us in Riga, where we had to make connections from the suburban train to the luxurious international express train with separate sleeping compartments glittering with mirrors, and individual sparkling bathrooms with small sinks in every two-berth compartment.

It was the first time in my life that I saw a first class, sleeping railroad carriage with soft, comfortable sleeping sofas instead of wooden berths. My sister and I were standing with our mouths wide open, mesmerized by such fabulous regal splendor. Father brought us around shouting, "Close your mouths and go wash your hands!" So we did. That was also the first time that I felt like a fairy-tale princess in a castle.

Eight months later, we left Estonia on a freight train, together with thousands of military families, riding to nowhere, with no destination or a forwarding address — just eastward, as far as possible from the western border, away from the front line.

The country was not ready for war. Chaos, confusion and panic reigned at all levels of civilian and military bureaucracy. Thank God it was summer, and we were lightly dressed. I carried my new portfolio with all the textbooks for the third grade; my sister carried her doll and a small canvas bag with her favorite toys. We both wore personal hygiene kits made of fabric across our shoulders. Mother put in each one a toothbrush, a box of tooth-powder, a bar of soap, a comb and a white cotton handkerchief. Later, when we arrived at Grandparents' place, my grandmother reproached me saying, "You should have put an extra pair of shoes in your portfolio instead of the textbooks. Your sandals are almost worn out." It was true, but we children had our own priorities and values. The most important thing for me was my new oilskin portfolio with new textbooks.

During our trip, my sister and I were old enough to walk on our own, enabling our mother to carry two suitcases. Women with toddlers or small infants in their arms could carry only one suitcase each. There was no help, no appropriate services, no shelters with supporting medical staff, nothing at all to help us during our hasty, panicky escape from bombarded Tallinn to the east. We rode on the freight train like cattle. The train had no bathrooms, no running water — none of the simple primitive amenities, whatsoever.

We had nothing, nada, zero, only hurriedly put-together horizontal wooden planks at both sides of the doors almost reaching the ceiling. On those planks, we spent all the time sleeping, playing, eating, talking, quarreling, crying and laughing, while the freight train was rushing to nowhere, to uncertainty, with short stops only for nature's call for scared and exhausted women and children. It goes without saying that small children were not able to wait until the next train stop, so they used their potties instead. Sometimes, five or six toddlers were sitting in a row on their favorite potties. You don't need a vivid imagination to fancy the stench in that train car: a mixture of human excrement, sweat, dirty diapers, unwashed bodies and smoke from the locomotive. Back then, locomotives used coal as fuel. Its unbearable smell haunted me for a long time after the trip.

We suffered through it all. We were hungry and thirsty all the time. We didn't have any cold or hot water to wash our hands. When we stopped at a large railroad station, all the women rushed to the platform to get some boiled hot water for tea or cocoa from the special faucet on the platform of the big railroad terminals. Above the faucet there was an inscription in big letters — KYPYATOK — boiled water. Every woman held a tin or an enamel tea kettle. They had to stand in a long queue, sometimes without getting anything, because the lines were long, and the train stops were short.

Many times during our three-day trip our freight train had to wait at the stations with double tracks for a long time so the military trains carrying Russians and Estonian soldiers to the western front line could pass. The soldiers were also transported by freight trains, like prisoners. I still remember their smiling but frightened, blue-eyed faces as they waved at us and shouted farewell and good-bye both in Russian and Estonian, "*Do svidaniya! Yataiga!*" We also waved back and screamed our good-byes.

While screaming farewell greetings to the soldiers who were heading to the front, and probably to their certain death, I didn't realize at that time that I was saying

"Good-bye" to my childhood, which was associated in my memory with busy, but pleasant school days. Those days held memories of the divine scent of lilies of the valley, which we picked with our parents in the cool, spring forest; with the fragrance of the Persian lilacs, heralding the approaching summer school vacation; with children's snow games during the winter breaks; and the carefree life we had left behind. I didn't choose to say "Good-bye" to my childhood, being nine and a half years old. The war made that choice for me.

2. An Intermediate Stop at Gavrilov Posad

After the three-day agonizing trip from Tallinn, our freight train finally stopped not far from Moscow at a small railroad station with an antiquated name "Gavrilov Posad." In old Russian the word *posad* means "trading post or quarter." All we "evacuees," a new word in our war-era vocabulary, disembarked from the train with our bags and baggage.

From that moment, things started to develop so fast that I can hardly remember what was happening or the sequence of events. This was a completely new experience for all of us — for me, for my little sister, Louisa, and for my mother, Raisa. My childhood memory has retained only a few visual images from those hectic and uncertain days in Gavrilov Posad.

I remember the three of us together with other evacuees sitting or sleeping on the floor on mattresses filled with thatch in a big classroom at the local school. There weren't enough fabric mattress cases for every family; therefore, those families who didn't get them sat and slept on the floor covering the thatch with blankets, sheets or just towels, surrounded by suitcases and bags.

Unfortunately, we didn't get a mattress case, only an armful of thatch which we covered with our blue flannel blanket, and it served as a place to eat, to sleep and to sit on during the daytime. I remember the three of us sitting on the blanket like Gypsies, eating stale wheat buns and washing them down with lukewarm water from the teapot. We had only two enamel mugs, and we had to take turns drinking.

Another vivid scene which has been imprinted on my memory was a small and shallow flat-country river with steep banks running through that small town. As soon as the evacuees had settled down at the local school, they rushed to the river. The water in the river was warm. The summer of 1941 was hot as it usually is in the middle part of European Russia — about ninety degrees Fahrenheit.

Evacuees from our train bathed themselves and their children in the warm summer waters; some of them did laundry, while squatting or kneeling on its lower bank, using the wash basins and wash-up bowls, borrowed probably, from the locals, because I had not seen such household items previously on our train.

Our life as evacuees was getting more complicated every day. There was no information about the situation on the front, no telephone communication, no central newspapers in that small railroad town, only the local radio station which transmitted local news and victorious military marches. There were no supportive services for the evacuees during the first months of the war.

We were the first avalanche of evacuees from the border area whom the residents of Gavrilov Posad had seen, and surely, would not be the last one. The authorities of the town were not ready to cope with the influx of evacuees, nor to provide appropriate services for them without governmental financial help. The government, in its turn, was in disarray because of the sudden and unexpected attack by Germany with whom, ironically, the Soviet Union had a non-aggression pact.

Many evacuees were eager to seek refuge in Moscow, but the national Capital was closed. Only trains and transports with military personnel and equipment were allowed to enter Moscow. However, several families from our train, wives and children of high-ranking military personnel who had close relatives and connections in Moscow, obtained permission to go to Moscow. Our relatives in Moscow didn't have a phone, so we couldn't reach them and ask for their help or advice. Moscow was inaccessible to us. So, we had only two choices: to be evacuated behind the Ural mountains, to Siberia, or to go to the place of my maternal grandparents who lived in Southern Ukraine.

At that time, all the evacuees were disoriented and in the state of complete ignorance. Nobody knew anything about the development of the war, and there was nobody to ask for information. The general consensus among evacuees was that the retreat of the Soviet Army was temporary, that the Germans would be defeated very soon by the "invincible" and "legendary" Soviet Red Army, as we were taught in school.

My mother, a young, inexperienced woman, was for the first time in her adult life, at age thirty-one, facing hardships alone: her country at war, without her husband's support, without parents close by, with two small children and almost without money. My sister and I were not toddlers, but we were too small to understand what was happening. Our mother had made the decision herself — to go to her parents' place in Southern Ukraine.

As we found out very soon, it was the wrong decision. But in July of 1941, at the very beginning of the war, nobody believed that the war would last for a long time. In addition, Mother didn't dare evacuate behind the Urals, with its harsh Siberian winters without proper clothes, and with the little money we had. Looking back, I can't blame her for that.

3. At Grandparents' Place

*I*n mid July 1941, we arrived at the big railroad station in the town of Dolguintsevo in Southern Ukraine. The passenger train was overcrowded, and we were packed like herrings in a barrel. We all slept in a sitting position, which made all our limbs ache.

Late afternoon, tired and weakened from the heat, stuffiness and tightness of the passenger car, we disembarked from the train. For a while, we stood on the platform looking around, as if we didn't believe that our trip had come to an end. There were no taxis, no buses in the town. So, we picked up our luggage and headed along the familiar street in the direction of Grandma's house.

The weather was hot, and there were few people in the streets. We walked slowly. Mother carried two heavy suitcases and got tired very fast. We stopped to rest, then moved on again. We crossed Main Street and approached the farmers' market square where everything looked the same as before the war. Life was going on here as usual. The market place was almost empty at that time of the day. We saw a few vendors at counters selling the local delicacy — slightly salted fried sunflower seeds. A small group of men were gathered around the newspaper stand reading and discussing something with great animation.

Mother put our suitcases on the dirt street and said, "Wait for me here and watch the luggage. I'll go to see what they are reading about. Maybe there is some good news from the front." Louisa and I sat on the suitcases and watched Mother as she approached the newsstand. We saw her talking to a tall, elderly man. Very soon she returned accompanied by him. The man greeted us, smiling and said, "Good day, girls! You've grown up!" He was Grandma's neighbor and had known our mother since she was a little girl. He picked up one of the suitcases, and we continued our walk.

Soon we reached Grandma's house. The man stretched his hand over the gate door and opened the inside hook. Then he put the suitcase inside the yard and said, "Say hello to your grandparents for me and have a nice vacation," and he left. We entered the yard and latched the gate with the hook from inside. Finally we were at Grandma's place!

I remember we used to come to Grandmother's place for summer vacation. It always was a joyful trip for all of us. The climate in that area is hot. There were plenty of tasty fruits, berries and vegetables which we enjoyed, as well as the tender and caring hands of Grandma Anastasia. She adored and spoiled us children, indulging our every whim in every possible way. At the same time, she still remained demanding, but fair. She was a retired school teacher, tall and slim, very good looking, with a salt-and-pepper braided bun on the back of her head.

Grandma allowed us to participate in small household chores. When she baked, we cut cookies with small and large glasses. We sorted out red and black currants, gooseberries and raspberries. She also asked for our help during food preparation for lunch and dinner. She trusted us to wash the fruits and vegetables: apples, potatoes, carrots, lettuce, spinach, green onions, parsley, dill and celery. We were very slow and not too dexterous while peeling and cutting, but we had a great desire to learn how to do it, and we wanted to feel needed and helpful.

Before the war, our mother, an elementary school teacher, was very busy taking care of all of us, doing chores, as well as working. She never allowed us to take knives or scissors in our hands. She told us more than once that she was scared that we could cut ourselves and become cripples. She preferred to do everything herself, instead of watching us slowly and clumsily helping her. She had very little patience. During this time, our father was at his military unit all day. He returned home late, when we were already sound asleep. He helped our mother do the chores on Sundays. We all spent Sundays together. It was our favorite day.

Grandma was trustful and self-assured. Unlike Mother who had little patience with us, Grandma never admonished us when we made mistakes, and I don't remember her losing patience even in critical situations. As I was two years older than Louisa, Grandma trusted only me to peel potatoes, beetroots and carrots for her famous Ukrainian *borscht* (vegetable cabbage soup). I did it with pleasure with a short dull kitchen knife. We had no special paring knives for different kinds of vegetables and fruits.

I still season my *borscht* the way Grandma taught me. I chop fresh dill, garlic and pieces of pork fat or bacon

13

into small pieces. I still have that recipe imprinted in my head.

Grandparents had a small orchard and vegetable garden in the backyard of their five-room house. In the orchard were a few apple trees, two apricot trees, three pear trees and several bushes of red and black currants and gooseberries. My favorites were the two mulberry trees. The yellow and purple berries, sweet and juicy, fell almost straight into our mouths and on our laps if we only slightly shook the tree. It was delightfully pleasant and funny. Birds and spring chickens liked mulberries, as well. Even our dog, Sharyk, a squeamish mongrel, was not shy about treating himself to mulberries.

The vegetable garden was Grandma's domain. In separate patches she planted green onions, radishes, lettuce, parsley, carrots, tomatoes, garlic, and celery. It's strange that in both Russia and Ukraine we used as an herb only the green leaves of celery, but not its stalks. Grandma showed us how to take care of the growing vegetable plants, how to water them, to weed, to harvest and to store them for winter. She also tried to teach us to be careful with different simple utensils: knives, scissors and hammers. She taught us how to be useful, helpful and, at the same time, feel safe in the small town environment unfamiliar to us, big city children. She was very skillful and patient doing that.

Grandma Anastasia was the first person among my relatives who shared with me the tragic story about her father, my great-grandfather, Constantine Tsitovich. Before the October revolution, he was a rich merchant living in Byelorussia with his wife and six children. When the revolution took place, the Soviet authorities confiscated all his properties and money, leaving him with nothing. In despair, he hanged himself in the barn. His desperate wife, fearing persecution, had fled Byelorussia with her six children, including my grandmother, and went to Ukraine where nobody knew them and where their distant relatives offered them shelter.

Unlike Grandma, Grandpa had never confided family secrets to me. At that stage in my life, I became interested in family history and secrets. I didn't realize until later how depressing and sometimes unbearable the burden of those secrets could be.

I could have found out a lot of interesting facts about the genealogical tree of my family from Grandma Anastasia. She remembered many family events, all her relatives, and was eager to talk about them. But I was too young to comprehend the importance of such information. I couldn't ask appropriate questions, and I wasn't able to put all the tiny bits of that valuable knowledge together in order to depict a bigger and more complete picture. I was too young to think analytically.

My maternal grandfather, Ivan Danilovich, was a taciturn and unsociable person. I never heard Grandpa having a long conversation with anyone or telling stories about his parents, siblings or other relatives. His younger brother Vladimir, Uncle Volodya, as Grandma called him, lived in the same town where my grandparents lived, but the families didn't socialize.

Many years ago, the brothers had a falling out, and they did not even say "hello" to each other. I tried to find out why, but Grandma didn't want to give me any explanation. She secretly maintained friendly relations with Vladimir's wife, Alexandra (we called her Shura), and we visited her on a regular basis. I always accompanied Grandma when we visited and picked up aromatic, juicy pears and plums in their large and nicely cared-for orchard. We made those visits when Uncle Volodya wasn't at home.

According to Grandma Anastasia, when Grandpa was young, he was a good-looking man: tall, well-proportioned, with a dark complexion. From his large portrait hanging in the "big room," as we used to call the largest room of the house, he looked at us with his serious, penetrating eyes without a trace of a smile under his thin, stylish moustache. His short hair, with a part in the middle, was a typical man's hairdo for that time.

When we arrived at Grandparents' place that tragic summer of 1941, Grandpa still was tall, dark, but not as handsome as Grandma used to depict him. I noticed that he always held himself straight and walked fast as if he were marching in formation.

By profession, Grandpa was an engine-driver and worked for the state railroad department all his life. He had lived through three major train crashes and had suffered serious head injuries, which, according to my grandmother, drastically changed not only his behavior, but his character, as well.

He was very demanding of us children, and treated us as if we were adults. He tried to impose a strict discipline on us. If we misbehaved, played pranks, disobeyed or neglected his orders, he easily became angry. His deep brown eyes sparkled fiercely and, what was even more frightening, he used to put his tongue out, while pretending to search nervously for the stick to punish us. As soon as we saw his tongue between his teeth, we would run away like scared rabbits, crying and screaming for help under Grandma's protective wings. Only she knew how to calm him down.

"Ivan Danilovich, don't scare the children, I beg you," she would say to him in a low and quiet voice. "They are still too young to know what head injuries could do to a person. Calm down, go and have a glass of cold *"kvas."* (*Kvas* is a homemade cold drink processed from rye bread and hops.) "For God's sake, leave the poor children alone!"

Sometimes, Grandpa retorted, reproachfully, "You have spoiled the children, defending them. They should know their place and do what they're told!"

"They will," responded Grandma. "They still have time to learn, but scaring them will teach them nothing; they could become stutterers for the rest of their lives." Grandpa always followed Grandma's advice. I don't remember him punishing us; he only threatened to do it.

Grandpa Ivan took care of all the animals of the household: a cow, a pig and two dozen chickens. The cow stall occupied the left part of the barn; the hen-coop was located in the right part of the same barn. The pig sty was outside of the barn. Every day, Grandpa cleaned the cow stall and the pig sty.

Every morning, about five o'clock, Grandma milked the cow. Then Grandpa took the cow to the community herd outside of the town limits, about three miles from the house. From there the shepherds took the herd to the pasture. In the evening, after sunset, Grandpa brought the cow back home.

When the cow was back home, the evening milking took place. Grandpa also knew how to milk the cow. He substituted for Grandma on those rare occasions when she was sick or for some reason couldn't do it. Grandma wanted to teach me that great art, but the cow didn't like children and kicked me with a hoof as soon as I tried to touch her. I was scared to death and simply quit trying.

At midday, Grandma, having put a white cotton shawl on her head for protection from a scorching southern sun, with a big white enamel bucket in her hand, headed to the place where the herd was brought from the pasture for the midday milking. Grandma tried to force me to wear a white cotton hat, but I looked so funny in that childish headdress that I preferred to walk with my head uncovered. It's a pity that we had no sunglasses back then. We didn't even know that they existed.

According to the community arrangements, one day a month everyone who owned a cow had to bring lunch for two senior shepherds and two teenaged herd boys. When it was our turn to feed the shepherds, Grandma asked me to help her carry food: a pot of borscht or soup, boiled potatoes, some fresh tomatoes and cucumbers, boiled eggs, pieces of chicken or other meat, and, of course, some seasonal fruits for dessert or a piece of fruit pie.

While Grandma was milking the cow, the shepherds would have their lunch, sitting in a circle on the grass. The food was served on a piece of oilcloth put in the middle of the circle. I don't remember bringing napkins or knives. I do remember bringing salt and a big loaf of fresh rye bread. I still have that picture in front of my eyes: one of the shepherds is cutting large hunks of bread with his knife while pressing the round loaf against his chest. After lunch, we picked up the dirty utensils and headed home. On our way back, Grandma carried a bucket with milk, about nine or ten liters. I carried dirty utensils in a cloth bundle.

At home again, Grandma strained the milk through cheesecloth, poured it in separate bottles and ceramic containers and distributed it for separate purposes: to make sour cream, butter and yogurt. She made us children drink a glass of milk fresh from the cow. We didn't like it, but Grandma considered it very beneficial for our health and made us drink it anyway. I never had the chance in my later life to drink milk fresh from the cow ever again.

Both Grandma and Grandpa took care of the cellar. It was located in the barn. Grandparents stored in it fresh vegetables: potatoes, beetroots, and carrots for the winter. Barrels with salted or marinated vegetables were also stored in the cellar. There was always a big wooden barrel with sauerkraut, another big one with pickled cucumbers, yet another with salted red tomatoes, a smaller one with marinated eggplants, and a huge barrel with salted watermelons. Only small, ripe watermelons were selected for salting. I tasted different kinds of marinated and salted vegetables from different countries throughout my life but nothing has tasted better than a salted watermelon served with homemade fried potatoes. It has an exquisite and unique taste!

Rows of bottles with homemade tomato sauce and homemade berries and fruit liqueurs sat on the side shelves. Grandma kept homemade fruit and berry jam in the pantry, inside the house because they could be stored at room temperature.

However, she always kept separately jars with raspberries and black currant jam. She never served those jams for the evening tea. She used them only for medicinal purposes. She considered that those jams had healing qualities and helped treat colds, flu and other diseases. She kept those jams in a separate section of the sideboard and didn't trust anybody to get them. She always did it herself. As the jars had no lids, Grandma covered them with oilpaper and tied them with a special little bow her style which was difficult to imitate, like she used to say. But not for my favorite, resourceful aunt Valentina. Sometimes, when Grandma was not at home, she secretly got the jam out and treated us children with a teaspoonful. Then she licked the teaspoon, smacked her lips and skillfully tied the small bow exactly the way Grandma did.

"Don't you dare tell Grandma," she warned us. "Because if you do, you will never have a chance to treat yourselves to these gorgeous jams." We promised on oath that we wouldn't tell anybody no matter what. We missed sweets in our diet because there were no candies, no cookies and no cakes in the stores during the German occupation.

4. The End of the Summer of 1941

*E*verything seemed to go on as usual that first summer of war — the same hospitable house, the same caring and loving grandparents — but something definitely was not the same. We were not the same people as before. This time, we were not on vacation; we had come here as evacuees having left everything behind, fleeing from the front zone and hoping that the war would not reach us in this peaceful and prosperous corner of Southern Ukraine.

How wrong we were!

Events developed so quickly that we children didn't have enough time to adjust to our new status as evacuees and to digest the meaning of everything that was happening. There was no way to get information, because newspaper reports often were confusing. They didn't mention the exact location of the front line. Maybe they did it for security reasons; maybe the reports were lagging behind the actions in the battlefields. Rumors picked up at the farmers' market, which Grandpa called "Market News," were our main source of information. According to the rumors, the front line was rapidly approaching our newly-acquired refuge.

Suddenly the local Soviet authorities announced by radio and in the local newspaper the start of the evacuation. The same day, Grandpa brought from the farmers' market shocking news: "The Ryabushkyns are leaving tomorrow," he said. They were our neighbors across the street. I knew well their twin teenaged sons, Elias and Boris. Sometimes Boris gave me a ride on his bicycle to the Town Park where the ice-cream kiosk was located.

"They are doing the right thing to leave," Grandma said, "because the Germans could kill them. There are rumors that they kill Jews and Gypsies."

"Why do they kill them?" I asked.

"Nobody knows, but the rumors are persistent about the killings of Jews, Gypsy people and Communists."

At the family gathering in the evening, it was decided that my mother, Louisa and I had to evacuate, as our father was a Soviet officer and a member of the Communist Party. It was dangerous for us to stay under the German occupation. Nobody knew how Germans would treat the families of the fighting Soviet officers. Our relatives and friends collected winter clothes and footwear for us as winter was fast approaching.

We were almost ready to leave when Louisa fell sick with diphtheria. Her disease determined our destiny. Mother didn't dare abandon Louisa because the local town hospital and its medical personnel, including doctors and nurses, had to evacuate, as well. She didn't dare evacuate with a sick child, in a freight train on the threshold of winter. So, we were stuck at our grandparents' place, and the future looked uncertain and threatening.

The German airplanes commenced air raids during the nights and dropped bombs aimed at the railroad station and the locomotive depot. The long drawn-out sound of air attack sirens was so scary that we immediately sought refuge in the empty damp cellar like everyone else in the town. If we had no time to reach the cellar, we just crawled under our beds, praying and hoping that the bombs would not hit our house. Our actions were naïve and silly, but there were no bomb shelters in the town. There was no place to hide. There was nowhere to run.

I feared for our lives. Somehow I understood that we could be killed not only by German bombs, but by the German soldiers, as well. It was an unpleasant and overwhelming discovery which made me suffer during sleepless nights.

We were nervous, confused and scared to death. The adults felt helpless. My sister, Louisa, cried and screamed at every sound of air attack alarm. She was still a child and didn't understand anything. As for me, the war made me feel more mature. I started to understand the meaning of many things. The war pulled me out of my protected child's environment. I was forced to socialize with strange adults and participate more actively in everyday chores.

The air raids intensified, accompanied by the rumors that the Germans if not today, then tomorrow, would reach our town. Our house was located in the downtown area, close to the railroad station. So, our family decided to spend the approaching night at the place of our distant relatives, several miles away from downtown. Only Grandpa stayed in the house to watch it and to take care of the animals. Grandma wanted him to come with us, but he insisted on having it his own way.

"Don't worry about me, Anastasia. The Germans aren't fools. They need the railroad to transport their troops and military equipment to the front line; there is no other way. They won't destroy the station." He put his hand on her shoulder and kissed her on the cheek. It was the only time I saw him kiss Grandma.

The same night, two bombs hit the railroad depot. We didn't close our eyes that night; we sat fully dressed in the darkness and listened to every sound of the night and shuddered at the rumble of every artillery salvo. The adults tried to distinguish by the sound of the aircraft whose bombers or fighters were flying overhead in the night sky — German or Russian. It was a warm night, yet we shivered with fear.

At dawn everything became strangely quiet. We came out of the house and stood at the fence, at the gate, looking up and down the street. The morning was sunny, the sky was extremely blue, the trees were still green, and the flowers in the front gardens, freshened with the morning dew, smelled especially sweet. Our neighbors on both sides of the street also stood at their front fences, watching the street, as if they were expecting something to happen.

We looked towards the direction of a distant rumbling and were paralized with fear: a column of military trucks full of German soldiers, sitting on benches and holding sub-machine guns between their knees came into view. The column was moving in the middle of the wide, unpaved suburban street bordered with gorgeous poplar trees. A motorcycle with a side car, a technical wonder we had never seen before, rode at the head of the column. Not a single shot was fired. There were no screams, no cries, no shouts — only eerie, alarming silence, broken solely by the rattle of the motorcycle and the rumble of the trucks. I heard a man's voice commenting gloomily, "Yeah, here are the Germans."

It was the end of August of 1941.

5. Life Under German Occupation

$\mathcal{T}$he German occupation was a landmark in our new lives as evacuees. We were uncertain of everything. Nobody knew what to expect from the new authorities. As the rumors said, the Germans wanted to establish "a new order" all over the conquered territories, but no one understood what that meant.

I was worried about school classes. The school year, according to the calendar, had already started. I had all my new textbooks for the third grade neatly packed in my new portfolio. All I wanted was to go to school and to study.

Right after the arrival of the Germans, there were rumors that classes probably would start in a week or two. Several weeks had passed, then several months, but there was no school. Then the news came like a bolt from the blue: there would be no school.

Grandma Anastasia, who lived through the hungry, devastating years of WWI, the Civil War and the October Revolution sarcastically commented on the news, "Germans don't need educated slaves; they only need people able to do hard manual labor." That was the first time in my life that I heard the word "slaves."

"What are slaves?" I asked.

She explained to me, "Slaves are people who have to work for other people, but they are not paid for their work. They have no right to go to school or to go to the movies. All they have to do is work." I felt perplexed and scared because I didn't want to be a slave. I just wanted to go to school, to the third grade, and after the third grade to go to the summer Pioneer Camp. I was so upset by the terrible news that I hid in the barn hayloft and cried the whole day.

In the evening, Mother called me, "Come down, Nina, go wash your hands. Supper is ready!" I was hungry and quickly descended from the loft by way of the wooden ladder. When Mother saw my tear-stained, swollen face and red eyes, she asked in disbelief, "Have you been crying about school? Don't worry, silly girl. I am a teacher. I will teach you and Louisa myself. We'll do just fine without school. Promise me not to cry anymore. Promise?" I nodded in response.

Since then, every day after breakfast, when Mother was free from domestic chores, we sat at the square table in the big room, and Mother taught us both, Louisa and me. While I was writing exercises or copying texts, Mother taught Louisa to read and to write letters and syllables. Louisa had to start the first grade that fall. When she was doing her written assignments, Mother was taking care of me. She reviewed arithmetical rules with me, and I practiced them, solving problems.

My favorite task was to read aloud and to retell different stories from the textbook reader. It was an assignment for both of us: Louisa had to listen to the stories while I was reading and retelling them. After that, Mother used to ask us the W-questions (Who? What? Why? Where? When?) about the events and the characters of the story. At the end, she always asked us whether we liked the stories or the characters or not, and why. She asked me first, giving Louisa the chance to listen to my answers and to make up hers.

In the beginning, Louisa's slow reading annoyed me a lot. In two or three months, she started to read faster and actually enjoyed it.

When Mother was busy doing chores, we sat alone in the big room reading stories from the textbook, writing exercises or just copying sentences or short texts. On such occasions, Mother entrusted me to help Louisa and supervise her. If Louisa misspelled or mispronounced unknown words or had difficulty identifying letters, I made her read and write those words again and again. With time, she learned to read and to write, and proudly recited all thirty-two letters of the Russian alphabet. Those after-breakfast classes were the highlight of my day, and I enjoyed them immensely.

Schools, kindergartens and day nurseries were closed. All the public institutions and services remained shut down: the library, the hospital, the pharmacy, the stores and the bakeries. There was no transportation of any kind for civilians: no trains, no buses. The movie theatre was closed; the radio station stopped broadcasting. The post office was closed, and no mail was delivered. There was no electricity in the houses and in the streets. The public baths were also closed.

Several weeks before the Germans' arrival, when the front was approaching our region, people started to panic and began to buy everything from the stores: salt, sugar, household soap, matches, oil lamps, candles, oil for lighting and kerosene for cooking stoves. Vodka and wines evaporated from the stores at the speed of lightning.

The shelves of the pharmacy were emptied in the

twinkling of an eye. The people grabbed everything: aspirin, iodine, crystals of manganese, bottles of hydrogen peroxide, cotton bandages, packs of gauze and even enemas, as if everybody was expected to be wounded, bandaged and constipated. People were buying everything for emergencies, just in case, even if they had no need for them at that precise moment.

Whatever wasn't sold out before the arrival of the Germans was looted from the stores and warehouses in the short period of anarchy between the Soviet troops' withdrawal and the Germans' arrival. Luckily for us, the front line passed by our town.

Nothing was left. Every public building was looted and wrecked by the daredevils who were not afraid to go on looting raids under the cover of night despite the crazy artillery salvos and uninterrupted rumble of the Soviet and German military planes.

When the Germans arrived, the first thing they did was to open the church which had been closed in 1917 by the Soviet government immediately after the triumph of the October Revolution. The Orthodox church building, used for a quarter of a century as a high school sports facility was reopened. It was as a shaft of light on the horizon for the scared, desperate people. Grandma proudly extracted a modest set of icons, which she kept hidden in the small attic of the pantry room and solemnly hung them in the right corner of the big room, according to the Orthodox tradition. She also began to wear a small metal cross on her neck. She told me with sadness that before the October Revolution, she and all her sisters had golden crosses, but during the hunger years of the Civil War, they has swapped them for several loaves of bread.

Gradually people — especially the older generation — started to go to the church services. Even the young people who were raised without religion went—some of them for curiosity, and others, maybe, for the desire to demonstrate loyalty to new authorities.

Church weddings, christenings and funerals became very popular. It was something new for the young people, something which had been forbidden before. For the older generation, like my grandmother, it was a revival of an ancient tradition. In comparison with the cheerless and boring civil marriage registration procedure in the Town Hall, a church wedding ceremony was now more spectacular: the bride in a white dress with a veil on her head; the groom in a black suit with a white or ethnic Ukrainian shirt embroidered in black, red and white cross stitching; all the attendants to the bride and groom—all dressed up.

Children's christenings also became popular. Everybody, as if on fire, rushed to baptize their children, including teenagers. Even young adults were baptized. Every religious ceremony was the occasion for family gatherings and celebration. The Soviet National holidays were abolished, and there were only two major religious holidays—Christmas and Easter. People needed some positive motivation for celebration, and what occasion was better than weddings and christenings.

Our family was no exception. It was Grandma's idea to baptize the three of us at home, for privacy reasons. The family decided that we were too big for the public christening at church: I was almost ten years old, Luisa was eight, and our cousin, Zhanna, was six. Zhanna was the daughter of Valentina, Grandma's youngest daughter. Valentina and Zhanna moved in with Grandparents soon after our arrival when Valentina's husband, Dimitry, Uncle Mitya, as we called him, was drafted.

Grandmother and our mothers selected godmothers

and godfathers for us according to their own criteria. We were not allowed to participate in the selection process. As a result, my godmother, who was my mother's cousin, was a young beautiful woman. My godfather was an old, ugly, even scary man, who happened to be the husband of my grandmother's best friend.

There was no problem with my name, Nina, which is of Greek origin and is officially registered in the Church Calendar, but the names Louisa and Zhanna were not in it. Therefore, the new names sounding as close as possible to their old ones, had to be selected for Louisa and Zhanna. After a short consideration, Louisa's chosen church name was Lydia, and Zhanna's was Eugenia, the diminutive of which, Zhenya, sounds close to Zhanna.

It was not easy for Louisa and Zhanna to react properly to their new church names in a short period of time. As a result, they experienced moments of slight embarrassment. Luckily, it happened at the very end of the christening ceremony, when the priest had to ask us, one by one, our new church names, and we had to answer him.

At first, he asked me, "What is your name, my child?"

"Nina," I answered without hesitation.

When Louisa was asked the same question, she opened her eyes wide and her mouth even wider, staring at the priest as if he had bewitched her, and with difficulty tried to articulate the first syllable of her name. Then she suddenly stopped as if she had been struck and shouted with relief "Lydia." Our cousin, Zhanna, also stumbled her name, but then took a deep breath and with fear in her eyes almost whispered "Eugenia." They both felt ashamed that they couldn't memorize their new church names straight off, without hesitation.

There was a consolation prize for all that anguish: Grandma sewed for us new dark blue polka-dot cotton dresses with frills and flounces and short bell-shaped sleeves, and we had colorful bows in our pigtails. We also received small metal crosses to wear around our necks, gifts from our godmothers and some sweet treats from Grandma.

The table for the priest and guests was placed in the big room, with a large bottle of *samogon* — homemade vodka — standing out in all its splendor in the middle. Several big, oval plates, full of small browned pies stuffed with green cabbage, rice with dried apricots, meat and with sour cherries, surrounded the bottle. But we were too excited to sit quietly at the table. We were eager to get out of the house, to go to the street and to show off to our friends and neighbors our new dresses and bows, our new metal crosses, and our new names.

The new names didn't stick to my sisters, and the whole family continued to use their old names — Louisa and Zhanna.

After we became adults, at any occasion when the three of us had the chance to get together and reminisce, our memories infallibly recalled that funny scene from our childhood, when we three lanky girls stood at the three washbasins with water, in front of the priest, surrounded by family and guests where two of us couldn't recall the simple Russian names — Lydia and Eugenia. Nowadays, when I call my cousin Zhanna in Moscow and greet her with my usual *"Privet, Eugenia,"* meaning "Hello, Eugenia," she laughs unrestrainedly, regardless of her mood. I visualize how her face lights up with the joy, recollecting those difficult and unforgettable years of our war childhood.

"Only you call me Eugenia; nobody else does," she told me once.

6. Everyday Activities for Survival

*R*eligious holidays, church weddings and christenings were the highlights of everybody's life during the occupation period. Unfortunately they didn't happen very often. The rest of the year, people had to face the gloomy reality of a conquered country: life without jobs, without paychecks, without public and communal services such as health care, utilities, postal services, and without shops and all those small things which before we took for granted. We couldn't get a new pair of sandals and socks for summer, or a new toy for birthday, or an ice cream on Sunday, or just to be photographed on our birthdays by a professional photographer at the tiny photo shop of the farmers' market. All those small pleasant and necessary things didn't exist anymore.

In order to survive in such a desperate plight, people had to work very hard in order to feed their families and provide for them at least the bare essentials. The only way to do that was to double or even triple the efforts in cultivating vegetable gardens located outside of the town. Thank God, the age-old, pre-revolutionary tradition of distributing community land for its cultivation among the citizens was not abolished by German authorities. So, people tried to get as many pieces of land as possible for vegetable gardening.

Before the war started, my grandparents usually cultivated one piece of land (a one hundredth part of the hectare) for their own consumption. "Now we have seven mouths to feed," Grandma Anastasia said. There were seven of us: Grandma, Grandpa, my mother, my sister Louisa, my aunt Valentina, her daughter Zhanna, and me.

In spring of 1942, my grandparents managed to get six pieces of land for vegetable gardens instead of the usual one. Everybody in our family, except for little Louisa and Zhanna, took part in planting, weeding, harvesting and transporting the vegetables. After everything was harvested, we had to clean, to dry and to sort out potatoes, beetroots and carrots before storing them in the cool cellar. Large potatoes were stored in one corner of the enclosure and small potatoes in another. I asked Grandma why we did that. She explained to me, "I will need less time to fill up a bucket with small potatoes if I want to sell them in the farmers' market in spring when they cost more because they are good for planting. That way I don't have to stay for a long time in the cold cellar."

Cultivating vegetables is not the easiest work. Grandma prepared lunch for us to take to the field. We covered our heads with white cotton square shawls for protection from the sun when we were ready to leave.

We had no transportation, not even bicycles, so we had to walk about three or four miles to the vegetable garden, carrying shovels and hoes, our lunch, and several bottles with water and milk. I was the oldest granddaughter, so I was allowed to participate in the field work.

One of the women—Grandma, my mother or Aunt Valentina—always had to stay home to watch and feed

Louisa and Zhanna and to take care of the animals. She also had to prepare supper for the family. Sometimes, I stayed home, too. But I preferred to go to the field.

At the field, Grandpa and one of his daughters dug holes in the soil with a shovel; Grandma and I put one potato or several seeds which we were planting such as beans, pumpkin seeds, sunflower seeds or others in the holes. Then we covered the potato or seeds with the soil, and that was it. Planting potatoes was the most difficult job, as Grandpa had to carry several buckets of potatoes in a burlap sack on his back, and the load was heavy.

At midday, we had lunch: boiled eggs, cold cooked potatoes, marinated or fresh cucumbers and cold pancakes. Grandpa enjoyed a sandwich with salted pork fat and onions or garlic on a slice of rye bread. We all drank milk or water and rested for a half an hour. After lunch, we continued our arduous work till sunset. Then, sweaty, hungry and exhausted, we went home. That routine lasted for a week, sometimes longer.

After the planting was finished, we waited for the spring rains to arrive. In a month, we had to hoe up the weeds around every individual plant. It was tiring work under the hot spring sun. Then, we had to wait again for the next rain. After the rain, in a week or two, we had to weed again and to mound up every plant.

Finally, in early September, we had to gather the harvest. Everything would be taken from the field, including the stems of the corn and the sunflowers. The most difficult job was to transport all the harvest home by hand, on the handcart which had two heavy metal wheels, a wooden body and had to be pulled by two people. Those handcarts were not manufactured by industry; they were made by the people themselves.

Before the German occupation, people had the opportunity to hire a coachman with a wagon or even a teamster with a truck to transport their harvest from the fields, but the Germans confiscated all the horses and used them as local means of transportation. People had no choice: they pulled those handcarts themselves instead of the horses. Two adults pulled the cart by the front handle; older people and children pushed it from behind.

After the harvest was delivered to the backyard of my grandparents' place, it had to be processed and properly stored. First and foremost, potatoes, beetroots and carrots had to be sorted out, cleaned, dried and stored in the cellar. Meanwhile, beans, peas, sunflower heads and corn-cobs dried in the sun or in the hayloft of the barn. After that, they had to be shelled, sifted and winnowed. Grandpa had a set of sieves of different sizes; they were our only supporting tools for harvesting.

When all the vegetables were cleaned and dried, they were stored in the cellar. Beans, peas, corn grains and sunflower seeds were stored in big and small canvas bags in the pantry. We had only wooden boxes and bins, canvas bags and ceramic vats for storage.

Traditionally, we used corn only to feed domestic animals and poultry. As feeding for pigs, for example, corn was ground down, cooked in water, and mixed with bran; then some slop was added for taste. Every now and then, certain types of wild grass, such as goose-foot, were added to our pig's rations. Grandma entrusted the children to provide the grass.

Stocking up produce for winter was the most important task for the summer and the fall seasons. During the summer, we dried seasonal fruits: apples, pears, apricots, plums and sour cherries. We dried them on the tiled roof of the house and in the hayloft. It was always hot and dry there, and there were no flies, no bees, no bumble-bees, and no wasps which usually were attracted by the smell of the sweet ripe fruits on the roof.

When we still had sugar, we prepared homemade jam of strawberries, raspberries, gooseberries, red and black currants. When sugar disappeared completely from the rations of the general population, people became proficient in preserving berries and fruits with the help of ordinary aspirin. However, the usage of aspirin in the preserving process required precise measurement of water and aspirin. There were accidents when the incorrect dosage of aspirin caused the explosion of the glass jars, with tragic consequences.

We also cooked tomato sauce and stored it for winter in the beer and wine bottles in the cellar. We salted and marinated green cabbage, cucumbers, tomatoes, eggplants and watermelons, and we stored them in wooden barrels in the cellar.

In order to provide meat for their own consumption, every family bred chickens, ducks, geese and rabbits. Every family had at least one pig, which was usually butchered a week before Christmas. As a rule, a butcher was hired to kill a pig. He cut up the carcass, cutting out two front and two back legs which were slightly salted and smoked. Every part of the carcass, with the exception of hooves, teeth and, of course, the contents of the stomach and intestines, was thoroughly processed and used.

The stomach and intestines were cleaned, then washed many times with cold and warm water. After that, the intestines were stuffed with ground sausage-meat seasoned with salt, black pepper and garlic. No drop of pork blood was wasted; it was saved to make blood sausage. The intestines were stuffed with blood mixed with seasoned sausage-meat. Wonderful headcheese, stuffed with pieces of pork, pork fat, and seasoned with spices, was made from the pig's stomach.

No refrigerators existed back then in the Soviet Union, so the headcheese and the sausages were stored in big ceramic vats, and hot lard was poured over them. They could stay fresh for a long period of time, actually up to Easter. Smoked bacon and salted pork fat were stored in square wooden boxes and also stayed preserved for a long time.

The butcher was paid with a good piece of fresh pork, a piece of pork fat and a promise to get a ring of fresh sausage for Christmas.

The entire family worked hard for several days processing the pork meat. The only equipment we had were sharp knives and a big hand-operated meat grinder which Grandma borrowed from our neighbors. We had no running water, not to mention hot water, so it took us great amounts of time and hard work to do the job. As a consolation prize, those days we ate mashed potatoes with tasty pig liver fried with onions and sour cream, and ravioli stuffed with ground pork and freshly chopped onions, seasoned with black pepper and chopped fresh dill.

For Christmas, Grandma cooked our favorite dish— pork jelly. We children helped her to separate cooked meat from the bones, and we sucked around the bones. We also chopped the garlic and decorated the plates filled with hardened meat jelly with the rings of hard boiled eggs and carrots.

For us children, it was the first Christmas celebration in our lives.

7. Our Moonshine Adventure

*C*ultivating vegetable gardens, raising pigs and poultry were the most important legal activities for survival which the civilian population of Ukraine undertook during the German occupation (1941–1944). However, because of the shortage of bare essentials, people were forced to resort to different kinds of illegal enterprises. One of the most widely-spread activities was the production of *samogon* or *samogonka* — homemade vodka.

Moonshine fever engulfed almost every household because it was possible to distill homemade vodka literally from everything: from white, sweet beetroots, from any grain, including corn, and from apples, plums and apricots. Vodka was in great demand. It wasn't produced commercially because all the liquor and wine production factories were closed. What is more, the shortage of sugar didn't permit people to produce wines with sugar, fruits, cherries, and berries to satisfy their drinking needs. Thus, vodka, though illegal, was a saleable product at the farmers' market, and it wasn't cheap. So, production of vodka was worth the risk. Like others, our family distilled *samogon* for sale.

One dark, autumn evening, Grandpa brought home in a sack a big, strange apparatus made of meandering metallic tubes. The next morning, he installed it above the stove over the big pot with some mixture that had been fermenting for a week in a small wooden barrel on our veranda, emitting a strong, unusual smell. He heated the concoction, put the tube in it, and several hours later, a transparent liquid began to drip from the glass tube into a three-liter glass milk jar. Drop by drop, the jar filled up to the brim; then another one began to fill. With amazement and acute interest, my little sister, Louisa, my cousin Zhanna, and I, watched the magic happening in front of our eyes; we had never seen such an apparatus before. Grandpa took a jar in his hands, looking at it approvingly and said, "What a beauty! Splendid! Clear as a tear-drop."

The entire house was filled with the smell of alcohol. The smoke from the chimney also smelled of alcohol, and probably attracted uninvited visitors to our house. Grandma later said that she suspected that one of our envious neighbors had reported our illegal activity to the police. Things like that had happened before, as informing had become popular in those days. When our illegal ordeal was almost finished and all the adults were gathered in the barn, the divisional inspector of police, one of the locals who was collaborating with the Germans, appeared at our back door, accompanied by his deputies.

Louisa spotted them while they were walking by the small bedroom window. She grabbed the heavy three-liter glass jar filled with freshly distilled vodka, took it to the next room, and hid it under the bed. I was surprised that she managed to do it because the jar was heavy, especially for the eight-year old, fragile Louisa.

The policemen dismantled and confiscated the apparatus and the second jar of vodka. The hard labor of several weeks went down the drain, together with our hopes to make some money from the sale of *samogon*.

To my great surprise, I overheard Grandpa complimenting my mischievous sister Louisa for her resourcefulness. "*Molodetz*, Louisa, good girl," he said, stroking her blonde hair sticking up in all directions. "You did the right thing that you have hidden the jar. At least, we have something to sell at the farmers' market, and we'll make some money." Louisa was all smiles. It was the first time that Grandpa didn't admonish her, but praised her behavior.

Our illegal moonshine adventure was not a big success, but it didn't stop us from trying again. Life was getting harder. All the pre-war reserves of food and other essentials made by my thrifty grandmother were almost exhausted, and our family, in despair, clutched at every straw to survive.

8. Soap-Boiling

*O*ur second illegal enterprise was neither envisioned nor planned. It happened in late fall, a year after our moonshining misadventure. Unexpectedly, our pig got sick. In the morning, the pig didn't eat its food. This was surprising because the pig usually had a great appetite and devoured everything in its feeding tub. Preoccupied and nervous, my grandparents decided to wait until noon to call the vet. But it was too late. By midday feeding, the pig was already dead.

All the family was in despair. Nobody knew what to do — whether to go to the authorities to report the death of the pig, as required by law, or just to get rid of the pig's dead body secretly, under the cover of night. The pig's death caused a huge financial loss to the family. It was too late to buy and bring up another piglet before Christmas. Besides, piglets were more expensive in the fall than they were in early spring, at the height of the birthing season. Worried and desperate, my grandparents couldn't see their way out of the situation.

We children cried loudly, mourning the death of our pet. We loved our pig. We used to pick up grass for it, and we helped Grandpa bathe it during the summer time. He scratched the pig with a brush, while we poured water on it from the watering cans. The pig liked it and grunted with delight.

Grandpa was inclined to go to the civilian authorities to report the pig's death, according to the local ordinance, but Grandma stopped him.

"Listen, Ivan Danilovich," Grandma said, addressing him by his full name as she used to do during serious conversations, "what will we gain with your report? They will come, and they will take the pig's body away on the pretext of some infectious disease. We actually don't know what has happened to the pig. Do we? The pig just could have had a heart attack. If animals have hearts, they could also have heart attacks. Am I right?"

Grandpa retorted with irritation, "What shall we do with the pig's body, then? We can't eat the meat of a pig that died from, God only knows, what devil's disease!"

"Give me more time. I'll think of something!" Grandma promised, trying to persuade Grandpa and to calm him down.

Grandma kept her promise. She talked to some of her close friends and with their help, she came up with the idea of soap-boiling, which was another illegal activity the people resorted to because of the soap shortage.

The German authorities had officially banned soap-boiling because of its main ingredient—caustic soda. The only way to get caustic soda was to steal it from the metal works located about ten miles from my grandparents' place. The Germans put it in operation and hired local labor to do the work. Caustic soda was one of the chemicals used in manganese ore processing.

The local workers knew all the ins and outs at the works which occupied a huge territory. Security was provided by the locals and supervised by the Germans.

So, it was not beyond workers' ability to take out several kilos of caustic soda secretly and to sell it at the farmers' market, under the counter, of course.

Grandpa was hesitant; he wanted to report the death of the pig. Grandma tried to insist on having her way.

"We need soap. Look at your granddaughters. The girls scratch their heads all the time because they have lice. We all scratch ourselves because we also have body lice, to say nothing of the bedbugs. Don't you understand that? We need soap, and we need it quickly; otherwise, the horde of these damn insects will eat us alive!" Grandma said, almost crying. "Besides, we need soap for laundry and washing. There are seven of us, and we have a pile of laundry every week. Homemade soap is very expensive at the farmers' market. Now we have a chance to make our own soap. We didn't plan that—it just happened. It was God's will," Grandma sighed. "It's true, that every cloud has a silver lining."

It was the truth. The hair lice were eating us ruthlessly, despite the desperate efforts of my mother to comb our hair with a fine-toothed comb several times a day. My braids, my pride and beauty, were the first victims of the lice invasion. Then Louisa's and Zhanna's hair was also cut short in order to get rid of the nits and lice.

I sobbed uncontrollably when my mother cut my hair with a big tailor's scissors, but she threatened to cut it close to the skin if I didn't stop crying. I did stop, but I couldn't forgive her for a long time. I grumbled at her, and I spent a lot of time in the hayloft, my favorite hiding place, consoling myself with reading and rereading my beloved *Anna Karenina*.

One afternoon, Mother climbed up to the hayloft. "Are you hiding, Nina, because you are angry with me? Don't worry, *dorogaya*, honey. After a haircut, hair grows even faster. In no time, you will have longer and thicker hair. You will see! By the New Year, you will have wonderful pigtails. Stop grumbling at me. I had to do it; we have no soap to keep your hair clean and free of lice." Her tone was conciliatory as she tried to justify herself.

Tears streamed down my cheeks, but I didn't know why I was crying. Was I crying because of my lost braids, or was I mourning the tragic fate of the beautiful Anna Karenina who had committed suicide and had died a terrible death under the wheels of a train?

Mother and Aunt Valentina supported Grandma's decision to do the soap-boiling because it was getting harder to fight hair and body insects without soap. Finally, we became soap-boilers. Grandma managed to get some caustic soda. Grandpa himself cut off the fat from the pig's body. He put the remains of the pig's carcass, with all the meat on it, into burlap sacks, put the sacks on the handcart and covered the load with a piece of tarpaulin. Then he took the cart far away to the forest plantation and buried what was left of our beloved pig.

The soap-boiling process didn't require special equipment as moonshining did. The small pieces of pork fat were put in a big zinc vat, then water and caustic soda were added in certain proportions. The vat was put on the stove, and the soap-boiling began. It lasted the whole day. When the nasty-smelling mass was completely dissolved and started to get thicker, Grandma poured into it half a flask of her favorite lavender oil for fragrance. Then, it was poured into two zinc washtubs, and left to cool and harden.

When the mass hardened, Grandma cut it with a knife in small, square pieces. That freshly boiled soap looked very strange. Every piece consisted of three grayish layers, from dark grey to light gray. It also smelled strange.

Obviously, half a flask of lavender oil wasn't enough to counteract the strong, persistent smell of the caustic soda.

Despite the unusual odor of our homemade soap, it enjoyed a great success at the farmers' market. Maybe it happened because Grandma enhanced the sale of every bar of soap with a beautiful tale about the acquisition of that flask of lavender oil. According to her story, Grandpa had bought it for her as a gift when they had vacationed at the coast of the Black Sea many years ago. Now she had to sacrifice it all for a good cause, for the soap which we all needed so badly.

Grandma's behavior surprised me. I had never heard her telling a lie, and I knew for sure that she had poured only half a flask into the soap. When I confronted her and asked why she had lied about it, she answered, smiling gently, "You know, *detka*, child, I wanted to pour the whole flask. I knew that half of it wasn't enough for that amount of caustic soda, but I couldn't do it. That flask of lavender oil is very dear to me. Its smell always reminds me about that one and only summer vacation we had with your grandfather. Someday, you will understand and forgive me!" I didn't understand her then, but now I know what it means to live on memories.

Grandma sold only half of our homemade soap at the farmers' market. The other half was used by the family for laundry and bathing.

On Christmas Day, we sat at the table, all dressed in freshly-washed clothes. Our hair was clean and shining. But instead of our usual Christmas treat—pork sausage, headcheese and our favorite pork jelly—everyone had a small portion of fried chicken. There were seven of us to share one chicken butchered for Christmas. Grandpa wanted to butcher two, but Grandma didn't allow him. She said softly, "Spring is getting closer every day. The chickens will lay more eggs in spring. The more chickens we save, the more spring chickens and eggs we'll have. We can survive without meat, but in no way can we make it without eggs!"

Bozhe moy! My God! My prudent and wise Grandma was right, as usual.

9. Uncle Mitya's Ingenuity

*A*nother type of illegal activity practiced by many people during the German occupation was caustic soda purification. The result of the chemical reaction was baking soda, which was in great demand at the farmers' market. Only one local bakery was in operation to provide sufficient amounts of rye and wheat bread for the German troops who worked at the railroad station and at the depot. After their need for bread was satisfied, the small amount of square-loafed rye and wheat bread was sold to the locals in the bakery, at the farmers' market.

The bakery opened at seven o'clock in the morning. In order to get at least a half of a loaf of any bread, people had to get in line at dawn. The bread was sold out in less than an hour. More than once, Grandpa returned from the bakery empty handed. In that case, Grandma had to bake pancakes or round crumpets as a substitute for bread. Baking soda was handy on such occasions; baking with yeast dough needed more preparation, more time and effort.

Our family had been involved in caustic soda refinement activity indirectly, through Uncle Mitya, Aunt Valentina's husband. He was a chemical engineer. Before the war started, he had worked as a shift foreman at the famous local metal works. He was tall, lean and, according to my Aunt Valentina, "handsome like a young Greek God." That phrase didn't mean much to me then. All adults considered him hardworking and skillful. At that time, Valentina, Uncle Mitya and Zhanna lived in a new two-room apartment built for metal works' employees, not far from his work place. They even bought a gramophone, a luxury item at that time. Aunt Valentina worked at the pharmacy as an assistant to the pharmacist, and little Zhanna went to kindergarten.

Then, one fateful day in 1937, a disaster struck. A serious industrial accident happened at Uncle Mitya's shop, during his shift. It was the bloody year of 1937, when Stalin undertook his ideological campaign of purging the Communist party and the Soviet society from extraneous elements, from "enemies of the people."

There wasn't a single family in the Soviet Union that didn't suffer during Stalin's repressions in 1937. Innocent people who had never committed any crime, were arrested, prosecuted and thrown into jails at the slightest suspicion of conspiracy, plot or sabotage against the Soviet state and the Communist party. Proof of the crime wasn't needed; slander or mere accusation was enough to put the people in prison for decades.

In this atmosphere of suspicion, fear, and betrayal, even a simple industrial accident was considered an act of sabotage. Uncle Mitya, together with all the workers of his team, was arrested, accused of sabotage and prosecuted. After his arrest, Valentina with little Zhanna, moved in with Valentina's parents.

A year and a half later, in 1939, to everybody's surprise, Uncle Mitya and his team were released from jail because of the lack of evidence. Uncle Mitya told our family that the public prosecutor and the investigators tried to force all of them to confess to sabotage which they allegedly had committed in order to damage the technical equipment at the metal works, one of the first industrial giants of the newly developed Soviet industry. The prosecutor tried to force them to admit that they were spies and, therefore, enemies of the people. The punishment for that crime was a firing squad or, at best, decades of imprisonment in exile, in Siberia.

The jail supervisors kept the "accused," as the defendants were called in the Soviet judicial terminology, in overheated and overcrowded cells. They were deprived of sleep and forced to stand all night long. Sometimes, the jail guards didn't allow them to sit or to lie down for hours.

The workers didn't understand why they were treated in such a way. They hadn't committed any crimes, they hadn't plan any acts of sabotage, and they hadn't been involved in any plot against the peoples' state or against the government. It was just one of the common industrial accidents which had happened at the metal works for obvious reasons, as Uncle Mitya explained to us. The equipment was obsolete and worn out, safety rules didn't exist, and programs to train and retrain young workers didn't exist either.

Both prosecutors and investigators, with all their might, tried to extract a confession from the defendants, but Uncle Mitya and his team fought for their lives. They insisted that the accident was just that—an accident, an unplanned industrial accident, and nothing else. They refused to sign the confession, despite the tortures to which they had been subjected.

In summer of 1939, when Uncle Mitya returned from jail, it was the first time that I had the chance to become acquainted with him. I was seven and a half years old. I was sure that I had met him before, but my memory didn't register that previous encounter. I was too little to remember. Mother, Louisa and I, as usual, were spending the summer vacation at grandparents' place. Aunt Valentina with little Zhanna lived there too.

That late afternoon, I found myself sitting on the sofa in Valentina's room. The window of the room faced the street. We wound up the gramophone and listened to my favorite record, the foxtrot *Rio-Rita*, which was very popular that year. I was enchanted with the gramophone. Gramophones had just appeared in the Soviet Union. They were considered items of prestige; everybody wanted to have one, but not everyone could afford one. My family didn't have one, so it was a novelty for me which I enjoyed immensely. I listened to that tune again and again, and joined in singing the refrain of *Rio-Rita*. I was singing and looking at the window. Valentina's back faced the windows when she tried to put on another popular record, the tango, *The Tired Sun*.

Suddenly, I realized that the same man was walking back and forth in front of our window, and I said, "Look, Valentina, why is that man walking back and forth under our window?"

Valentina looked up, then jumped from the sofa, and dropping my favorite "Rio-Rita" record, she screamed, "Oh, my Mitetchka, my Mitetchka!" Then she stormed out of the room. I stood looking in awe at the pieces of the broken record, and I couldn't understand a thing.

Very soon, Valentina came back accompanied by a tall, young man with tired eyes and a timid smile, and said, "This is my husband, my Mitetchka, Zhanna's father. He has returned from jail." Then she started to cry. Looking at her, I started to cry myself. Valentina's tears were tears of joy. Why was I crying? Being seven and a half years old, I hardly understood the meaning of the word "jail." Was I crying because of my favorite, broken *Rio-Rita* record, or just to keep company to my beloved aunt?

Later, I asked Grandma, "Why didn't Uncle Mitya take the liberty of entering the house?" The wooden gate was locked from inside with a hook. We children couldn't reach it from outside, but he could. Grandma told me that there was some bad blood between Grandpa and his son-in-law, but she didn't elaborate.

Although his knapsack was almost empty, Uncle Mitya didn't come home empty handed. He brought presents from jail for his wife and his daughter: three sofa pillowcases embroidered by him in a cross-stitch style. On one pillowcase, the name "Valya," the diminutive of Valentina, was embroidered in red on a blue background. Another pillowcase, done in green on a yellow background, said "Zhanna." The third one, symbolically embroidered in white on a black background, read "Mitya."

We all were surprised. I was amazed, because I didn't know that men could embroider. We didn't understand how he could accomplish that without needles and thread. In Soviet jails, prisoners were not allowed to have any sharp objects or acquire thread and patterns for embroideries.

Uncle Mitya explained to us that he and his cellmates had made the needles themselves. It was not for nothing that they were engineers and technicians. As for the patterns, Uncle Mitya designed them himself. In order to get threads for embroidery, they unraveled all their colored T-shirts, then wound the threads into skeins and shared them.

51

They made embroideries in order to occupy their time and not to lose their minds. Books and newspapers were also forbidden in the Soviet jails in 1937. They had to be careful and hide their work from the jail guards. For that reason, one cellmate was always on watch, listening to the approaching steps of the jail guards while the others were doing embroideries. If the guard was close to their cell, the look-out signaled, and everybody had to hide his work and pretend to look idle. They did it in turns.

Upon his return from jail, Uncle Mitya got back his job, and soon, he, Valentina and Zhanna moved into a new apartment with all the modern amenities, in the same apartment building where they had lived before his arrest. Everybody was happy. Even the broken *Rio-Rita* record couldn't spoil my joyful mood because Aunt Valentina promised to replace it with a new copy as soon as they would get some money. "Don't worry, Ninochka," she said, "next year, when you come to Grandparents' place on vacation, I will have a lot of new records. Uncle Mitya likes music, and he likes to buy records. By the way, it was he who bought *Rio-Rita* in the first place."

I was happily lost in dreams about the next summer vacation, about listening to the new records and learning the new songs. Anticipating that something nice would be happening in the future, we soon left Grandmother's place. The school year approached, and Mother had to return to work.

We managed to see Mother's relatives, including Uncle Mitya, only two years later, in 1941, when World War II reached the Soviet Union.

On Sunday, June 22 in 1941, the German troops crossed the Soviet-Polish border. Uncle Mitya, like all young men of his age, was immediately drafted and sent to the front. Several weeks later, his unit was surrounded by enemy troops, and they were taken prisoners by the Germans. In chaos and confusion of those first months of the war, he and one of his fellow soldiers managed to escape from captivity. They didn't know what to do and where to go. They didn't have a map, and they had no information about the German or Soviet positions. They had no radio, not even watches, as German soldiers had confiscated all their modest possessions, including hand watches.

They decided to walk only at night, avoiding people and major roads. They walked through forest plantations, through corn and sunflower fields in Ukraine, staying as far as possible from towns and villages, moving in the general direction of the southeast. At dawn, they hid in fields and slept the whole day. They did it by turns: one slept while another watched and listened for every suspicious sound.

They were guided by the artillery fire and by the direction in which military aircrafts flew. They flew to the front line, to the East. It was dangerous for them to walk during the day because they didn't know who they might meet: groups of Soviet soldiers, lost or fallen behind, or German patrol units. Every encounter presented danger. They ate fruits and vegetables which they stole from the orchards and vegetable gardens, and drank water from the community wells at night.

It would be dangerous for them to be caught by Germans or by Soviets—both presented threats to them.

53

They tore their documents to pieces and burned them, just in case. They had a very simple plan if anything cropped up: if they were caught by Germans, they would play the roles of Soviet deserters; if they were caught by Soviets, they would pose as escapees from German captivity. Language was a serious obstacle in their perilous scenario, as neither one of them spoke German. So, they relied only on Providence and on their lucky stars. The flashes of the artillery fire and the explosions of the bombs on the dark night sky were their compass.

Finally, one starless fall night, they reached the city located not far from Grandparents' place where Uncle Mitya's sister, Faina, lived with her family. The next evening, Uncle Mitya arrived at Grandparents' house. He was thin and exhausted. He had managed to wash up and to put on a clean shirt and pants which his sister had given him the night before. His hair was cut; his face was clean-shaven. His sister was afraid that his untidy appearance might attract the unnecessary attention of the neighbors or the German military police.

Later that night at Grandparents' house, the family decided that it would be better for both Uncle Mitya and the family if he stayed at his sister's place, at least for a while. She had a bigger house, in a large city, where it was easier to be unnoticed in a crowd. In the tumultuous, uncertain times of German occupation, people didn't know whom they should fear more: their neighbors or the Germans. The new reality unleashed the best and the worst in people's behavior. It was better for Uncle Mitya to be as far as possible from Grandparents' place where everybody knew him and his family.

German authorities demanded that all young men of military age be registered in the City or Town Hall offices. If they avoided registration and were caught later, they could be killed on the spot. From time to time, Germans conducted night raids and searches of the private houses. It was safer to stay at home because the police checked the documents at public places such as the farmers' market, as well. There was no place to hide from the police, or from the vigilant and curious eyes of the neighbors.

In that situation, Uncle Mitya decided to register at the City Hall office and to pose as a deserter from the Soviet Army. He was offered a job at the same metal works where he had worked before the war. If he refused to accept the job, he would be sent to Germany as a work slave. He chose the lesser of two evils — he took the job.

That was how he gained access to the caustic soda. His salary was pitiful, but, like many others who worked there, he was able to obtain the caustic soda and process it into a valuable product — baking soda. But it was a dangerous and risky venture.

The process of caustic soda purification looked like a simple one. I saw it when we visited Aunt Valentina and her family. The wardrobe in Valentina's tiny bedroom was strategically placed against the corner, producing a triangular empty space behind it. A big glass laboratory vessel was hidden there. Some white, dry substance was slowly passed through the filter into the lower, wider part of the vessel where the new product, the baking soda, was slowly accumulating. There was no noise, no smell, nothing at all.

Before we left, Valentina used to give us a small bundle of baking soda which Grandma later would sell at the farmers' market, as there was a great demand for it. It was widely used to prepare pancakes, flat cakes and crumpets as a substitute for bread. Baking with yeast takes more time and effort. So, baking soda was a hot commodity, but a dangerous one, because it was produced illegally from a product stolen from the German-owned metal works. Uncle Mitya risked his life in order to help our families survive during the harsh years of the German occupation.

10. The Farmers' Market

*A*ll the roads and paths of socio-economic activities of our town, Doguintsevo, led to the farmers' market located on the Bazaar Square. The home address of my grandparents was 34 Bazaar Street. That street led directly to the market square which was one block away from my grandparents' house.

Several rows of wooden counters stood in the center of the market square. There were special counters for all kinds of produce: meat and fish, grain, vegetables, fresh and dried fruits, dairy products, eggs, and dry substances. Only a few counters had wooden awnings; the rest of them had no protection from the scorching summer sun, spring rains and winter snow. In a separate section of the market, live animals and poultry were for sale: cows, goats, pigs, piglets, rabbits, chickens, baby chickens, ducks and geese. A special area was assigned for horse carts and wagons because on Sundays, the busiest market day of the week, people from the nearby villages brought to the market their produce, cattle and poultry.

On the sly, it was possible to buy and sell many different things: old clothes and shoes, small domestic appliances such as oil lamps and stoves, pots and pans, and, of course, homemade vodka, *samogon*. German cigarettes, matches, flint lighters, candy, soap, even soldiers' mess tins and military uniform belts could be bought. We suspected that the German soldiers exchanged all those things for fresh eggs, milk, homemade salted pork, sausage and homemade vodka, which they liked very much.

The farmers' market functioned seven days a week. On weekdays, it started around 5:00 a.m., and was over by noon. On Saturdays and Sundays, by 6:00 a.m., it was swarming with people, and its selling-buying activities were in full swing. For me, the market was an unusual and attractive place. There, I could see different people and watch them interact and socialize. These weekend market activities lasted till late afternoon.

At the end of the summer, the market looked like a painting: the fruits and vegetable counters were iridescent—red, green and yellow apples, juicy green and yellow pears, meaty greenish, yellow and violet plums, piles of green, red and plum grapes, huge piles of ripe watermelons and sweet-scented melons. Everything attracted my eyes and made my heart rejoice.

Every time Grandma planned to go to the market, I volunteered to help her and to keep her company. On those days I had to get up before 5:00 a.m., and I was ready to make that sacrifice for the sake of my irrepressible childish curiosity.

Our everyday routine was monotonous and boring: we had no radio, we didn't go to the movies, we didn't walk in the park, we didn't listen to the brass band music anymore. We were not allowed to go to our playmates' houses or yards because adults were afraid that we children could accidentally blab out about illegal dealings of our family. Even entirely innocent things could be used against our family by malevolent neighbors. Going to the farmers' market on weekends was a fascinating adventure to me, and I never missed the opportunity to accompany Grandma.

Before the war, the small shops and stalls stood along both sides of the market. They provided such services as alterations, shoe-repair, key-making and knife-sharpening. There was a special shop where small appliances such as electric irons, radios, oil lamps and stoves could be fixed. My favorite was a photo shop where Louisa and I had our photos taken at a very young age. The bicycle shop was very popular. At that time, bicycles were the only personal means of transportation, an item of prestige and envy.

During the German occupation, almost all those shops and stalls disappeared. Only three of them were still in operation—the shoe-repair stall, the knife-sharpening stall, and another one which rented scales and weights to the vendors The inventory of scales, however, was limited; therefore, those vendors who didn't get the scales and weights had to use other means to measure their produce, including spring balances.

A vendor fee had to be paid for a space at the counter. Those who didn't get a counter space put their produce on the ground, forming rows, but they had to pay the vendor fee, all the same.

Some traditional ways of measurement were also used. Eggs, for example, were sold by tens. Apples, pears and plums were sold by tens, as well, or sometimes, by the piece. Berries were sold by the glass. Dry substances such as flour, buckwheat, semolina, oatmeal, pearl-barley, millet, beans, dried fruits and berries, and sunflower and pumpkin seeds were measured by jars or by large or small glasses.

Green onions, parsley, dill, celery, carrots, beetroots and radishes were sold by bunches. By request of the customer, beetroots and carrots could be sold also by the piece. However, during the harvest season, sweet and sour cherries, apples, apricots, plums and pears could be sold by buckets like potatoes, tomatoes and cucumbers.

At the height of the harvest season, at the end of August, people had no time and no sugar to process all the fruits and berries to make jam, especially if there was a good year for harvest. There were no opportunities to store the extra amount of fresh vegetables without salting or marinating them, and everybody tried to sell all the fresh fruits, berries and vegetables which they could not process.

Spinach, sorrel and hops were sold by the handful. Of course, those traditional popular measurements were quite arbitrary, but they had their advantages. On occasion, a vendor could lure the customer by adding just a little more to the offered amount. Green lettuce and green cabbage were sold by heads; so were melons, watermelons, and pumpkins.

Dairy products, such as milk, sour cream and homemade yogurt, *ryazhenka,* were measured by a liter or half-liter jars or by glasses. Fresh homemade butter and cream cheese were sold by the piece; each portion was wrapped in gauze.

Wine and beer bottles were worth their weight in gold because all the stores were closed, and there was no place to buy bottles. Bottles were used to measure milk, homemade tomato sauce, sunflower oil, homemade wines and homemade vodka, illegal but the hottest commodity at the farmers' market.

All the customers of the market had to bring their own packaging materials and containers for all kinds of produce. The vendors couldn't provide them, but they, in turn, had to bring the measures for the produce they wanted to sell.

Every time when Grandma needed to go to the market, I always helped her put all the things into a rectangular shopping bag called a *kosholka*, which was made of wicker straw and had two handles. If we had milk to sell, we used to put two jars into the bag—a half-liter jar and a liter jar. Just in case, we always put a funnel for measuring purposes along with a half-liter and liter bottles.

Usually, Grandma carried milk in two big three-liter tin milk cans with handles. Sometimes, Grandpa, Mother or Valentina helped her carry one milk can. When Grandma had to sell baking soda, she used a teaspoon and a tablespoon for measurement. She carried baking soda in a small, white cotton homemade sack. If we had any paper at all, Grandma asked me to cut it in square pieces and put them into the bag They served as packaging material for those customers who didn't bring their own but wanted to buy baking soda. Grandma made small cone paper bags and poured baking soda into them.

Grandma also put in her shopping bag a small sack of white beans and a glass to measure them. "Just in case if the policemen will show up," she used to say. German authorities prohibited the sale of baking soda which was produced from raw materials that had been stolen by local workers, including my uncle Mitya, from metal works.

At the market, Grandma always instructed me, "Don't stand gaping. Please, be all eyes. You are young, and your vision is sharp. As soon as you see the police at the far end of the market, just let me know at once. We'll hide the baking soda, and we'll pretend we are selling beans!" I was proud of that assignment and tired my eyes out and almost broke my neck trying to locate the policemen on time. Thank God the police never caught us.

Once, when Grandma had baking soda for sale and I was keeping my usual watch, a woman about Grandma's age came up and cordially greeted her, "Good day, Nastenka!" I rarely heard somebody calling Grandma that name, the diminutive term of endearment for Anastasia. As it turned out, they knew each other very well. They talked for a while, swapping family news and gossip. Grandma's friend complimented me saying, "*Molodchinka*, good girl! You are doing the right thing helping your grandmother at the market."

She bought some baking soda from Grandma and left. I was surprised that she didn't bargain about the price like others customers did. She didn't take advantage of being Grandma's friend. I noticed, however, that she had paid only for one tablespoon of soda, although Grandma gave her two and a half tablespoons.

"*Babushka, babushka!* Grandma, Grandma! She paid only for one tablespoon, but you gave her two and a half spoons," I said with alarm when the woman left.

"That's all right, *detka*, child!" Grandma tried to calm me. "I know that I gave her an extra spoon of soda. She was my close friend and a good neighbor when we both were young and good-looking. She met a handsome young man and fell in love with him. They got married and moved to another place. They had seven children, but her beloved husband became a drunkard. All their children got married and moved out. Her husband recently had died because of drinking too much. Now she, *bednyaga*, the poor soul, lives with two teenage grandchildren abandoned by their parents, surviving the hardships of war without any assistance. I just wanted to help her a little," Grandma said with deep sorrow in her voice.

I hardly believed that the poorly but neatly dressed woman, with a bun of grey hair on her neck and lifeless, tired eyes could have been good-looking at one time. Grandma saw disbelief in my eyes; she always read me like a book. She added with great pity, "They don't even have milk because they had to sell their she-goat. They are so poor now that every day they eat only *mamalyga* without milk."

I knew that *mamalyga* was a Moldavian dish cooked with coarsely ground corn, well-known in Southern Ukraine. However, only very poor people ate it before the war. I didn't like that dish. To my taste, even seasoned with butter or fried pork fat and fried onions, it was tasteless. Grandma seldom cooked it, as nobody in the family liked it. We all preferred fresh corn ears. Grandma, however, considered that dish healthy food and, from time to time, cooked it with milk for supper.

The length of our market day depended on what we had to sell and on the season of the year. In spring, for example, the people came to the market to make a quick sale of produce they had and to buy what they needed. Then they returned to work in their vegetable gardens and orchards, and to take care of their domestic animals.

If Grandma had only baking soda to sell, our market day could be over early, around eleven o'clock, sometimes even earlier when the market square was still full of people.

In summer, when cows produce more milk, it was harder to sell fresh milk because many people were selling it. Then we had to stay longer to make a sale, till one or even two o'clock in the afternoon. The market was emptying slowly; the janitors were sweeping the grounds covered with a thick, grayish layer of sunflower seed shells.

Sunflower seeds fried with salt were a local delicacy which enjoyed great success with people of all ages. Young boys and girls would stroll along the rows, exchanging smiles and greetings, laughing and talking loudly, while nibbling sunflower seeds from the paper cone bags, and nonchalantly spitting out the shells on the ground.

Grandma and I put everything in our shopping bags, said "good-bye" to our companions at the counter, and headed home. "Thank God we made some money, and God willing, there will be another lucky market day for us next week," Grandma would say, sighing with relief.

11. Meat and Fish Trade Row

*D*uring the occupation period, there was only one row of counters where meat and fish could be sold. Actually, there was very little meat for sale, and no fish at all. The residents of our town, Dolguintsevo, raised pigs, chickens, ducks and geese for their own consumption; domestic animals and poultry were their only source of meat. In case of extreme need, if they had nothing else to sell, they were forced to sell poultry and pork to supplement their income.

As for the poultry, customers had a choice: they could buy fresh chicken, goose or duck meat, or buy live chickens, ducks and geese. Buying live poultry cost less because customers had to process it all themselves. Without running water, electricity and heating oil, it was a time-consuming operation.

Fresh pork was usually for sale several weeks before the winter holiday season when almost everybody butchered pigs bought as piglets in spring to raise them and have pork for Christmas and New Year's celebration. Very little pork was for sale because people processed all of it as salted and smoked ham, salted pork fat and homemade sausage. Those products lasted almost till late spring. Summer was a meatless season, when only poultry was used for cooking. Nobody butchered pigs in summer because they were still small, with little meat and fat on them.

We children liked to go to the farmers' market in spring when the air was filled with familiar, cheerful sounds of domestic animals and birds: the squealing of piglets, the chirping of baby chickens, the quacking of ducklings, the cackling of goslings, the bleating of lambs and kids, and the mooing of calves.

We liked to walk through the market crowd from one group of animals to another, from one box with baby chickens, ducklings and goslings to another, feasting our eyes on those fluffy yellow balls with tiny beaks and delicate feet. We tried to touch and to pat those wonderful creatures, to stroke their small, bobbing heads. The baby chicks tried to flap their tiny wings as if they wanted to fly.

Every spring, we had two brooding hens with their own hatched baby chickens. We helped Grandma feed them with boiled eggs sliced in tiny pieces. We watched our cat while the baby chickens were still too small and could not run fast or fight our old cat, the cunning Vaska.

Vaska tried to hunt baby chickens every chance he had. That is why Grandma asked us children to watch and protect the brood with her chicks while they were in the yard. She allowed us to scare the cat away and even to hit him with a switch if the baby chicks were in danger. We were on the alert all the time.

Once, when our playmates distracted us, disaster struck. Vaska seized a moment, grabbed a baby chick, jumped over the fence and disappeared as quickly as lightning into the thick orchard of our neighbors. When Grandpa finally caught him, the poor baby chicken was dead.

Grandpa was angry. So, too, was Grandma. Louisa and I were scared and crying. That was the moment when Grandma finally made the decision to get rid of Vaska who had already killed our neighbor's two baby chicks. In the evening, Grandpa put our treacherous cat in a sack and took him far away, about ten miles from our house, and let him go into the forest plantation.

Three days later, Grandma and I woke up very early to get ready for the market. First, Grandma had to milk the cow. She went out of the house, then suddenly, from the porch, she quietly called me, "Come here, Nina, look who is here!" I hurried to the porch, and there he was, our naughty, but still loved Vaska, dirty and emaciated, sitting on the porch as usual, ready to accompany Grandma. She always treated him with a saucer of fresh morning milk. Unlike us children, Vaska liked the fresh milk from the cow.

The cat rubbed his head against Grandma's ankle as if he were asking for her forgiveness. Grandma lovingly patted him on the back, and he gleefully purred in response. "Watch out, Vaska!" she said. "Next time, Grandpa will take you so far, you won't be able to find your way back. So, behave yourself, *druzhok*, old buddy!" Grandma admonished Vaska without any trace of anger or irritation. Then she headed to the cow stall, and the cat followed her, most likely hoping to get his usual morning treat.

After that, Vaska tried to avoid encounters with Grandpa. Sitting on the high fence, squinting from the sun and thoroughly licking his paws, Vaska would wistfully watch the newly-hatched brood of baby chicks swarming around the yard and joyfully chirping with their mother-hen.

From force of habit, people called that section of the farmers' market "Meat and Fish Row," but the fish row didn't exist as such, because we had no rivers or lakes in our area, and, therefore, we had no fish at all. Before the war, fish was delivered from other places. According to Grandma, herring and sea products, for example, were brought in from Astrakhan, from the Caspian Sea, or from the Black Sea.

In some villages around our town, there were natural and man-made ponds. By their own initiative, the villagers bred river carp in those ponds. By the end of the summer, the carp was big enough to put it for sale. On the horse-driven wagons, in big wooden barrels filled with water, the villagers delivered the load of live carp to the farmers' market.

During the short fish season, all the people ate only fish. It was cheap and delicious. In our family, we were treated with a variety of fish dishes because Grandma liked fish herself and loved to cook it. We ate fish soup, *ukha*, fish stew, fried and boiled fish. My favorite were fish balls and fish hamburgers which we called "fish cutlets," *rybnye kotlety*. The recipe is simple: ground fish meat, chopped yellow onion, nicely chopped dill, an egg, and salt to taste. All the ingredients were thoroughly mixed. Then, cutlets of desirable size were made with the palms of both hands. Sunflower oil or pork fat was used for frying the cutlets.

Grandma even managed to bake a fish pie, which was quite a delicacy. When she baked it, all our neighbors, as if by accident, called on us. Grandma, blushing with pride and embarrassment, whole-heartedly treated them with a piece of her famous fish pie and a cup of tea.

However, nobody knew how to preserve carp so that it could be used for a longer period of time. We didn't have refrigerators back then; we had no commercial ice, either. We didn't know if it could be preserved by being salted or dried. Therefore, the fish feast was delightful but short, and we had to wait till the next year to enjoy Grandma's fish pie.

12. Schoolless, Shoeless, Toyless, Joyless and Photoless

*L*ike Louisa and Zhanna, I was a little girl whose childhood coincided with and was affected by the unexpected outbreak of war and subsequent deprivation caused by the German occupation. The three of us liked to play games, to enjoy toys, to listen to fairy-tales, and we believed in magic. We had few old toys. All the shops in our town, including the toy shop, were closed. Besides, we had no money to buy toys even if there were toys available. We didn't have children's books or games, either.

The absence of all the above pushed us out of the house into the backyard. From early spring till late fall, we stayed outside all day; we used the house only to sleep in. We ate outside, under the old apple tree. Its fruit was sour, but the shade from its branches was comforting. The wooden table stood next to the summer makeshift kitchen under the awning, with a two-ring stove made of fire-clay. Grandpa's responsibility was to stoke it with bricks of homemade pressed dry cow dung. It took time and effort to kindle the fire with the homemade "shit fuel," as Grandpa called it. He couldn't do it without losing his patience.

We all liked to eat outside. For breakfast, we had eggs cooked in the samovar, fresh cucumbers, tea for adults and milk for children, and yesterday's pancakes or bread. Grandma had unusual taste: she liked to eat fresh cucumbers smeared with honey. I didn't like it then, but I do now. The combination is refreshing and healthy. For lunch, we had *kasha*, oatmeal, boiled rice or buckwheat with cold milk.

For supper we had *borscht* (cabbage soup with red beetroots) or vegetable soups. Sometimes, soups were cooked with chicken or pork meat, or without any meat at all. Such meatless soups were seasoned with fresh dill, parsley, sunflower oil or pork fat, fried carrots and onions. During the season of field work, supper was the only hot meal we had.

For the second course, we liked dumplings. Ukrainian dumplings were cooked in boiling water, seasoned with butter, sour cream, cracklings or honey, depending on the stuffing. Every member of the family had his or her favorite stuffing. Grandpa preferred his made of mashed potatoes mixed with ground fried liver and fried yellow onions, seasoned with a generous portion of cracklings. My favorite stuffing was fresh sour cherries seasoned with granulated sugar and sour cream. Grandma prepared only one stuffing at a time. On Sundays and holiday dinners we had a choice of two stuffings.

Another popular second course dish was fritters, *blinchiki*, thin pancakes wrapped with different fillings. The most popular fillings were cottage cheese or cooked ground pork. The fritters were like oriental egg rolls, but square and flat in shape, fried in sunflower oil.

Our days were regulated by meals. We played, studied and did our chores before, between and after meals. Louisa and Zhanna liked to play with their shabbily dressed dolls. I tried to find a secluded corner to read. In summer, I preferred the barn hay loft. It was hot there, but at least I had some privacy, and I liked the smell of fresh hay.

From time to time, I joined my little sister and cousin in the yard, when they were skipping rope or throwing a rubber ball over the clothesline, as we had no volleyball net. Our jumping rope was homemade. Grandpa cut off a piece of a clothesline so that we could jump. He also brought several loads of sand in his wheelbarrow and made a sandbox for Louisa and Zhanna. The girls liked to spend their time there sharing toy buckets they had and the only sand scoop which belonged to Zhanna. That scoop became the bone of contention between them. The girls quarreled and cried because of that sand scoop. One day, Grandma had enough. She gave Louisa an old tin tablespoon, and peace was made. Now both girls could dig the sand together.

Zhanna, the youngest of us, had a tricycle which was too small for her. So, the girls transported their dolls on it. Once they even offered a tricycle ride to our cat Vaska. The cat didn't like it. Fighting vigorously, he extricated himself from the seat, and, in the heat of the battle, scratched Louisa's face and hands.

From the hay loft, I heard some commotion in the yard and hurried to the door. When I looked out, the skirmish was approaching its "grand finale." Mercilessly scratched, Louisa was screaming as if someone was cutting her in half with a saw. Desperately meowing, Vaska tried to get out off the tricycle seat, but Louisa, scared and disoriented, wouldn't let him go. Finally, Vaska managed to get out of her hands. In one split moment he leaped over the fence and was gone.

For a week, Louisa's face was covered with Zelenin's

green iodine. She wore her battle scratches proudly. To me, she looked more funny than miserable. Zhanna, teasingly called her Green Frog.

As a punishment, Grandma prohibited us from playing with animals, even with kittens. "They are animals; they don't understand children's games. Leave them alone, and play only with your toys!" Grandma eyes glittered with anger. "You should have watched them as they played, Nina," she admonished me. "They are still little children and don't understand a lot of things. You are the oldest. You should keep an eye on them when the adults are busy."

I didn't say anything, but I didn't like the idea of babysitting my sister and cousin, being stuck with them all the time. I wouldn't have time to read. I didn't object, because I didn't want to disappoint Grandma or to make her more angry. Besides, she made sense, and I felt guilty.

Bicycles were an object of envy among us children. Only few had them. One of our playmates, Rimma, had a bicycle, but she didn't allow anyone to ride it. Her mother prohibited her from sharing the bike with other children, regardless of who they were and where they lived. That bike made me envious for the first time in my life. I even saw it in my dreams. It was my second obsession after books.

I liked reading and studying, but because the school and its library were closed, we had no children's books to read. During the spring and summer, all the adults worked the fields. Mother could do the schooling for us only once a week, but sometimes none at all. So, I read a lot instead. After I read and reread my third grade reader, I started to borrow books and school readers from my friends and neighbors.

I read all the school readers both for the fourth and the fifth grades by the time I was eleven years old. In our home library — four shelves of the open bookstand in the living room — I discovered such treasures as Leo Tolstoy's *Anna Karenina* and the poems of Alexander Pushkin.

I managed to get popular children's fairy-tales such as *"The Three Little Pigs," "Ivan, the Little Fool,"* and *"The Fairy-Tale about the Fisherman and the Golden Fish."* I read them to Louisa and Zhanna with feelings, making faces and modulating my voice, depending on the role. I read every fairy-tale to the girls until they memorized them. After that, we acted out the tales. I always played the bad, grey wolf, because Louisa and Zhanna were scared, and neither of them wanted to be a wolf. Louisa wanted to be the grandmother, while Zhanna preferred the role of her loving granddaughter in a red-hooded bonnet.

In summer, I didn't read much. The weather was wonderful, it was hot and sunny, and the sky was cloudless. The flowerbeds were gorgeous and fragrant. We had the opportunity to run and to play outdoor children's games. We wore cotton sundresses and walked barefoot. We put on sandals only when we went to church on Sundays or on religious holidays.

Footwear stores didn't exist during the German occupation, and that was a real problem for us children. Our feet grew fast, "faster than their brains," as Grandpa put it. Our sandals, shoes and boots were burning out under our feet. The shoe stand at the farmers' market did repairs only. The shoemaker didn't have material to make new footwear.

When I outgrew my sandals or shoes, Mother took them to the shoe repair stand and then gave them to Louisa. Zhanna got Louisa's old repaired sandals and shoes.

I had to wear my mother's used footwear, but her foot was larger than mine. Otherwise, I wouldn't be able to step out of the door when I needed to go to the outhouse.

As we walked barefoot all summer and the streets were covered with locomotive slag, our feet and knees had cuts and scratches which sometimes got infected. As a result, the three of us often had abscesses on our feet and toes. Once I had an abscess that covered the whole sole of my foot. I couldn't walk for two weeks. The pain was unbearable, I couldn't even read. Grandma treated my abscess with her famous home remedies: putting a plantain on my foot after a hot bath. Nothing helped. Then Mother took me to her friend who was a nurse. She opened the abscess and dressed my suffering foot. During the procedure, I wept bitter tears, as the lancing was done without anesthesia.

Our barefoot season ended with the arrival of fall with its rainy, overcast sky, gusty winds and low temperatures. We had to stay inside, because we didn't have winter clothes and footwear. Under the circumstances, Grandma, Mother and Aunt Valentina tried to do whatever they could.

Grandma's strategic reserves, however, came to the rescue. She had lived through and survived World War I, the Civil War, the October Revolution, the post-revolution man-made starvation in 1921 and later in 1932 and 1933, the Communist party political purges, the mass forced collectivization of the farmers, the expropriation of the *kulaks* (rich farmers), the merciless industrialization of the country, and other ideological, economic and social "experiments" conducted by the Communist government which later would be described as "twists" and "leftist deviations" from Soviet policy.

Life and personal experience had taught Grandma to have an emergency reserve of supplies and goods—just in case. It became her rule to which she strictly adhered.

When in July of 1941, two daughters and three granddaughters arrived at Grandparents' place, it was stocked with food supplies and different goods. A big sack with salt and another with sugar, boxes of matches and candles, packs of tea and cocoa, and two boxes of toilet and laundry soap were sitting on the floor and on the shelves of the pantry. Rolls of fabric, mostly cotton, dozens of cotton and wool head shawls and cotton stockings for Grandma, as well as dozens of cotton shirts, pants and socks for Grandpa were packed in Grandma's trunk. It seemed as if those domestic reserves would last forever, but they were saved for two people, not for a family of seven. It became obvious that those reserves wouldn't last long. That's why Grandma established new rules and limitations. We children had to wash with soap our faces and hands, but not our feet. We also received one cube of sugar for our morning tea, while adults got a cube and a half.

From time to time, in winter, Grandma drank tea with dried apricots instead of sugar and encouraged us to do the same. We had to do our reading and writing in the daylight in order to save candles and lamp oil.

Grandma made the decision not to touch any of the new fabrics until she with her daughters examined and utilized all the used clothes that had been accumulated for years in the chest sitting in the corner of the second veranda and in the three old-fashioned suitcases hidden under Grandma's bed.

Every free moment, Mother, Valentina, Grandma and I were undoing, cleaning, brushing and ironing the used woolen clothes. Special attention was given to coats and jackets. We prepared them to be turned on the reverse side and, with the help of Grandma's old *Singer* sewing machine, to be transformed into new outfits: a winter coat for me from Grandpa's used long coat, and a cozy winter jacket for my mother from Grandma's used woolen winter coat. Altering used clothes occupied a lot of our winter time.

In addition, Mother, Aunt Valentina and I had to spend hours and hours after every laundry day darning everybody's socks and stockings, patching and mending our clothes, bed linens and towels. I didn't remember Mother doing such things before the war. Now I helped my mother with darning and mending.

I also learned to edge white cotton handkerchiefs in chain-stitch with a rosy thread and gave one as a birthday gift to Grandmother. I couldn't tell who was prouder — Grandma or me. She always had that handkerchief under the cuff of her long-sleeved white blouse when she went to church on Sundays.

It took me time and effort to undo used knitted pieces of clothing, to tie the torn ends, to rewind the used yarn into hanks. Later, in the skillful hands of my mother and Aunt Valentina, that yarn was transformed into new knitted sweaters, head scarves, socks, and mittens for all the members of our family.

In late fall, Mother resumed our home schooling. Every day, we spent several hours after breakfast reading aloud, writing dictations and exercises, solving math problems and memorizing poems from the school readers.

On one hand, I liked winter because Mother had more time to take care of our home schooling. On the other hand, I hated winter because we couldn't go outside and play in the yard or walk in the streets, as we had no winter footwear. We children were in a hopeless situation. Our growing bodies needed fresh air and physical activities.

Grandma came up with the idea to sew for us long, up to the knee, quilted boots, which we had to wear with rubber galoshes. Those boots with galoshes were heavy and didn't look very nice, but we didn't care, and were happy to have them. We suffocated in the house where the stove burned almost all the day to heat the premises and to cook the food for the family of seven.

I wish I had a photo of me in those boots with galoshes. However, not a single photograph was taken of any member of our family during the occupation. The photo shop, together with its photographer, disappeared from the face of the farmers' market. Not a single person among our relatives, friends, neighbors or acquaintances had a photo camera. Photo cameras, radios and gramophones were considered at that time luxury items in the Soviet Union. Very few people had them. Upon their arrival, the Germans had confiscated all radios and all photo cameras. The last photo of my mother, Louisa and me was taken on the first of May of 1941, in Tallinn, two months before the start of the war. The next time I was photographed was three years later, in June of 1944. It was a group photo of my sixth grade.

During the cold season, every chance we had we put on our homemade quilted boots with galoshes and went to play outside in the yard or to accompany adults to the farmers' market. We could wear these only when the weather was cold and the streets and dirt roads were deeply frozen. As soon as the thaw began in late February, it became impossible to use those boots because the galoshes got stuck in the deep, black mud. We children didn't have strength to pull them out of the mud without somebody's help. We had to stay inside till the streets and dirt roads dried out later in the spring.

When I wasn't busy doing household chores, I liked to join Louisa and Zhanna and cut out paper dresses for their paper dolls. We colored the dresses with the few colored pencils we had, folded them, and put them on our paper dolls. We truly enjoyed making those doll outfits. We had one pair of dull scissors that Grandma gave us, and we took turns using it.

We needed school supplies, especially paper and pencils, but we couldn't get them because all the stores were closed. We liked to write with a pen, but we had no ink. So, we fabricated ink from indelible pencils which were worth their weight in gold. We borrowed colored pencils from our friends and neighbors every chance we could.

We liked to play children's table games. We had two of them — dominos and lotto. We learned to play simple card games with such strange names as "*A Fool* " and "*A Witch.*" I don't remember the rules of those games. What I do remember is that while playing cards, we used multi-colored sheets of paper for chips.

Once, while reshuffling her shoe-box where she kept her documents and personal papers, Grandma discovered a pack of colorful money-like papers. I was nearby, helping her.

"What is this? Old Russian money?" I asked in disbelief.

"No, *glupyshka*, silly, these are *obligatsyi*, bonds," Grandma said. "They were issued by our government before the war. They cost us a lot of money! The government forced us to buy them. The payments were subtracted from our salaries and later from our pensions on a monthly basis. Now these bonds are worthless. You

79

can take and play with them if you like, Nina. Look how beautiful they are! The colors are so bright and fresh." The glossy government bank-notes, with their colorful pictures depicted the gigantic construction projects of the Soviet era. In contrast, every-day reality could be depicted in dark gray, deep brown and black colors, because the Germans not only occupied our country, they invaded our houses and deprived us of the little comfort and privacy we had.

I hurriedly grabbed the pack and rushed to show it to Louisa and Zhanna. On the spot, we divided the bonds equally among the three of us.

My war childhood years were the only period in my life when I played cards. I never had a chance to learn how to play serious card games in my adulthood. I never had time for that.

The occupation period wasn't only shoeless, toyless and joyless, it was photoless, as well, but it had left an indelible imprint in my memories.

13. Uninvited House Guests

*T*he word "invasion" was not just a figure of speech, it was a harsh, sobering reality. As soon as the front line moved forward in the eastern direction, a lot of supporting German troops arrived at our town. They were railroad specialists who had to work at the railroad terminal and at the locomotive depot. They supervised the maintenance work provided by the locals. A considerable number of German medical personnel for the newly organized military hospital arrived, as well. The military hospital occupied the premises of the former civilian hospital which was evacuated with all its equipment and personnel before the arrival of the Germans.

As no military barracks or other premises were available for quartering the arriving troops, the German authorities decided to billet supporting military personnel in private houses, located within walking distance from the railroad terminal and the locomotive depot. Our house wasn't exempt from billeting as it was seven blocks away from both strategic places.

One summer afternoon, a group of German military accompanied by the divisional inspector of the local police and his assistant appeared uninvited at the yard gate of our house. They checked all the rooms, walked behind the barn and asked how many people lived in the house. The inspector's assistant served as an interpreter.

The Germans conferred among themselves. Then the inspector told Grandma that a German doctor would be quartered in our living room. He ordered Grandma to put clean bedding on his bed. He also told Grandma to warn the children not to make noise when the doctor was at home resting in his room. Later that afternoon, the doctor's orderly brought his suitcase and his backpack and put them in the living room. Grandma instructed us children not to enter the living room at any time and not to touch the doctor's things.

We seldom saw the doctor. He always left very early and returned from the hospital very late when we children were already asleep. Sometimes, he didn't return until the next morning. In such cases, Grandma told us to stay outside and be quiet.

That doctor didn't socialize with us; he didn't speak Russian, and none of us spoke German. Grandma had studied French and German half a century earlier at the grammar school. She remembered several words and phrases such as *Danke,* (Thank You), *Bitte,* (Please), *Guten Morgen,* (Good Morning), *Guten Abend* (Good Evening), and some others.

Often, during his lunch break, the doctor brought a young nurse to his room. Once, I was in the living room mopping the painted floor with a cloth and a small bucket of water when they entered the room. I crawled on my knees under the table covered with a big tablecloth which reached almost to the floor, so they didn't see me.

I heard some commotion in the room, but I couldn't see anything. When I crawled out from under the table,

I saw the doctor and a young German woman in a cute military nurse uniform, embracing and kissing. They were surprised to see me, but looked at me as if I were an insect. Then they laughed joyfully and started to kiss again. I was scared to death. I grabbed my bucket with a cloth in it and hurried from the living room as if the devil were chasing me.

I was frightened and told everything to Grandma. As usual, she tried to calm me. "Don't worry, *detka*, child! They probably have forgotten that silly episode already. They have a very short lunch break, and time flies quickly!"

Being nine and a half years old, I didn't understand the connection between the short lunch break and fast flying time. I was surprised and shocked. I thought that during a war soldiers had to shoot and kill, not hug and kiss. I didn't dare ask Grandma about that. Since then, she was always on guard when I had to mop the living room floor.

During the doctor's stay in our house, Grandpa was attacked and bitten severely by our neighbor's unfriendly dog. The dog grabbed him by the calf and bit several times before Grandpa managed to get away from the infuriated animal. When Grandpa, pale and nervous, got home with his trouser-leg torn to shreds, his leg bitten and bleeding, Grandma cleaned his wound, treated it with iodine, dressed it and told him to stay in bed.

Several days later, Grandpa's medical condition worsened; his temperature increased, his bitten leg turned blue and became swollen. The pain was unbearable, and he suffered a lot. We all got scared and didn't know what to do. The former civilian hospital was now occupied by the military one. Several civilian retired doctors who hadn't managed to evacuate on time were in hiding or on the run from the authorities because the Germans could force them to work in the military hospitals either in Ukraine or in Germany.

The situation was critical as Grandpa's life was hanging by a thread. It pushed Grandma to the edge. In despair, she pulled together the fragments of the little German she remembered and, with tears in her eyes and repeating *Bitte, Bitte* (Please, Please) after every Russian word, she led the doctor into the bedroom where Grandpa was lying, almost unconscious, on his single sofa.

The doctor looked at him, nodded his head, and left without saying a word. We didn't know what to think nor how to interpret his behavior. Grandma started to sob softly, drying her eyes with a corner of her kitchen apron; we children cried as well. Mother and Aunt Valentina tried to calm us.

In an hour or so, the doctor returned, accompanied by another, older doctor, who wore gold-rimmed glasses. He examined Grandpa's leg, shook his head disapprovingly while repeating *Sehr Mal! Sehr Mal!* (Very bad!) Then he put some ointment on the wound and put fresh dressing on it. He gave Grandma unusually looking dark orange tablets which were called "red streptocide," the latest innovation in war era pharmacology, and repeated *Sehr Gut, Sehr Gut!* (Very good!)." Grandpa had to take one pill every four hours.

When the doctor was leaving, Grandma gave him as a token of our appreciation, a piece of salted pork fat, about a pound, and ten fresh eggs, all neatly wrapped in a clean linen kitchen towel. We had no packaging materials back then, and we had no other means of paying for the doctor's services.

The doctor took Grandma's gift with a mild smile and a look of embarrassment and said *Danke!* (Thank you!).He visited Grandpa several times, bringing more dark orange tablets and the linen kitchen towel in which Grandma regularly wrapped another piece of pork fat and ten eggs.

The red streptocide pills did wonders for Grandpa. His urine turned dark orange, but he felt better. He was on the road to recovery. His temperature normalized, he started to eat food, and the swelling in his leg disappeared. His wound healed nicely. In two weeks or so, he started to walk around the house and resumed his regular household activities.

Soon after Grandpa's recovery, the doctor who was quartered in our living room was sent to the front line — *Nach Front* — as he told us. He had stayed at our house about two months. We never saw him again; we didn't even know his name.

The red streptocide, the dark orange magic pills which had saved Grandfather's life, turned out to be a double duty product. I remember that immediately after the war women used those pills to dye their hair, and the red colored hair looked gorgeous!

14. August and Otto

After the departure of the German doctor, nobody was
stationed in our house for some time. Mother and
Luisa returned to the living room where they both slept
in Mother's double bed. I slept with Grandma in her wide
and comfortable bed. Grandpa occupied a single sofa
in the same bedroom where Grandma and I slept. Aunt
Valentina and her daughter Zhanna slept in the double
bed in Valentina's bedroom. For a while, we all enjoyed
the privacy and comfort of our house. However, our
enjoyment didn't last long.

By the end of Spring, two German military railroad
specialists were quartered in our house. They occupied
Grandma's bedroom which had one bed and one single
sofa. I moved to the living room and slept on the big
trunk. Grandma used the sofa in Valentina's kitchen. That
sofa was ages old and uncomfortable, but Grandma didn't
complain and stoically slept there for four months. Poor
Grandpa had to sleep in the hay loft of the barn.

The German railroad specialists were of low military
rank. It was difficult for me to identify their exact ages.
One of them, whose name was August, was middle-aged
and unfriendly. In the morning, he always said *Guten*

Morgen (Good Morning). When he returned from work he said *Guten Abend* (Good Evening). That was it. He never smiled and spoke very little, even to his roommate, Otto.

Otto was younger and taller than August. He was blond, smiled a lot, and tried to be as sociable as almost a zero possession of Russian vocabulary allowed him to be. He addressed us by name. He liked Grandma's name and called her *Frau Anastasia*, making her blush.

Both Germans worked at the locomotive depot, supervising local workers who did the hard and dirty work of cleaning the furnaces and ash-pits of the locomotives, loading coal and refueling the locomotives with it. The local workers repaired locomotives, freight wagons, tank cars, flat wagons, and replaced the damaged rails and ties. It was hard, physically exhausting work.

By railroad, the Germans transported to the front line their heavy military equipment, weaponry, ammunition and personnel. At that time, the German Air Force didn't have large transport aircraft. So the Germans could move their army and its machinery only by railroad or by highways. As to the latter, those were scarce and in deplorable condition.

Both August and Otto got up very early and went to the locomotive depot. Before leaving, they washed up in the yard washstand. Grandpa always kept it full of fresh water. The Germans did their morning exercises in the yard. They had breakfast, lunch and supper in the soldiers' mess-hall at the railroad station terminal.

They returned from work in the evening bringing a square loaf of rye or white bread and several cans of sausage each. Sometimes, they gave Grandma half a loaf or even the whole loaf of bread, but they never gave us a single can of sausages.

In return, Grandma treated them with freshly fried salted sunflower seeds or with a mug of fresh cold milk each. They always said *Dankeschön* (Thank You Very Much), and with great pleasure drank milk and nibbled sunflower seeds. From time to time, they gave us children caramel candies, and we said *Danke*. Those German caramels reminded me of candies made of saccharine which I had tasted in Lithuania when we lived there before WWII started.

The behavior of both Germans shocked me. First, both August and Otto brushed their teeth with soap, not with tooth powder as we all did. Second, with undue familiarity, they farted publicly, without blushing or even saying "Sorry!"

Mother and Grandma always taught us and often reminded us to leave the room and go outside or to another room if we felt the need to pass gas. If the accident happened, we had to say "Sorry."

So, when for the first time, I heard Otto farting loudly while washing up at the kitchen washstand, I was stunned; I couldn't believe it. I rushed to Grandma and whispered in awe, "*Babushka, Babushka*! Grandma, Grandma! Otto *puknul* (farted)!"

She hushed me up and said quietly, in a delicate yet serious tone, "Just pretend that you didn't notice it! Maybe he has an upset stomach."

August and Otto, stayed in our house about four months. As the front line moved forward to the east, all the supporting services also moved to the east. However, after the crushing defeat that the German troops had suffered at Stalingrad in 1943, they started to retreat.

We had no information about the situation at the front. We didn't know that the German army under the command of General Paulus was defeated and surrendered at

Stalingrad. The first signs that something was wrong in the front for Germans were the endless rows of military echelons with wounded German soldiers passing through our station day and night. They made short stops to take coal and water and hurried to the west, to the border with Poland.

Then, one warm autumn afternoon, Otto, the German railroad worker, after being gone for six months at the front, opened the gate and entered our yard. We all were surprised. He appeared embarrassed, smiled awkwardly, and his eyes looked sad. For a long time, he relaxed on the bench under the apple tree, and Grandma treated him with a glass of cold milk and a piece of freshly baked apple pie which she managed to bake without sugar.

Otto was the first person who mentioned the word "Stalingrad" together with the word *Kaputt!* (The End!). Grandma asked him about August. He told her that August was at the station but couldn't come. As Otto was leaving, he stopped at the gate, waved and said *Aufwiedersehen!* (See you later!). We also said *Aufwiedersehen!* We all knew, however, that it was not *Aufwiedersehen!* It was Farewell!

15. The Military Art of Marauding

*T*he retreat of the German army in fall of 1943 was not as fast as its offensive at the beginning of the war, in the summer of 1941. The Germans moved back, conducting fierce battles and suffering huge losses both in personnel and weaponry. They did it under the constant barrage of the Russian bombers and newly invented *"Katyusha"* rockets.

Russian military aircraft waged night air-raids against our railroad station. Grandpa explained to us that both the Germans and the Russians wanted to save the railroad terminal and the locomotive depot. The Germans needed them for retreat and the Russians for offense. Consequently, they avoided hitting those strategic locations. They bombed adjacent areas instead, spreading fear and creating panic among the civilian population.

"What will they do without the railroad? How will they move their troops and machinery?" Grandpa asked rhetorically. From the military point of view, according to Grandpa, our house was in danger because it was close to the railroad terminal and the locomotive depot.

As soon as the air-raid warning sounded, we tried to find a place to hide. It was late autumn, and our cool cellar, *pogreb*, in the barn was full of fresh, salted and marinated vegetables in barrels—our winter reserve. We couldn't hide there; nor was there a bomb shelter in our town, either. We understood that it was useless and silly to crawl under the beds, but we did it all the same. Grandpa was the only one who didn't move from his sofa. He covered his head with a pillow in order to muffle the air-raid's shrill siren, and slept.

In addition to the artillery shelling and bombing, alarming rumors spread like forest fire that German soldiers were on the prowl, conducting raids and searches of private homes in order to take away all the men, regardless of their ages. We were scared and stayed inside, quiet as mice. Grandma told Grandpa to stay in the hay loft, no matter what. Grandpa was so frightened that he didn't poke his nose out of his hiding place.

One unlucky day, when two low-ranking German soldiers with their automatic weapons across the shoulders entered the house, Grandpa was in the kitchen. He had gotten cold in the hay loft and had come down to drink some hot carrot tea.

One of the soldiers, without wasting a moment, concentrated his attention on Grandpa, who hurriedly put on his glasses, extracted his medical disability certificate, written in Russian and handed it to the soldier. With trembling lips and shaking hands, Grandpa tried to explain to him, in Russian, that he had been disabled at work. The soldier listened, understanding nothing. Grandma said, with tears in her voice, "Invalid, invalid, he is an invalid."

Meanwhile, the other soldier was trying to push his way through the narrow folding door of the living room. His automatic weapon, hanging across his shoulder, caused him to get stuck in the narrow door. He struggled for a moment, then lurched back, freed his weapon and said several phrases to his partner who was examining Grandpa's papers. The soldier returned the papers to Grandpa, and both soldiers made off in an unusual hurry, without saying a word.

We all breathed a sigh of relief — Grandpa was saved! Grandpa told us that he was surprised that the soldiers were not accompanied by an officer like they always were. Grandma was shocked that the soldiers didn't check the living room.

Everything became clear later in the evening, when Mother, as usual, wanted to wind up her gilded wrist watch and couldn't find it. She always kept it together with her gold wedding ring in the bowl of the samovar, on the night stand, next to the living room door.

When the German soldier pretended to get stuck in the door, he, in a split second, scouted the living room and discovered his award — Mother's gilded watch and her golden wedding ring under his nose. Just stretch your hand, grab it and hide it in your pocket.

No doubt, it wasn't the first time the soldiers played out that scenario. They did it quickly and skillfully. We didn't even have time to come to our senses before they were long gone.

The night when the looting occurred, Grandma, already in bed, told me that before the October revolution, being a young woman with two small daughters, she had quite a bit of gold jewelry: several gold rings and earrings, a gold cross with a gold chain, and two silver brooches with semi-precious stones — one with a garnet, another with an aquamarine. Grandpa had a gold wedding ring, a gold cross on a golden chain, a silver cigarette case, and a silver pocket watch. Their little daughters, Valentina and my mother, Raisa, both had gold crosses with gold chains and a silver teaspoon.

During the October revolution and the post-revolutionary years of man-made hunger of the 1920s and 1930s, the family had to swap all its jewelry, piece by piece, for bread, flour, sugar and other groceries in order to survive. Grandma told me that she had sobbed while she was exchanging her favorite golden earrings with Persian turquoise for a sack of wheat flour. Those earrings had been a gift from her parents on her sweet-sixteenth birthday. Grandma never had the chance to acquire golden jewelry again. Since then, she wore on her neck a silver cross on a ribbon.

Several days later, our neighbors told Grandma that the same couple of German soldiers had robbed them, too. The Germans caught them off guard. In a hurry, the looters unceremoniously took off the gold wedding ring from the neighbor's finger, made her daughter take off the silver cross with the chain from her neck, and effortlessly pulled out by the hanging chain the silver pocket watch from the side pocket of her father's pants. That watch was the object of pride for the eighty-year-old man who couldn't understand anything and was shaking like a leaf in the presence of the German soldiers.

The farewell looting was the good-bye salute of the retreating German troops. Before they attacked the Soviet Union on June 22 in 1941, the German troops had marched triumphantly across Western and Eastern Europe. In 1943, they suffered a crushing defeat on the bank of the Russian Volga River, at Stalingrad. In 1956 the city was renamed Volgograd.

16. Misbehavior is Contagious

*I*n the winter of 1944, during the interval of two or three days between the retreat of the Germans and the arrival of the advancing Soviet troops, a period of anarchy and chaos flourished. The Germans has already left, but the Russian troops hadn't arrived yet, as the crucial battle had taken place twenty miles away from our town. We heard and watched the battle from a distance.

That was a scary and unpredictable span of time. Days and nights, the newly invented Russian rocket launchers called *Katyusha* thrust their lethal charges upon the German positions and their retreating troops. It was more frightening at night when the multiple lines of rockets cut the dark sky, followed by frightening explosions.

Nobody knew why the Germans didn't blow up the warehouses alongside the railroad station. According to rumors, they had planned to do it before their retreat. Maybe they didn't have enough time as the Soviet troops were close on their heels. Grandpa stated they didn't do it because of the warehouses' proximity to the railroad itself.

Germans feared that the blasts could damage the tracks and cut off their hasty retreat.

We lived in a state of complete ignorance — without a radio and without newspapers. Nobody knew where the front line was, or in which direction the Russian troops advanced. News spread that Germans had already left without blowing up the warehouses. The unexpected calm followed that news. Not a single artillery salvo was heard. Inspired by the puzzling silence, people crawled out from their shelters, rushed to the warehouses, and indulged themselves in the old-fashioned craft of looting.

Grandma, finally, allowed us to play in the yard. Curiosity pushed us to the street, where we met a couple of our friends. They carried sacks and bags and headed to the German warehouses. They told us in strict secrecy that they had decided to check the warehouse for office supplies. Somebody had told them that in that building were stored supplies which we all needed for school.

Without hesitation, Louisa and I joined them. We did it without asking Grandma's permission because we knew that she wouldn't allow us to do that. The temptation was stronger than common sense or even fear. Our life under the German occupation had become so monotonous and boring that even stealing looked like a fascinating adventure.

When we reached the warehouse, we saw several teenagers, all equipped with sacks and empty wooden boxes. They were filling up their containers with small cardboard packages of regular, colored and, oh my God, our favorite indelible pencils which we needed to make ink.

We hadn't seen new pencils or notebooks since the start of the war. Louisa and I were mesmerized just looking at those treasures, sitting orderly on the shelves, neatly packed in cardboard boxes of different sizes and colors. The boxes seemed to be smiling back at us. Having feasted our eyes on the shelves, we selected several small boxes with colored and indelible pencils and two packs of notebooks each. That was all we could carry in our hands. Happy and overwhelmed with excitement, we rushed home to get some sacks and return to replenish our non-existing inventory of school supplies. We badly needed more notebooks.

"As soon as the Russian Army is here, the schools will be reopened," said one of the fellow looters, a tall, pimpled-faced boy about fifteen years old, who walked next to me carrying a heavy sack of stolen goods across his shoulder.

"Oh, *Bozhe*, God, schools will be reopened." That thought warmed my heart. For three and a half years, I hadn't been at school. I realized that soon there would be some changes in our lives, and I felt happy. We had enough pencils to make fresh ink, but we needed more notebooks. "More notebooks, more notebooks," I repeated like a parrot.

However, our plans were not destined to come to pass. From afar, I saw Grandma at the gate turning her head to all sides like a weather-vane as if she were trying to spot us. My heart skipped a beat. We had been absent for a long time and we had left the yard without permission. I slowed down and said to Louisa, "Look, Grandma is waiting for us. *Derzhis, sestrichka!* Hold on, little sister."

When Louisa saw Grandma, she rushed towards her, beaming with joy and screamed, "*Babushka, Babushka!* Grandma, Grandma! Look what we have: new pencils, colored, indelible, and new notebooks. We can bring more, but we need sacks and bags."

Grandma, pale as a ghost, let us into the yard, then stopped, turned to me and asked sternly, "Where have you been? Whom did you ask permission to leave? We were worried sick about you! Grandpa and your mother are still looking for you in the neighborhood. Now I have to worry about them too? They asked all your friends and playmates. Nobody saw you, nobody knew anything." Grandma didn't smile and looked dead serious. It scared me, and I was completely taken aback. Louisa, who didn't understand the seriousness of the situation, answered Grandma's questions.

"We went with our friends. They knew the building where we could get new pencils and notebooks. We didn't have sacks like the other children. We came back to get sacks. We want to go there again. We need more notebooks for school," Louisa jabbered, without pausing.

I was surprised that my little mischievous sister managed to pronounce so many phrases at once. She always spoke, using simple, short sentences. The shock of seeing so many new objects had loosened her tongue, and she was prattling nonstop.

"*Babushka*, Grandma, listen please," I interjected. One boy told us that as soon as the Russian Army is here school will be reopened. That's why we need more notebooks and pencils."

"Maybe it's true, but the Russians are not here yet, and this lull in the fighting is temporary," Grandma said. "Both Russians and Germans can start to bomb and to shoot at any moment. Do you understand that?" She almost screamed in rage. "You could have been killed. Then you would not have needed new notebooks and pencils, *glupyshki*, silly you! Your mother was crying, and

Grandpa was angry as hell! So, give me your loot and don't tell anybody about your foolish deed. Now, go wash your hands! We'll talk about this later when Grandpa and your mother return home."

Grandma hid all our stolen treasures in the small attic of our veranda. Then she said, "What you did is very bad. You have stolen those things. They don't belong to you. It is a shame for all our family." I felt guilty because I knew Grandmother's motto by heart: "It's better to be poor but honest."

I objected timidly, "We didn't steal, Grandma, we just took them like everybody else. Those things are nobody's. We need notebooks, pencils and metallic pens to write."

Grandma interrupted me with metal in her voice, "Don't worry about school supplies, Nina. If, with God's help, school is reopened, it will provide everything for all of you. Like they say, 'God will give us the day; God will give us food.'" As a rule, I believed in Grandma's wisdom, and I trusted her gift of foreseeing. She trusted me, and I betrayed her. I had left the yard without asking permission and had set a bad example for Louisa.

As soon as Grandpa and our mother returned from their searching expedition, everything began again. Mother cried with joy and repeated all the time, "You could have been killed! You could have been crippled! The war is not finished and the front line is approaching, even as we speak. A stray bullet, a shell or a bomb could kill anybody. Anywhere! Anytime! It's a miracle that you have returned safe and sound." As if in confirmation, we heard several distant bomb explosions and the increasing din of the *Katyusha* rockets.

Grandpa looked tired. He was angry and insisted in disciplining us the old fashioned way — with the belt. Grandma, as usual, took us under her protective wing.

Thank God, she was a compassionate woman and always was against corporal punishment, which, according to her opinion, cripples the soul.

As a punishment, we had to stay inside for a week. So, going back to the warehouse to pick up more school supplies was out of the question. The only house we were allowed to visit was our old wooden outhouse behind the barn.

Mother was right. The explosions occurred more often as the battle-line approached our town. The Russian Army advanced under the cover of the avalanche of *Katyusha* rockets. The Germans fought fiercely, covering the retreat of their troops.

The majority of the people didn't dare leave their houses and stayed inside, not that staying inside presented less danger. However, the terrifying noise of approaching hell of the front line didn't stop some desperate but daring people from going on looting expeditions, even under the artillery bombardment.

Through the living room windows facing the street, we watched the people hurrying in the direction of the warehouses. Everybody carried sacks, buckets, carts, even wheelbarrows. Some rode bicycles with small homemade trailers.

Everybody knew that the German warehouses for food supplies were located on the other side of the railroad station. Nobody knew, however, if the Germans had mined them. In order to reach the warehouses, people had to cross more than twenty railroad lines which could be mined, as well. Several hours later, we saw the same people returning from their looting expedition with sacks of flour and sugar on their shoulders, on their carts, on wheelbarrows and on bicycle trailers.

In the evening, during supper, one of our neighbors, a sixteen-year-old girl, knocked at our door. She was crying bitter tears and asked Grandma for any medical supplies. Sobbing uncontrollably, the girl told us that her mother and she had gone to the food warehouse and got two sacks of granulated sugar. They put them on the wheelbarrow and started on their way home. Suddenly, an artillery shell exploded near them. The girl was thrown and deafened by the explosion, but she was alive, with cuts and bruises only, while her mother was not as lucky. The fragment of the shell hit her leg and cut it off below the knee.

With the help of other looters, the daughter unloaded the sacks with sugar from the wheelbarrow, put her mother in it, and brought her home, more dead than alive. The girl was crying and begging for any medical supplies.

Grandma, with shaking hands, tried to cut two clean white bed sheets for bandages. With tears in her eyes, Mother helped Grandma. Grandpa took from his hiding place a half of a liter bottle of *samogon* for disinfection.

The three of them hurried to the neighbors' house. Grandpa carried a teapot of boiled water; Mother had the bottle of vodka in her hands, and the girl carried a big roll of cut clean white bed-sheet bandages with both hands pressed to her chest. That was all we could offer to our neighbors.

When Grandpa and Mother came back, they told us that our wounded neighbor was bleeding profusely. "She is white as a sheet. She lost a lot of blood; we didn't manage to stop the bleeding. She won't survive the night without a doctor's help and medications," Grandpa said, shaking his head.

"Don't prophesize ill, Ivan Danilovich," Grandma said, her eyes swimming in tears. "She is young and strong; she might survive, God willing."

Everybody knew that there were no hospitals, no doctors, no nurses, no medications, nothing at all. So, there was little hope for our suffering neighbor. We all felt helpless and prayed, crying quietly.

Grandpa's prediction came true: by morning, our neighbor had died leaving behind her husband, two teen-aged children, and her old parents. Her name was Ann, and she was forty years old. Ann was the only one whom we knew personally.

As we found out later, there were a few more deaths and severe injuries due to the artillery shelling that day. Grandma and Mother were right. Our looting spree which we undertook without permission and enjoyed so much was a risky endeavor. It could have cost us our lives. Only by a miracle, we returned home safe and sound.

17. The Perpetual Cycle

*T*he winter of 1943–1944 was saturated with different events. First, the Germans started to retreat along the all front lines, from the south to the north. Second, the Soviet Army freed our town — *Ura! Ura! Ura!* Thrice repeated Hurray! The Soviet soldiers and officers paraded the streets showing off their new uniforms with the shoulder straps instead of tabs like our father had on his collar before the war.

In order to rekindle the patriotic spirit of our suffering nation which had been undermined by the mass extermination of *kulaky* — the rich peasants — by Stalin's repressions of 1937, and by extermination of the high-ranking military leaders which the Red Army inherited from the Tsar's Army, the Kremlin decided to reintroduce the uniform and insignias of the old Tsar's army. According to the new army regulations, the senior officers had special messengers at their disposal to run both their official and personal errands.

We were full of hope and impatiently waited for any news from our father. For me, that winter was not only a period full of joy and expectations, but a time of revelation, as well. The unexpected, tragic loss of our neighbor, Ann, was my first close encounter with the death of a familiar person during the war. I was shocked and dispirited.

We heard the fighters flying over our heads. The bombers dropped bomb days and night. We heard the artillery shelling and their explosions, sometimes very close. I understood that soldiers and officers, both Russians and Germans, were wounded and were dying in the battles, but I didn't see them die.

For the past three and a half years, since the start of the war, we hadn't been to the movies, we hadn't watched the war news chronicles, and we hadn't read the news reports from the fronts in the Soviet newspapers. So we didn't see soldiers fighting, wounded and dying in the battlefields. We hadn't listened to the radio either, as the Germans, immediately after the occupation of our town, had confiscated all the vacuum-tube radios.

When the war started in June of 1941, Aunt Valentina with her daughter Zhanna moved into Grandparents' place and brought, among other things, a brand new vacuum-tube radio. At that time, it was a novelty, and everybody tried to acquire one. Her husband, my uncle Mitya, was a passionate amateur radio operator. As Aunt Valentina told us, he had bought that radio and the gramophone at the eve of the war. He was very proud of those purchases but didn't have time to enjoy them. Like many others, he had been drafted during the first weeks after the declaration of the war.

The German authorities immediately ordered the confiscation of all types of radios. People had to bring their radios to the collection points and hand them to the Germans. Failure to comply meant death. We found out much later that the latter phrase wasn't just a figure of speech, but a harsh reality.

Grandpa made his own decision as to Valentina's radio. He carefully unscrewed all the tubes from the radio and dismantled all the metallic parts. Later, in the night, he drowned all the radio parts in our outhouse. Then, with a small ax, he chopped the empty wooden radio box and used those chips to kindle the samovar. Grandpa never commented on nor explained his destructive impulse. Nobody asked him for an explanation, either. Grandpa didn't allow the Germans to use that radio.

To balance my face-to-face encounter with the death of our neighbor, I learned that we would soon be getting a new baby in the family: my new cousin, Aunt Valentina's child.

When the Soviet army freed our town, Valentina lived with her husband and nine-year old Zhanna in a large industrial city, Krivoy Rog, ten kilometers (about 6.5 miles) from Grandma's place, and she was pregnant with her second child. When the Germans retreated, they forced Uncle Mitya and many other workers to accompany their heavy equipment which they transported to Germany by railroad. Nine months' pregnant Aunt Valentina was left alone, with little Zhanna, without a hospital, doctors, without a telephone, and without any social and financial support.

Grandma decided to help her daughter in her time of need, and she took me to assist her. Valentina's apartment consisted of a tiny bedroom, a living room and a small kitchen. It had no indoor plumbing, no hot water, no heating system, no amenities at all. The wooden outhouse was in the backyard. The winter was brutally cold. It was the end of January of 1944. I was twelve years old.

When we arrived by foot at Valentina's place, she and Zhanna were squeezed into their tiny bedroom and the kitchen. The living room was occupied by Soviet soldiers who, without taking off their boots and overcoats, slept side by side in a row on the floor without pillows, blankets or mattresses. They used their winter soldier hats or their knapsacks in place of pillows.

Aunt Valentina gave herself up to despair. She cried all the time. She was worried sick about her husband; she didn't know if he was dead or alive. Grandma, energetic and active as usual, took charge. She calmed Valentina. She sent me to the barn to bring some coal; she heated the stove and cooked a hearty vegetable soup. Then we all had lunch. We had brought some bread and marinated vegetables from Grandma's house. For dessert, we all drank carrot tea with dried apricots.

After lunch, Grandma ordered Valentina and Zhanna to take a nap in their small bedroom. Valentina obeyed. Doing the dishes in the kitchen, I heard Valentina reading a book to her daughter. At least, she wasn't crying.

Grandma took care of the Soviet soldiers housed in the apartment. She took pity on them and decided to do something to make their stay in Valentina's living room more comfortable, as there were no barracks to quarter the soldiers in our town. She went on a mission visiting our neighbors, asking them for extra pillows, pillowcases, and old blankets. Almost every household hosted soldiers; therefore, our neighbors couldn't offer much.

Grandma managed to collect several items and brought them to Valentina's apartment with the help of two teen-aged boys. They helped us fill the donated empty pillowcases with dried straw and dried corn husks, also donated. Grandma offered those pillows to the soldiers, and they accepted them with gratitude She also got from the neighbors several homemade matting floor coverings and homemade rugs which she put on the living room floor instead of mattresses; the floor was chilly as the winter months of that year were unusually cold. The heat from the kitchen stove hardly reached the living room.

Grandma asked me to make a list of the donated items, so that we could return everything to the owners as soon as the soldiers left. She asked the soldiers to bring several buckets of water from the well and put them in our kitchen where the temperature was warmer. By morning, the water had become lukewarm. It was too cold to wash up in the veranda in the middle of February.

Grandma invited the soldiers, one by one, to wash up, to brush their teeth, and to shave in the kitchen, using our washstand. She also heated a tea kettle of hot water for shaving. Some of the soldiers had no toothbrushes. Grandma offered them tooth powder and some used toothbrushes which she found in the kitchen table drawer. She also gave them several clean towels to dry with, as their own towels were filthy.

We didn't have much food, even for ourselves, but Grandma treated the soldiers with our local delicacy — fried salted sunflower and pumpkin seeds. The soldiers accepted the treat gratefully. In the evening, sitting or reclining on the floor in our living room, they nibbled sunflower and pumpkin seeds and watched Russian movies and war chronicle news, using the small narrow-film movie projector which rattled like a machine gun. From time to time, the projectionist had to stop the camera in order to change the reels.

It was the first time since the war started that I watched a Russian movie, but I was so nervous and excited about Valentina's forthcoming childbirth that I only remember a few scenes depicting wounded soldiers and brave caring nurses dressing their wounds at the height of the severe, bloody battle. In that movie, however, for the first time, I saw the famous *Katyusha* rockets in action. Before, I had only heard them discharging their lethal load from a distance. The picture fitted the sound. Not without reason, during WWII, the artillery was called "The Goddess of the War."

Unexpectedly, one of Valentina's neighbors brought a big bowl of homemade pickles. Handing it to Grandma, she said, "This is for your soldiers. Most likely, they haven't eaten homemade pickles for a long time. Let them feast on mine. They are especially good this year — zesty and crunchy." Grandma thanked her and decided to treat the soldiers with potatoes boiled in their skins.

The soldiers were pleasantly surprised when Grandma asked one of them to carry into the living room a big, heavy pot of steamy potatoes, generously seasoned with fresh chopped dill. They ate potatoes and pickles with delight, and, to my great amazement, they didn't even peel the potato skins.

The soldiers told us that the field kitchen where they got their meals three times a day cooked mostly different types of *kasha*, such as oatmeal, buckwheat, millet, and rarely macaroni or rice. They were happy to have pickles with freshly cooked potatoes which they dipped into the saucer of fresh sunflower oil. One of the soldiers confessed to Grandma that he hadn't eaten such tasty potatoes since he had been drafted at the start of the war. He kissed Grandma on the cheek. She kissed him back on the forehead, saying, "May the Lord help you, Sonny!" I had noticed the tears brimming in the corners of her eyes.

Then, the time came for Valentina to give birth to her child. In the morning, she was well and in good spirits. After lunch time, Grandma noticed that Valentina was pale and looked exhausted. Grandma asked her, "Are you all right, Valya?"

"No, Mother, I am not. I feel a sharp pain in my lower back."

"Go to the bedroom and lie down; you need rest," Grandma ordered her. Then she whispered into my ear, "It has started! We have to be ready, Nina! Don't get scared, *detka*, child. There is nothing to be scared of, believe me. Just help me a little bit, and after that you and Zhanna will spend the night in our neighbor's house. She offered to shelter both of you." As always, Grandma tried to calm me. She saw the fear in my eyes. I must have looked like a scared, hunted rabbit. I was really terrified.

Grandma started to boil water and to save it in all available containers. She prepared two piles of clean bed linens and towels, and asked me to iron them. Several hours later, when the ironing was finished I mopped the painted floors in the bedroom, in the kitchen and in the small hallway leading from the veranda to the apartment. At the end, I dusted everything with a moist cloth.

Valentina stayed in bed. Her moaning and groaning became louder, but she tried to restrain herself from screaming. Grandma asked me to sit for a while at her bedside and to wipe away the perspiration from Valentina's forehead. She also instructed me not to allow Valentina to drink too much water.

I was in an unusual and enigmatic situation. I hadn't the slightest idea about the process of childbirth. I was scared. I didn't dare ask Grandma. She was very busy with preparations, and she was a nervous wreck. I didn't want to distract and annoy her with my silly questions.

In the hustle and bustle of the preparations for the birth of the child, we both forgot about little Zhanna. She was quiet and looked scared, too. In her own way, she tried not to bother anybody. She hid herself in the dark corner behind the kitchen table and sat there, without making a sound. Only once she asked Grandma in a weeping voice, "Why is my mother crying and moaning? Is she sick? Is she going to die?"

"No, no," Grandma answered hurriedly. "Your mother's groaning is temporary. She will be fine very soon, and, *detka*, honey, you are going to have a little brother or a sister. Don't you worry, Zhannochka, just think about a name for your little sibling, any name you want," Grandma said joyfully, but I detected concern in her trembling voice.

After the preparations were finished, Grandma sent our neighbor's teenaged-son to bring the midwife and waited impatiently for her to arrive. The midwife was late, and that made Grandma more nervous. She looked anxious and desperate as Valentina's birth pangs became more frequent, and she was already screaming at the top of her lungs regardless of the presence of a dozen young soldiers behind the thin wall of her bedroom. I felt terrible that the soldiers could hear Valentina's moans and screams.

Finally, the midwife arrived. She was a middle-aged plump woman, with kind eyes and a tired smile. She inspired confidence, and I immediately liked her. "She will help Valentina, and she will save her from death," I said to myself and breathed with relief.

The midwife took control of the situation. She checked Valentina's pulse, her temperature and the frequency of her contractions. Then, she advised Grandma to take Zhanna and me to the neighbor's house, across the yard, for a pre-arranged sleepover. I didn't know why, but no Soviet soldiers were quartered in her house although it was spacious and warm. She lived alone, and she looked very old.

Zhanna, with a tear-stained face, kissed her mother and, crying, left the bedroom. When I held my aunt's hand and kissed her on the cheek, I felt that her face was sweaty; the grip of her hand was also sweaty, but firm. I tried not to cry, but I was choked with tears. I was scared for Valentina's life. I thought that she might die. Grandma accompanied us to our neighbor's house. I carried the bundle with our nighties wrapped in a towel.

That night in our neighbor's house, I couldn't fall asleep. I helped Zhanna undress and put on her nightshirt. Then I took off my shoes and lay down next to Zhanna in our neighbor's wide bed, on the soft down pillows. The neighbor entered the room and saw that I was lying fully dressed, only without shoes.

"Oh, no, Nina, that won't work. Take off your dress and your stockings and put on your nightshirt. Otherwise, you won't be able to relax. You need to rest," she said. "Grandma will need your help. You are a big girl, Nina. So, lie down and sleep tight. *Spokoinoy nochi!* Good night!" She left the room and closed the door.

Zhanna slept quietly, but I couldn't. I was thinking about my aunt loudly screaming in her tiny bedroom, about young soldiers sleeping on the cold floor in our living room who could hear Valentina's moaning. I was also thinking about Valentina's husband, my uncle Mitya, who was somewhere in the battle zone. Nobody knew where he was. I was thinking, as well, about my father fighting in the front. We hadn't heard from him since the war started. I was tired and overwhelmed with emotions. I felt miserable, helpless and abandoned, as if I were alone in the whole world and there was nobody to help me. Engulfed in the comfortable cloud of self-pity, sinking into the cozy and warm down pillow, I began to cry softly and, finally, cried myself to sleep.

18. Acquaintance With a Newcomer

$\mathcal{T}$he next morning, Grandma came across the courtyard and cheerfully woke us, "Get up, *sony*, sleepy heads! You have overslept and have missed everything. We have a new baby! He is big and strong and has a good appetite. You'll love him. He will be a military man because today is February 23rd, our National holiday — Red Army Day," she said with excitement.

Zhanna and I could hardly wait to see the newcomer. We hurriedly put on our clothes, and without washing our faces or combing our hair, we rushed across the yard to Valentina's apartment to see the baby. I had seen small babies before, but this was my first face-to-face live encounter with a newborn, my new cousin, Zhanna's baby brother, Oleg.

Grandma told us that the midwife had already left. Her mission was successfully accomplished; the baby was delivered without complications. Grandma told us that she had paid for her services with a bucket of fresh potatoes, a half-liter bottle of sunflower oil, and a three-liter jar of her famous homemade sauerkraut. It was a heavy load to carry. Grandma offered the midwife our children's sled

111

to transport it. That winter was snowy, and the sled was an appropriate means of transportation. Between the two of them, they put everything on the sled and fastened the load with a rope. The midwife promised that the next day her teenaged-son would return our sled.

Zhanna and I hesitantly approached the bed where Aunt Valentina was lying with huge dark circles around her kind blue eyes. She was smiling. Her left arm lovingly embraced a swaddled bundle tightly wrapped in a faded, used flannelette blanket, a gift for the baby from our neighbors. First Zhanna, then I kissed Valentina on the cheek and said, as Grandma instructed us to do before we entered the bedroom: *Pozdravlyayu!* Congratulations!

We looked at the tiny creature wrapped up to his neck, peacefully sleeping in Valentina's arm. The bundle looked like a cocoon. I couldn't see his eyes, but I liked his tiny nose, eyebrows, eyelashes and lips. He made soft smacking sounds in his sleep. His toy-like face, framed in a cotton baby bonnet, was so cute and charming that I liked him immediately. "What an angel!" I said. Valentina smiled tiredly in response.

Since then, our daily routine revolved around the needs of that greedily sucking and nonstop peeing little angel whom everybody adored from the day he was born. As soon as he started to groan, to wheeze or to grunt, it always meant something: he was hungry, or wet, or totally immersed in smelly feces, and, therefore, was uncomfortable. So, his swaddling clothes had to be changed, he had to be washed with a warm flannelette cloth, and after that he had to be fed.

Before the war, it was possible to buy simple items for newborns. But even after our town was liberated from the German troops, the stores remained closed. Grandma and Valentina sacrificed several used bed sheets, cut them in square pieces and used them as swaddling clothes. Valentina sewed a cotton bonnet for the baby, more like a little triangular scarf to put on his tiny head and several loose cotton jackets. That was all she could afford.

As we had no indoor plumbing, no hot water, and no electricity, it wasn't an easy task to take care of the newborn. We had to heat up water on the coal stove. Irons were also heated on the stove. The stove was always in operation from early morning until late night. It was hellish work to maintain the fire in the stove, to do the baby's laundry, to dry it on the clothesline stretched along the kitchen and to iron everything. We had to dry the laundry inside, as the weather was cold and snowy; besides, the laundry could be stolen.

The four of us—Grandma, Valentina, Zhanna and I—felt like caged hamsters on a treadmill. My morning responsibilities were to bring coal from the shed and water from the well located, thank God, in the front yard of our neighbor's house. I carried coal in a wicker basket and water in a small zinc bucket. Sometimes, Grandma also shared those chores with me. She took care of the cooking and the laundry for the baby, and for all of us, as we all needed to eat and to have clean clothes. Zhanna and I helped her in the kitchen. I washed and peeled vegetables, washed beans, dried fruits and did the dishes. We dusted everything; we swept the floors and washed them almost every day. Zhanna was nine and a half years old, and I was twelve.

Valentina's priority was her tiny newborn son. She was still weak and got tired very fast, but she took good care of her baby. She didn't trust anybody. She changed his nappies, his loose jackets and bonnets. Every morning, she washed his face and eyes with a soft, warm cloth. Every evening, she bathed him in a small zinc washtub put on two sturdy wooden stools in the middle of the kitchen, the warmest room in the apartment.

It was our favorite procedure; and no matter how tired we were, we all participated in it. The baby liked being bathed from his first encounter with water. Grandma carefully held his head in her left palm; with her right hand she held the baby in the water so that he didn't splash. Aunt Valentina tenderly washed the tiny body with a soft cloth.

Zhanna and I were eager to participate in the bathing ritual. Grandma reminded us to wash our hands with soap and to warm them up in order not to scare the baby with cold hands. Then, we were allowed to pour warm water from a mug over the baby's belly, his tiny legs and arms, and slowly massage them with a warm cloth. While doing that, we admired his tiny ears, his neck, his fingers, and his toes.

Once, when I was washing his delicate hand with a cloth, he unexpectedly grabbed my little finger and squeezed it with such strength that I dropped the cloth. We wanted to wash the baby's face, but Valentina preferred to do it herself. She was afraid that we might be negligent with the soap, and it would irritate the baby's eyes and make him cry. After the bath, the baby was put on the clean bed sheet on the kitchen table, dried off with a soft towel and dressed in a clean loose jacket and bonnet. He was tightly wrapped, cocoon style, in freshly-ironed swaddling clothes. Then, he was nursed and put to sleep next to Valentina in her bed.

While my cocooned baby cousin slept like an angel, we all had supper. As a rule, we ate leftovers from lunch — a plate of pumpkin *kasha* with millet or a glass of milk or tea with homemade jam and pancakes. We always ate vegetables or hot cereal. We never had pork or chicken.

114

We were in the middle of the winter, the meatless season. We had to save the little salted pork we had for the spring work in the field; we also had to save live chickens so they could lay eggs, and so we could have more chickens later. We were so tired and sleepy by evening that we hardly talked during the meal. As we had no electricity, we went to bed early and got up with the cock's crow.

After supper, Zhanna went to bed. Grandma had to do the baby's laundry and to hang it to dry in the kitchen. Valentina had to do the dishes, while I mopped the kitchen floor.

The next morning, all the boring routine was repeated with mathematical precision.

Zhanna and I didn't have a free moment to go to the yard to play or for a walk. The winter of 1944 was extremely cold, and we didn't have appropriate winter clothes to stay warm outside. We were exhausted and sad, probably depressed, but this word was not a part of our vocabulary back then. Sometimes, in Grandma's eyes, I saw some inexplicable expression, a combination of tiredness and sadness which scared me. Now I know that it probably was despair.

Our life seemed grim and tiresome. We didn't laugh; we only smiled at the baby. He was our joy and consolation. He was so tiny and helpless; he depended on us. We had to keep him comfortable and to protect him, and we knew that there was nobody to help us.

Grandma's prediction turned out to be true. A quarter of a century later, my cousin, who was born on February 23, in 1944, and whom Zhanna named Oleg, became an Air Force

pilot. As to the National Holiday called Red Army Day, it had been renamed during WWII to Soviet Army Day. We didn't know that and used its old name. Several decades later, the word "Soviet" disappeared from the title of the holiday. Now it is called The Day of the Defenders of the Fatherland.

19. Post-Occupation Challenges

*A*t the end of supper, Grandma suddenly looked at us intently and said: "We can't continue like this! We have to do something. Spring is getting closer every day, and we have to think how we'll work our vegetable garden. There are rumors that the schools will be reopened soon. You children have to go to school. I think that you, Valentina, and your children, will have to move back home to my house. Being under one roof will make it easier for of us to take care of the baby and to deal with the domestic chores during the spring and summer field work.

Grandma's words were like a light at the end of a long pitch-dark tunnel. *Will I really go to school again?* I joyfully asked myself. Then I realized that it had to be true. The Germans had already retreated, and the Soviet soldiers were here, sleeping on the floor in our living room.

Then one unexpected thought warmed my heart: we have school supplies! Pencils, notebooks, indelible pencils to make ink. We have enough for Louisa, Zhanna and me!

Suddenly, I realized how much I had missed going to school every morning, preparing my *portfel*, as we called school bags back then, checking and rechecking if I put all the things I would need every day, arranging my notebooks in a special folder, putting my pencils and pens in a cute wooden pencil box together with a ten kopecks coin which Mother used to give me every morning for the school snack. The pencil box had a special coin compartment.

I wanted to read new textbooks, to write exercises. I wanted to solve math problems which I hated before. Oh, *Bozhe*! God! Now I can go to the summer Pioneer Camp, as I am twelve years old. I had been dreaming about the camp since the first grade. However, the students could not become members of the Communist Pioneer Organization until the age of ten. The war had cruelly interrupted my dreams, but now I could go to the summer Pioneer Camp. I heard a lot about Pioneer Camps from older children. They were located in the forest or mountain areas, near the rivers or lakes, on the shores of the Black and Baltic Seas and the Sea of Azov.

A lot of sports and recreational activities were available in the camps for the children of all ages: they had volleyball, soccer and swimming sections, hiking trips, dancing and singing groups, a lot of table games, art studios and children's theater. The pioneers spent a lot of time outside in the fresh air, enjoying nature and the company of one another.

My dreams about the Pioneer Camp took me far away from the dark, kerosene lamp-lit kitchen table where Grandma, with a serious expression on her tired face, explained to us her plans for our near future.

"Tomorrow, in the morning," she said to Valentina, "I myself will go and talk to the colonel of the unit whose soldiers are stationed in our living room, and I will ask him for help. They have military trucks coming and going from the unit all the time. It's only ten kilometers by highway. We have to take all your furniture and all your belongings by military truck. There is no other transportation right now. We can't postpone the departure. Spring will come soon and with it, the dirt roads leading from the highway to our town will be impassable. So, we shouldn't waste our time. We need to hurry."

Grandma kept her word. The next morning, she went to the house where the colonel with his entourage was stationed. She explained our difficult situation and asked him for help. The colonel listened to her carefully, thanked her for sheltering the soldiers of his unit, and promised his help.

He told Grandma that in a week a convoy of empty trucks would go in that direction. We could go on one of the trucks by the highway till the turn to the dirt road leading to our town. The trucks were on schedule and would not take the risk of getting stuck in the spring mud on the dirt roads. From the turning point off the highway to the dirt road, we were on our own. That was as close as the trucks could go.

20. At the Communal Grave

*G*randma and I had stayed at my aunt Valentina's place
for three weeks. A lot of things happened during
that period. The Germans retreated, the front line passed
through our area, like a wild fire through the steppe, the
Russian soldiers had been stationed in our living room,
and, finally, my little cousin, whom his sister Zhanna
named Oleg, had been born.

The rest of our family was just ten kilometers away
from us. However, we had no contact with them, as there
was no telephone connection, no postal service, no public
transportation—nothing at all. So, we were worried sick
about Grandpa, my mother and my sister, Louisa. The
three of them had to take care of themselves, of all the
domestic chores and of our animals—the cow, the pig, and
the chickens.

We could reach them only by walking over a frozen
dirt road covered by snow. We had to let them know about
our moving plans and our arrival at Grandma's place.
After short consideration, it was decided that Valentina
would go for one day with baby Oleg. She couldn't leave
him behind as she was his milk provider. Besides, she
herself wanted to ask Grandpa and my mother to help her

move and rearrange the furniture the way she wanted it in her room, at Grandma's place.

It was risky and dangerous for Valentina to undertake that journey alone. So, Grandma, solemnly looking at me said, "You, Nina, are twelve years old. You are not only the oldest of my three granddaughters, but the most serious and mature one. You will accompany Valentina and help her with the baby during that three-hour walk. It's the best arrangement we can do for now, child, *detka*. I hope you will get safely to the town."

I couldn't believe my luck. For several weeks, I rinsed, hung and ironed baby's cloth diapers in the smelly overheated kitchen. Now, I was desperately eager to get out of the small overcrowded apartment. I was ready not only to walk, but to run in any direction, especially to Grandma's town where Mother, my sister Louisa and Grandpa impatiently waited for any news from us. In short, I was happy as a bird. I gave Grandma a hug, kissed her on the cheek, and couldn't stop smiling looking forward to the next day's tiring trip being a wonderful, promising adventure.

As we had to carry a bundle of the baby's things, we decided to use our sled. On it we put a big down feathered pillow for the baby, a small cotton comforter and a pillowcase full of fresh, dry cloth diapers, loose jackets and bonnets for the baby. We had to return the next day, by evening. Grandma and Zhanna stayed at Valentina's home and had to start packing our more than modest belongings.

On the eve of that trip, we prepared the sled that could carry everything. That evening, we went to bed earlier than usual. The next morning, Valentina changed the baby's cloth diapers and nursed him. We had a quick breakfast, and said good-bye to Grandma and Zhanna.

We departed after Grandma, making a sign of the cross over us, said, "May God be with you!"

It was a bright, cold winter morning. The streets, the houses, the bushes, and the trees were covered with snow. It was quite a pretty picture. There were icy spots on the streets and on the sidewalks. During the last months of her pregnancy, Valentina was locked in her apartment and didn't walk much. After giving birth to baby Oleg, she mostly stayed in the apartment, taking him outside just for a quarter of an hour every day. So, now she was walking carefully, but briskly, obviously enjoying being outdoors and breathing the frost, fresh winter air. We, finally, had time to take pleasure in looking at the scenery.

I also felt great being outside, out of the stuffy kitchen, where wet cloth diapers were hanging to dry day and night, nonstop, as if it were an assembly line: do the laundry, dry and iron it, and then start again.

Baby Oleg was three weeks old; however, he displayed an exemplary behavior. He quietly slept wrapped in his comforter, his head covered with Grandma's downy headscarf up to his eyes. He enjoyed sleeping on the down-feathered pillow, breathing the fresh winter air. He too, was probably tired of staying all the time inside and breathing the humid, smelly air of the kitchen.

Very soon, we reached the outskirts of the city and saw the vast space of the empty fields stretching up to the horizon. The dirt road leading to Grandma's town, was hardy visible under the thick blanket of fresh snow, for very few people used it. We actually were alone on the road. For some reason, we were not scared and silently continued our walk. We were almost half way there when we noticed at a distance, on the left side of the road, a group of people. They looked like Russian soldiers, but it was not clear to us what they were doing.

We approached the group. The soldiers were standing, leaning on their shovels, at the top of a freshly dug pit. They were young. Their sweaty faces were red as a result of the frosty cold and physical effort. It was not that easy to dig a pit in the frozen, hardened winter soil.

Valentina was the first one to approach them. I walked behind her, pulling the sled with the sleeping baby prince. When I was close enough to see what was happening, I suddenly saw that she covered her mouth with one hand as if she were trying to stifle a scream. I also saw the tears in her eyes. At first, I understood nothing. Then I took several more steps, closer to the edge of the pit, looked down, and I almost uttered a shriek myself. I could not believe what I saw.

It was a communal grave for the soldiers killed during the offensive of the Russian troops which had taken place three days before. Three of the dead soldiers lay at the bottom of the grave, stripped of their military uniforms, all barefooted, wearing only white cotton soldier's underwear consisting of long-sleeved shirts and long underpants. Only one soldier, a red-haired young man with pronounced freckles on his pale dead face was still in his uniform. On the left breast pocket of his shirt was a small hole, pierced by a bullet, with coagulated blood around it.

One of the grave diggers unbuttoned the dead soldier's breast pocket and pulled out his ID — a small, thin red booklet. With a serious expression on his young face, he said: "It's a good thing that he had his *soldatskaya knizhka* (ID card) on his body. At least we can report his death to the unit. After that, the unit will report his death to his parents or to his relatives. His unit has already gone; they moved forward. It would not be possible to identify him without his ID, and he would be reported as *propuvshiy bez veste* (MIA)."

During WWII, the Soviet military didn't use metallic dog tag IDs which were used by the American and Allied military.

One of the dead soldiers looked very young, just a teenager. His blue, still eyes were wide open as if they were fixed on the pale blue winter sky. "He was only eighteen. He had been drafted last fall," said another soldier turning over the small pages of the dead soldier's ID. "He didn't even have time to fall in love or to taste the war."

Looking at the young dead soldiers in their white underwear and barefooted, I immediately imagined my father at the bottom of the communal grave, somewhere far away, during the cold severe winter, almost naked, without his high boots, and the tears started to stream down my cheeks. Valentina put her hand on my shoulder and said, "Don't cry, Nina, calm down, *milaya*, darling. Let's pray for their souls!" Then, to distract me, she asked the grave diggers why they had taken off the uniforms and boots from the dead soldiers.

"We didn't want to, but our commanders ordered us to take off everything, including foot bindings. There is a huge lack of military uniforms in the army. We have to take off everything from the dead, including officers' uniforms," said another soldier who looked like the leader of the funeral detail.

Valentina and I were shocked. We stood and prayed for a while. Before we said good-bye to the soldiers she shared with them a small bundle of dried apricots which Grandma had given us for the road. The soldiers thanked her and immediately started to chew Grandma's "fruit candy" as she used to call the dried fruits.

We made the rest of our trip in silence. Valentina carried her bundle of joy in her arms so that the baby could change position. I pulled the sled. Soon we reached Grandma's house where our mongrel dog, Sharyk, greeted us with his loud, joyful barking. It was such a relief to be back home, even for one night only and feel the warm embrace of Mother's kind arms. I even allowed my sister Louisa to kiss me on the cheek although I usually avoided her obtrusive, slobbery kisses.

That night, lying next to my mother in her comfortable bed, I had a terrible dream — a long, deep communal grave filled with dead young soldiers in the middle of snowy nowhere. In the morning, Mother told me that I had been crying and screaming in my sleep. That persistent nightmare returned to haunt me for a very long time.

21. A Short Visit to Grandma's Place

*G*randpa, Mother and Louisa were happy to see us. They had been worried sick about us. Grandpa was pleased to see his first grandson, as he had three granddaughters. Mother was charmed with her first baby nephew; Louisa was stunned by her baby cousin. She treated him as if he were a toy, and wanted to take him in her arms and play with him.

Valentina, however, was on alert. She, like a mother-lioness, vigilantly watched everybody who approached her baby cub. She didn't allow Louisa to hold him, because Louisa, in Valentina's opinion, wasn't accustomed to dealing with newborn babies.

Valentina unwrapped the baby's swaddling clothes and undressed him. Then she gave her son a sponge bath with a soft warm cloth and warm water. It was all she could do under the circumstances. As our visit was unexpected, there was no hot water to bathe the baby; it was too late to kindle the stove again and to heat the water.

Louisa helped Valentina with the sponge bath. She lovingly washed the baby's tiny fingers and toes and tried to kiss them. After the baby's wash up, Valentina told us that he was tired and needed to rest.

Oleg yawned so cutely, opening his tiny mouth like a nestling. I enjoyed looking at him when he was yawning and stretching. Valentina dried him with a soft towel, put the clean loose jacket on him and a pink cotton bonnet in which he looked like a doll. Then she wrapped him in fresh swaddling clothes, nursed him, and put him to sleep on Grandma's bed.

When the baby was asleep, we all had a late supper. We ate dumplings with homemade cottage cheese and drank milk with pancakes and sour cherry jam — leftovers from lunch. The adults shared news and gossip. The most stunning news was that the schools would be reopened soon. Mother, like other teachers, was doing preparatory work at the school, where she would work as a teacher. The post office, hospital, and other services, including electricity, would be starting to function very soon.

In spite of my tiredness, I felt agitated, excited and full of hope. I wanted to listen to all the news and rumors. I didn't want to miss a word of the conversation at the table, but my eyelids were sticking together, and I kept nodding. Mother noticed that and said, "Go to bed, *milaya*, honey, you are tired and you need a good rest. The three of you have been through a lot today. We'll have a very busy day tomorrow. We all need a good rest. *Spokoinoy nochi!* Good night!" She kissed me on the forehead and patted me on the back.

I undressed, put on my nightshirt, and stretched my tired, numb body on Mother's bed. I put my heavy head on the wide down pillow. I felt as if I was collapsing into warm, caressing waves. Suddenly, all my worries, terrible images and emotional sufferings of that long day started to vanish slowly as I was falling asleep. My last thought of that day was: "Those poor barefooted soldiers! They probably are very cold in their grave." Then, like a last ray of hope, a happy thought struck me. "*Bozhe!* My God! Let school start sooner!"

The next day, we all worked like slaves, without taking a moment off, cleaning Valentina's former room, taking out the old things and produce which had been stored in it, as the room was used as a pantry and a storage space. We needed to make a space for the furniture which Valentina had to bring. So, we stored some things in the barn. Mother promised Valentina to finish cleaning the room, to wash the windows and the floor in order to make everything ready for Valentina's move back.

We finished everything fast, and after an early lunch, we were ready to leave. Mother and Louisa volunteered to see us off as far as the outskirts of town. Mother carried the baby; she and Valentina walked in front of us. Louisa and I followed them pulling the sled. Louisa said: "I miss you and Zhanna, Nina. I have nobody to play with. Come back soon. I want to bathe the baby, too, I like him a lot." I felt a pin-prick of jealousy because I used to be the object of Louisa's adoration. Soon I forgot about that because I, myself, liked our baby cousin very much.

Having reached the outskirts of the town, we kissed each other good-bye. Mother and Louisa returned home; Valentina and I continued our walking journey. When we approached the familiar site of the communal grave, we saw a little sepulchral knoll and a simple wooden pedestal, with a red star on its top. The names of four buried soldiers were written with indelible pencil in the center of the pedestal. We stood for a while at the side of the fresh grave; then we crossed ourselves, and Valentina said in a low, trembling voice, "*Bednye deti!*" God rest your souls, poor children. Then we resumed our walk.

That evening, at Valentina's apartment, baby Oleg who had survived the two-day walking trip, received a good, warm bath and fell asleep as soon as he was wrapped in fresh swaddling clothes and nursed. After supper, Grandma said, "You had two difficult days. We all are tired. Let's go to bed, and tomorrow we'll start fresh, and we'll decide what to do next. As they say, "Things will always look brighter in the morning."

22. Post-Occupation Revival

*A*fter our one-day visit to Grandma's place, events developed as quickly as a sled rolling down a hill. The next day, under Grandma's supervision, we started to pack our simple belongings. We had no packaging materials such as cardboard boxes and plastic bags. We had only several pieces of old ropes, strings, and cords.

We used bed sheets to tie up our bedding, towels and clothes in bundles, large and small. Grandma told me and Zhanna to pack our clothes in separate bundles so that later we could easily find whatever we needed. The large bundle contained Oleg's swaddling clothes and all the rest of his clothes.

From Grandma's house, we brought several empty large canvas mattress cases. We threw out the thatch they were filled with, and used them to pack cotton comforters, blankets and pillows. Several burlap sacks were set aside to transport fresh potatoes, beetroots, carrots, and other produce from the kitchen cellar and the pantry, as well as utensils, pots and pans.

At the beginning of March 1944, the weather unexpectedly got warmer, and the spring thaw began. As a result of the fast snow melting, the dirt roads were covered with deep, sticky mud; they became almost impassible, even for the powerful military trucks. It was a real danger that our moving from Valentina's apartment to Grandma's place could be undermined by the warm weather conditions. Grandma and Valentina, nervous and worried, were eager to leave as soon as possible. Finally, the colonel's messenger told Grandma that the next day, there would be a big truck to transport us and all our belongings to Grandma's town.

Early in the morning, the soldiers stationed in our living room loaded our furniture and all our bundles on a big military truck. Valentina with Oleg and Zhanna got into the cab and sat next to the driver. Grandma and I had to climb up into the body of the truck. Before climbing up, Grandma thanked the soldiers for their help and gave them a canvas sack with dried apples, apricots and sour cherries as a token of our appreciation. We waved good-bye to the soldiers and our neighbors, and the truck drove away.

At that moment, standing in the body of a tall American military Studebaker truck, with the fresh spring wind blowing into my face, I suddenly realized that the German occupation was over for good, and that a new life had begun. I felt a wave of immense joy filling my heart.

It was about a ten-mile ride by highway. So, very soon we reached the fork crossing from where the narrow dirt road leading to our town began. The truck got off the highway. However, it managed to reach only the outskirts of the town and got stuck in the deep mud, next to the first house. The wheels were spinning in the deep, sticky spring mud.

The driver of the truck, a young soldier, with his cap cocked at a jaunty angle, was afraid of being stuck in the mud. So, together with the two men from the house, he helped us to unload the truck and to take our furniture and the rest of our belongings to the barn of the household. That was the last we saw of him.

Luckily for us, the owner of the house where we unloaded our furniture and bundles turned out to be an old acquaintance of our grandfather, a retired locomotive operator like him. He had a horse and volunteered to take us home in his horse carriage. We took several bundles with us and left the rest of our belongings behind. There were five of us including the coachman and the baby, and there was only one bony horse pulling the wagon over the treacherous dirt road.

We moved slowly along the washed-out dirt road. Several times the wagon got stuck in the deep, thick mud, and we all had to push it forward. Finally, we reached Grandma's place and all breathed a sigh of relief. Thank God we were home, although Valentina's furniture and most of our bundles were left behind in the friend's barn.

We were all together again under the secure roof of Grandparents' house like at the beginning of the war, at the crucial period of our lives. Now, it looked as if the inevitably approaching end of the war had united all us again, offering the same warm and reliable shelter as it had happened at the beginning of the war.

Grandpa was happy to meet his former co-worker. He invited him to have supper with us, but the coachman declined the invitation. He wanted to get back home before sunset. The two men talked while Grandpa treated the horse with a good portion of oats and a bucket of fresh water. The horse needed it. She was tired and hungry, as we all were.

Grandpa gave his former co-worker a half liter bottle of homemade vodka, which he had kept for special occasions hidden in a secret place, somewhere on the upper shelf of the pantry. His friend appreciated the gift and accepted it with an approving smile. He said, looking at Grandpa, "We'll drink it together when the war is finished. It will be soon. Don't worry, *druzhok*, my old buddy, I will try to bring your daughter's bundles as soon as possible. The furniture has to wait until the dirt roads are dried. You will need a small truck to transport it." He waved good-bye and drove away.

Grandma, Valentina, Zhanna and I were cold, hungry and exhausted from a long, hard day. Valentina gave a short sponge bath to baby Oleg, hastily changed his swaddling clothes, nursed him and put him to sleep. We washed up and had supper.

At the table, Mother looked at us and said with obvious joy in her voice, "I have good news for you children: school starts in a week. We have seven days to prepare everything for school — your clothes, your books, all you need for your classes. We all will be very busy."

I couldn't believe what I heard. I will be in school again! With other children, not with adults all the time. At that moment, I realized how hard it was to be involved in their world of domestic chores and affairs, no matter how simple they were. In my heart, I still was a child despite the fact that I had read Leo Tolstoy's novel *Anna Karenina* when I was eleven years old. As for Louisa and Zhanna, they had attended only kindergarten; they were not worried at all, just curious and uncertain about school. To me, they both looked somewhat indifferent.

That night, I couldn't sleep. I kept tossing and turning on the hard thatch mattress on Grandma's big trunk, which served me as a bed. I imagined my new textbooks, my new teachers, my new classmates. Because of the war, I had missed the third, the fourth and the fifth grades. If I would be accepted in the fifth grade, I would fall behind only one year. That would be great. But, would I be able to study in the fifth grade? Would I be accepted at that level? I didn't want to go back to the fourth grade. Who would be my new classmates? All those thoughts filled my tired, worrisome head, and prevented me from falling asleep.

23. Back to School!

$\mathcal{G}$randma and Mother spent the next few days sitting at Grandma's old *Singer*, altering skirts and blouses for Louisa, Zhanna and me from their own used clothes. As a result of their joint effort, a dark blue pleated skirt and a light blue long-sleeved blouse were made for me, and brown pleated skirts and light cream long-sleeved blouses were made for Zhanna and Louisa. The three of us were happy as clams with our new outfits. We didn't care that they had been altered from used clothing. It seemed to me that dressed in our new school outfits, we looked more serious and mature, even smarter.

The stores weren't functioning yet, even though the Germans had retreated. But the war wasn't over. All economic resources were still needed by the Soviet Army for its machinery and personnel. Therefore, there was not a single chance of getting new footwear for the three of us. So Mother washed, dried and cleaned our old worn-out shoes and boots and took them to the shoemaker's stand at the farmers' market for repairs. Then we polished them with a fervor until they shone like new kopecks and smelled like hell.

I was the lucky one as I had my leatherette school bag, which back then we called *shkolnyi portfel*. All those years, I kept it in my secret hiding place under the bed, next to Grandmother's small "suitcase for death." Grandpa had asked me several times to give him my school bag. He wanted to keep important documents and papers in it. I didn't want to give it to anyone. It was my talisman, my lucky charm, which reminded me of our normal, pre-war life and my happy, carefree school days.

I put several notebooks, pencils and a pen into my school bag; that was all I had. I didn't have a single textbook for the fifth grade. Mother, who had been hired for a teaching position in the same school, told us that some textbooks would be distributed among the students at school.

Louisa and Zhanna had no school bags. Grandma sewed for each of them fabric square bags with long shoulder straps, so that they could carry them across the chest. According to her age, Louisa had to go to the third grade. She had gotten all my third grade textbooks and put them into her bag together with notebooks, pencils and a pen. "Now these textbooks are mine," she said proudly, making a face.

Zhanna did not have textbooks; she put into her bag several notebooks and a pencil box with pencils and a pen. I gave her that pencil box as a gift because she was the youngest of us and was anxious about school. At least, we wouldn't go to school empty-handed: we had some school supplies, thanks to our looting expedition to the abandoned German warehouse during the hasty retreat of German troops.

School started on Monday. That day, we got up earlier than usual; we didn't want to be late for classes. Mother braided my long hair and tied a big bow at the end of each braid. As we had no ribbons, Mother made them from the same fabric as our blouses. Both Louisa and Zhanna had short haircuts, but they wanted to have bows on the crowns of their heads. Like little monkeys, they used to imitate my behavior and my taste to the point of absurdity. With the bows, they looked very funny, especially Louisa, whose bow was constantly slipping to one side. She tried to adjust it, jerking her head like a playful foal on a spring meadow.

On Monday morning, accompanied by Mother, we arrived at school, which was not far from our house. In the main street, leading to the school, we saw a lot of children walking in the same direction. Some had school bags; others carried their books and notebooks in their hands or under their arms. Some teenaged boys had their books tucked behind their belts.

In my fifth grade classroom, there were forty students between ages eleven and fifteen. As I found out later, not a single student had home schooling during the occupation as we had, thanks to my mother, a teacher. So, most of the students were afraid to go on to the six or seventh grade because they had forgotten a lot of the academic material, especially math. They preferred to repeat the fifth grade.

All my classmates were dressed in mixed, ill-assorted, worn-out, used, but clean, clothes, sometimes oversized. The shoes of the students were a disaster and left much to be desired. Some boys wore boots several sizes larger than they needed. Almost everybody was shod in his or her own way.

Nobody paid attention to one another's clothes or footwear. We were happy to be at school again, to be in the company of classmates, to do students' business—

studying and learning in order to determine what we had missed during those harsh and desperate years of the German occupation.

The teacher, a short, spry brunette, explained that we would start with reviewing the most important material at high speed: arithmetic, writing and reading in Russian and Ukrainian. We would study history, geography, botany, and the German language according to the fifth grade curriculum. By the beginning of the summer, the teachers would make their decision as to who would stay in the fifth grade and who would go back to the fourth or advance to the sixth grade.

Our teacher distributed textbooks during the very first lesson. There were forty of us, but only twenty sets of textbooks were sitting on the teacher's desk. So, one set of textbooks had to serve two students, depending on the location of their houses. The children who lived in the same neighborhood had to share textbooks while preparing homework. This way, students had, at least, one textbook for the desk, and everybody had the opportunity to work in class, doing reading, writing and math exercises. The teacher promised that as soon as the school received a new batch of textbooks, everyone would get an individual set.

There were several familiar faces from our neighborhood among the students, but I was meeting the majority of my new classmates for the first time. During the German occupation, we children had no opportunity to come together in public places such as libraries or movie theaters. There were no celebrations of National holidays, nor any other activities.

Our class equipment included a big blackboard and a box of white chalk which was in the teacher's possession and under her control. A damp cloth for cleaning the board completed the inventory. The only instructional aides were a big wooden ruler and a wooden pointer, which were, again, under the teacher's control.

Hung on the wall above the blackboard in every classroom was a big portrait of Stalin, the leader of the Communist party, and "the best friend of all the Soviet children." Although it was a cool early spring, the heating system of the school building was not yet in operation. The portrait of "the father of all the peoples of the Soviet Union," was supposed to warm not only our hearts, but our hands as well, so that we could write without putting our gloves on.

We hadn't been at school for three years, so it was pretty noisy in the classroom; we all tried to talk at the same time and loudly. Our teacher was not able to calm us down. Somehow, amidst that chaos, she managed to call the class roll and asked everyone if all the personal information on the roster was correct: full name, date and place of birth, and home address of every student. None of us had a telephone, with exception of two girls whose fathers worked for the local KGB Office.

That energetic, spry and patient brunette happened to be not only our home teacher but our Russian language and literature teacher, as well. She immediately assigned two students, sitting at the first desk to be on duty that Monday. They had to clean the blackboard before classes and after every lesson. At the end of every day the students on duty had to sweep and to mop the classroom.

We attended school six days a week, including Saturdays. We had five or six classes every day, depending on the schedule. All classes lasted forty-five minutes. After every lesson, we had five minutes' break to go to the restroom or to drink some water from the restroom faucet. We had no water fountains, no hot water, no toilet paper either. We had to provide it ourselves.

Every morning before we left the house, Grandma reminded us to put in our school bags, for use as a toilet paper — several square pieces of newspaper cut by Grandpa after he had finished reading it. Many times during the breaks, I watched the boys tearing off the pages of their notebooks, then crumpling and putting it in their pockets before going to the restrooms.

At that time, we had no slightest idea of the existence of toilet paper as such. The first time I saw the toilet paper in the stores was when I moved to Moscow at the beginning of the nineteen seventies. By the way, there was a huge deficit of that product during the Soviet era. I will never forget the picturesque scene I once witnessed at the bus stop near Patrice Lumumba University in Moscow where I worked. The bus was late, and the crowd of potential passengers was getting bigger and bigger. As a rule, the big crowd of people eager to get into the overcrowded bus looked decisively aggressive. But not this time. When I approached the crowd, I understood why. I saw a tall man in military uniform, joyfully retorting the comments of the crowd. A ring of toilet paper rolls hung over his shoulder reaching to his knees. With one hand he tried to prevent the rolls from sliding off his shoulder. In the other hand he held a string bag with two lemons and a bottle of Armenian cognac, marked with three stars for its high quality.

"You are well equipped, colonel," said a man in the crowd. "The three-star cognac is a classy drink. Only you made a blunder — where is the snack for such a beautiful drink?"

"I called my wife and told her about my lucky purchase of the toilet paper," the colonel said playfully giving a wink to the man. "Dinner is in the oven!"

As the bus approached the stop, the crowd, headed by the brave, resourceful colonel, stormed both the front and the back doors of the overcrowded vehicle.

After the third lesson, we had a big break—fifteen minutes of uncontrolled freedom during which we could even run out of the classroom into the school yard to play games or just run around, rain or shine. When it was extremely cold or rainy, we were allowed to run and play in the long, wide hallways of the school building.

That first Monday, at the end of the third lesson, our home teacher said in a somewhat mysterious tone, "Take your time to do what you need, but in five to seven minutes be at your desks. I'll be back with a surprise for you, a nice one!" Then she left smiling, with enigmatic sparks in her eyes.

Ten minutes later, she was back carrying a big metal tray covered with a newspaper. She put it on her desk and solemnly pronounced, "From now on, every day during the big break, you will get a snack for free. Today's snack is—" and, like a magician, she took the newspaper off the tray.

We were not sitting at our desks anymore. We stood with our necks stretched forward like geese, our mouths and eyes wide open, trying to see what was on that tray. Suddenly, the tallest guy from the last desk at the wall screamed, "*Ura! Eto sakhar!* (Hurray! It's sugar!)

We all gasped with surprise, as we saw square pieces of black rye bread sprinkled with granulated sugar which we called "sugar sand," sitting in even rows on the tray, causing our mouths to water. We hadn't seen sugar for a long, long time. We hadn't seen candies of any sort, either. We got sugar only from eating fresh and dried fruits; even homemade jams were cooked without sugar.

All the students got their snack treats; however, everyone enjoyed it in different ways. Some gulped it down and then enviously looked at those who were savoring their portions with gusto, biting off small pieces in order to prolong the pleasure. I was among the latter. During the breaks and even whispering during the lessons, we discussed the granulated sugar snack treats and guessed what else we might get at future breaks. *"Life is getting sweeter!"* I thought to myself. My heart was singing, and I felt happy and inspired. I immediately wanted to go home and do my homework, as if I were pushing the time forward, closer to the next day's school snack time.

After school, Mother had to stay for the teachers' meeting. I picked up Louisa and Zhanna, and we walked home. Even before the war, there were no school buses in the Soviet Union. We always walked to school, or used public transportation such as street car and trolley when we lived in Minsk. On our way back, both girls spoke breathlessly about the granulated sugar treats. They told me again and again how they ate their portions. Louisa said, "Tomorrow I will be smarter. I will eat my treat slowly like the other girls did. I won't swallow it all at once as I did today."

Back at home, Louisa and Zhanna repeated their stories before and after lunch, during their homework preparation, before and after supper. Even going to sleep, Louisa said, "I hope they will give us chocolate candy some day. I like chocolate candy, but I don't remember the taste of it." My poor baby sister was daydreaming about chocolate.

24. School Workday Routine

*S*chool days flew like arrows from a bow. We were busy all the time. I didn't even notice how quickly we had reached the beginning of June when we all were reevaluated and assigned to appropriate grades. I was accepted into the fifth grade. Summer vacation lasted through June, July and August.

School re-started on the first of September, which was in the Soviet Union and still is, in Russia and other former Soviet republics, the official beginning of the school for all grades — from the first grade through college and university.

We all received individual sets of books, and there was no need for us to share them anymore. Our class home teacher warned us not to write in the books, not to make marginal notes on the pages, not to underline sentences, even with a pencil. She explained that at the end of the school year, we had to exchange our fifth grade textbooks for the sixth grade ones. So our textbooks should be clean, neat and without missing pages.

Starting in the fifth grade, a new subject — a foreign language — was introduced in the school curriculum. It was German. We had it twice a week. At the first German lesson, I discovered that my classmates and I knew a lot of German words and phrases, as we children had been exposed to German speech for almost three years.

Twice a week, we had military physical training classes. We enjoyed them very much because sometimes those classes were conducted outside, weather conditions permitting. We marched in formation, we ran short and long distances, and we practiced high and long jumps.

In the Soviet movies that we could watch in the Park Movie Theatre Russian girl-soldiers dashingly and fearlessly handled handguns and rifles. We all dreamt and wanted to be like them. After all, the country was still at war.

During classes, our military instructor, a former Soviet Army officer, taught us to throw grenades, to load and unload rifles, hand guns, and even sub-machine guns. Actually, we never handled real weapons. We used only mock wooden rifles and guns. Our instructor fed us promises that as soon as the school management could afford it, we would have a shooting gallery, and he would teach us to shoot using real firearms. Everybody, including girls, wanted to learn to use weapons. Some boys bragged about their knowledge of using fire arms. The shooting gallery dream had never materialized in the three years while I attended that school.

At the military training classes, we sometimes played volleyball on the school yard grounds, during the early fall and late spring when the soil was dry and it was not raining. The school had no gym, for the hall where the gym was located before the war was now occupied by the church.

During the war, the Russian Orthodox church again, as before the October revolution, was an official, legal institution, and played an important role in consolidating all the nation and its patriotic forces. The church successfully collected money for the needs of the Soviet Army. The Soviet government reinstated its legal status, and the school management didn't dare fight for the church building.

In addition, the educational authorities didn't have financial means to build the gym for the school, as the priority for the Soviet government still was the victorious end of the Great Patriotic War II.

The church and the school were located on the same grounds. The church was in the middle, and two adjacent school buildings were on either side. They had to coexist side by side in the country where religion, according to the law, was separated from the state. The educational institutions, such as schools, were under the umbrella of the government, and legally, but not physically, like it was in the case of our school, were separated from the church.

25. After School Activities

*W*e had no gym or other large premises for our extra-curricular activities. They took place in the same lassrooms after the lessons were finished. We had a school choir, a folk dance ensemble, and a poetry recital group. We also had a volleyball team. During the choir rehearsals, we sang patriotic songs and Russian and Ukrainian folk songs. We also learned new modern popular songs which we hadn't had the opportunity to listen to and to learn during the years of German occupation. So we wanted to catch up—to learn and to sing the new Soviet songs.

It was not an easy task: we had no radios, no records, no tape recorders. We only heard them in the movies. We tried to catch the tunes and to memorize the lyrics. Sometimes several girls got together, recalled and put together the words of the songs, line by line, verse after verse. Boys also helped us restore the lyrics. In some cases, they remembered the lyrics even better than we girls, especially if they liked the tunes and the lyrics appealed to them.

At the dance ensemble rehearsals, we practiced simple dances such as Russian folk dance "Barynya," Ukrainian "Hopak," and the Moldavian folk dance "Moldavanesca."

We danced and sang to the music of an accordion or a bayan (a kind of accordion which had buttons instead of keys).

We made our own simple costumes for our performances—dark, fluffy skirts and white blouses embroidered with ethnic motifs. We wore garlands, decorated with long hanging ribbons of bright colors on our heads. We would have preferred to have red leather high boots to complete the costume, but that was an impossible dream. So we danced in our usual shoes.

At the choir, dance, and poetry recital rehearsals we practiced for the concerts dedicated to the next official Soviet holiday: Soviet Army Day (the 23rd of February), International Women's Day (the 8th of March), International Labor Day (the 1st of May), the anniversary of the October Socialist Revolution (the 7th of November), Soviet Constitution Day (the 5th of December), and, of course, New Year's Eve (the 31st of December).

At school, we never celebrated religious holidays such as Christmas and Easter. Our school choir, the dance ensemble and the poetry recital group performed at the matinee concerts for the students, teachers and parents. Those concerts took place on the eve of every official holiday.

We girls especially were eager to learn to dance modern ballroom dances which had become popular and fashionable in the Soviet Union before the war, such as the tango, foxtrot, classic Viennese waltz, and a slow version of it which we called the Bostonian waltz. The school, however, recommended traditional ballroom dances which were popular in Russia before the October revolution: the old-fashioned French minuet, the Polish mazurka, polonaise, cracovienne, polka, and quadrille, because those dances didn't require close physical contact

147

between partners, as opposed to the tango or foxtrot, for example.

Everybody wanted to learn to waltz, the most popular dance at that time. As to our male classmates, they were shy and clumsy, and were embarrassed to reveal their interest in social dancing. We girls were forced to pull the boys by the sleeves or push into their backs with our fists in order to make them dance. We even resorted to blackmail and threatened not to help them with math and physics tests, or with their vocabulary and spelling tests.

After every rehearsal, we asked our dance instructor to teach us, just for half an hour, the ballroom dances. We had to chip in fifty kopecks (the equivalent of fifty cents) each to pay the accordion player, as the school paid only for rehearsal time and not for the ballroom dancing practice.

So we started to dance the waltz, which I thought was one of the most graceful, elegant and delightful ballroom dances. Among the best old tunes of the waltz were such melodies as "On the Hills of Manchuria," "The Waves of Amur River," and, of course, the divine and unforgettable waltzes of Johann Strauss, such as "The Blue Danube," and "The Tales of the Viennese Forest." We learned the tunes and the lyrics of modern waltzes, such as "The Soldier's Waltz," "The Waltz in the Front-Line Forest," "The Forgotten Waltz," and "In the City Park," all written by Soviet composers.

We had more girls than boys in our volunteer ballroom dancing group. We girls, following the example of the girl-soldiers from the Soviet movies, cheerfully, with enthusiasm, waltzed with one another, and we were on cloud nine with joy. Even occasional wrong moves and stumbling couldn't spoil our wonderful mood and elevated spirits. Such fun for only fifty kopecks!

Finally, although with three years' delay, my dream to become a Pioneer, a member of the Communist Children's Organization, came true. All the students of school ages ten through fourteen, including our fifth grade, were officially admitted to the Pioneer organization at a solemn school formation ceremony where all the teachers and some parents were present.

The Pioneer leader of our school unit put red ties on our necks; after that, we took an oath. At the end of the ceremony, she greeted us with a Pioneer salute, raising her right stretched hand, bent at the elbow, to the middle of her forehead, addressing to newly admitted members, "Pioneers! Be ready to fight for the cause of Lenin and Stalin!" We saluted and shouted at the top of our young lungs, "*Wsegda Gotov!*" I am always ready!

The organizational structure of the Pioneers was very simple: the school was a Pioneer Unit, with a Pioneer Unit leader. It was a paid position, and, as a rule, was occupied by a young teacher who also wore a red Pioneer tie on the neck. Every grade represented a Pioneer detachment and had a detachment leader, one of the best students of the class. Every detachment was subdivided into four teams; every team had its team leader, also a student member of the team.

Detachment and team leaders had organizational and academic obligations. Every morning, they had to check if everyone was wearing a pioneer tie. Many teenage boys felt embarrassed to wear red ties like the third graders. They kept the ties in their pockets while they walked to school. At school, they put their red Pioneer ties on. However, from time to time, some of the boys forgot to do it. When that happened, the team leader reminded them to put the ties on.

For those who had difficulties or problems, team leaders also helped the members of the team with their homework. They reported to the home teacher the names of the students who, for different reasons, were absent at school. They oversaw the turns in class cleaning, and, sometimes, helped the students on duty to do the cleaning. Their most important task was to report to the home teacher the names of the violators of class discipline during the lessons, or cases of inappropriate behavior among the students, such as rudeness, fighting and secretly helping another student with tests. In sum, both detachment and team leaders, being home teacher's appointees, actually were teachers' assistants.

Finally, I became a Pioneer! *Ura! Ura! Ura!* It was one of my pre-war dreams come true.

26. My First Trip to Summer Pioneer Camp

I studied like crazy and finished the fifth grade with straight A's. I didn't realize I had missed my school routine so much. Studying was always a pleasure to me, and that's why it was easy and fast.

In winter, I had to do my homework in the house. There were three of us doing homework at the same time. We had to do it using the daylight, for there were still shortages of electricity from time to time. Louisa did her homework at the window table in Grandma's bedroom; Zhanna occupied the table in front of the window of her mother's bedroom. As for me, Grandma allowed me to do my homework at the round table in our living room which had two big windows. Usually, we children were not allowed there. We were allowed only in the kitchen and in the bedrooms.

In spring and in early fall, I did my homework in the barn hayloft. It was my favorite place, and I liked to be there — it was quiet, smelled of fresh hay, and I could concentrate, review and retell my oral assignments aloud, without imposing on anyone. The only inconvenience was that the hayloft had only one small window for ventilation located above the door in front of which I did my written assignments. I sat on the floor, Turkish style, with my legs crossed under me at a wide, low wooden desk which Grandpa made for me. Sometimes it was hot up there, but I didn't care because I enjoyed my hayloft privacy, and I was happy. Adults didn't disturb me. Louisa and Zhanna couldn't bother me with their silly questions and requests. I was in seventh heaven. Only my heaven was filled with hay.

By the middle of June, the school year was finished. The school administration gave my mother a free 26-day package to the summer Pioneer Camp for me. When she brought the news, I was ecstatic; I jumped and screamed for joy and couldn't stop smiling.

Louisa and Zhanna couldn't go to the summer camp. They were good students, but not straight-A students. So, Mother and Valentina would have had to pay for their packages, but they couldn't afford it. Valentina was not able to work; she had to take care of baby Oleg. Mother's salary was not enough to cover all our growing needs for shoes, winter boots, coats and clothing as we all grew very fast. We all wore hand-me-downs.

Over a year had passed, and we still hadn't heard anything from our father. We didn't know if he was dead or alive. Valentina and Zhanna hadn't heard from Uncle Mitya, either. We could only hope that both were alive and would return to us. At church, we always lit candles for our father's and Uncle Mitya's health. Grandma assured us that candles could create miracles. We believed her. We wanted to believe; otherwise, there would be nobody to help us. My father and Uncle Mitya were our only hope.

Both Louisa and Zhanna were disappointed and cried a lot, especially Louisa. Mother consoled her the best way she could, "Don't cry *milaya*, honey! Next year I hope you will be a straight A student, and I will get a free package for you, too. Maybe our father will find us and will send us money so that I will be able to pay for your package."

I was downcast because of my sister and my cousin. But I couldn't be sad for very long, as every string in my soul was playing a joyful melody with a refrain like this: "I am going to the camp! To the camp! To the camp! I'll be swimming in the camp! In the camp! In the camp!"

Looking at the tear-stained faces of Louisa and Zhanna, I promised myself that I would bring them some gifts from my camp trip. I said nothing to them because I had no idea what I could possibly bring to them from the Pioneer Camp. I had no money, and I knew nothing about the camp, its location and conditions. I told myself that I would figure out something to make my little sisters happy.

But it was not the summer Pioneer Camp I had dreamed about for all those years. This one was not located far away on the coast of the Black Sea or the Sea of Azov, nor in the wooden cabins in the mountain forest, among the beautiful pine trees. The Pioneer Camp occupied a four-story, red-brick school building, located on a desolate hill, at the outskirts of a small town which looked deserted. It was a miracle that the building itself had survived the war. Situated on the high hill, open to all the winds, without any natural protection such as deep forest or adjacent hills, it was an excellent target for both German and Soviet bombers.

In defiance of everything, the building had survived the perfidious German invasion, their hasty retreat, and the victorious advance of the Soviet troops. Now, it was ready to shelter the first war generation of young Pioneers who were eager to scream at the top of their young lungs our pioneer salute, *Wsegda gotov!* I am always ready!

153

There was not a single tree or bush around the school building—nor any sign of a stunted forest or, at least, a forest plantation, as was typical for that open steppe region of Southern Ukraine.

The train journey there took three hours. Then we drove half an hour more by camp bus to the building. There was no river on the horizon. Later, we found out that there was a small lake with silt banks, not far from our camp, about three kilometers. That summer, being twelve and a half years old, I planned to learn how to swim. I couldn't wait to get there. I had a feeling that it would be an interesting and entertaining time.

27. Pioneer Camp Routine

*T*here were thirty-five pioneers in our detachment. All the boys and girls were sixth graders, like me. We occupied three spacious classrooms on the second floor. One bedroom was for boys, another for girls, and the third was a game room. There was a night stand near every bed. One bed in the girl's bedroom was for our female teacher. The bathrooms were on the same floor.

The lives of the young pioneers were regulated by four meals: breakfast, lunch, after nap snack, and the evening meal which we called "supper." All our indoor and outdoor activities took place before, between and after meals.

At 7:00 a.m. we were awakened by the sounds of the pioneer bugle. We had to get up, to wash, to brush our teeth and to dress. We had to wear pioneer ties all the day. After that, we had to make our beds and be ready for the morning formation. That procedure always took place outside of the building on the sports grounds.

The detachments lined up in a perfect rectangle facing the senior chief pioneer leader. The leaders of all detachments reported to him or her about the readiness for the activities; they called the names of sick pioneers and those who were on duty, or who had violated the order or discipline in the camp.

The chief leader also announced the schedule of activities for every detachment for that day — which detachment was assigned to go to swim in the lake after breakfast, which in the afternoon. Every day, one detachment was on duty in the kitchen. He also announced the time and place of the rehearsals for the choir and the dance group, and the time for soccer and volleyball practice.

The camp opening ceremony was scheduled a week after our arrival at the camp. It would be held on the sports grounds. The preparation for that event was in full swing. The pioneers had to take part in the concert. Rehearsals of the choir and the dance group took place almost every day, sometimes even twice a day, after breakfast and after nap time. I participated in both of them.

We had breakfast at 8:00 a.m. As a rule, for breakfast, we had porridge with milk or cream of wheat, tea with two cubes of sugar, a small portion of butter and two slices of rye bread. Sometimes, we had cocoa with milk instead of tea. We never had coffee.

After breakfast, each detachment acted according to the schedule announced at the formation. Some detachments stayed inside in their game rooms and played dominos, lotto, and other table games. Playing cards was considered inappropriate for the pioneers. The detachments, in turn, spent scheduled time at the camp library reading books, children's newspapers and magazines. Volleyball and soccer teams practiced on a regular basis on the sports grounds of the camp.

Senior detachments were on duty in the kitchen and in the dining hall. In the kitchen, we washed and peeled vegetables. In the dining hall, we set the tables, served the meals, and cleaned the tables. After every meal, we collected and washed all the dishes by hand. We also mopped the floors of the dining hall. Sometimes, the cooks gave the boys on duty an extra glass of milk or a pancake as they always were hungry from running like crazy while playing soccer day long. I was not hungry; what they served us was enough for me.

The most desirable and exciting activity was, of course, the walk to the lake. We marched in columns, like soldiers, carrying the banner of our detachment, according to the pioneer ritual, while singing pioneer marching songs. It was our favorite activity. We were always ready to go to the lake, even in the middle of the night. Only two detachments were assigned to go to the lake every day: one after breakfast, another after the lunch nap.

The lake was too small to accommodate more than one detachment. It was hard for the teacher and for the physical fitness instructor to watch and properly supervise all the children when we were in the water. It was dangerous for the children who didn't know how to swim, which turned out to be the majority of us. I was one of them. But we were eager to learn.

On the bank, our instructor explained to us how to swim and showed all the moves. Then we entered the water up to the knees standing in the deep, sticky silt and practiced moving our arms for a while. After that, we moved farther into the lake up to our chests repeating the same moves with our arms.

Finally, the instructor made one boy lie in the water belly down while he held him with both hands from below. The boy started to move his hands and legs and slowly moved ahead; the instructor was still holding his body from below. Then, he took his hands away, but the boy kept swimming.

Suddenly, the boy realized that nobody was holding him, stopped moving his arms, and disappeared under the water. We opened our mouths; we didn't even have time to scream when he came up and stood right in the water which reached up to his neck. The lake was not very deep, but a danger of drowning for beginning swimmers was always there.

We spent more time on the bank listening to the instructor's explanations than practicing swimming. Besides, we had no swimming equipment such as ring buoys or other floating devices. Our only rescue equipment was a big, old, dirty truck tire which belonged to the instructor. I managed to learn how to swim "kitten style," as we say in Russia, which is the same as the "dog paddle" in America. I was immensely proud of myself. Since then, swimming became my favorite pastime, and it still is.

Lunch was at 1:00 p.m. We were served traditional three-course meals. As the first course, we always had some kind of soup: spinach, bean, cabbage, vegetable or borsch (beetroot and cabbage). For the second course, we had mostly canned meat garnished with cooked rice, buckwheat, mashed potatoes, cabbage, and carrots. Sometimes, we had traditional meat cutlets made with ground meat, hamburger style.

Dessert consisted of a glass of *compote* (a cool drink made of fresh or dried stewed fruits) or a glass of *kissel* (the same as *compote*, only made with the addition of some starch). From time to time, we had seasonal fruits for dessert: apples, apricots, plums or pears.

The mandatory after-lunch nap lasted from 2:00 p.m. till 3:30 p.m. We spent it in our beds. We had to sleep or just to stay in bed and rest. We were not allowed to read in bed or to talk. We had to be quiet. After nap time, we had to make our beds again, and wash our hands and faces.

At 4:00 p.m., we had the afternoon snack which was not served in the dining room; our teacher brought it to our game room on a simple, flat plate.

The first day of our arrival, she put the plate on the table and said, "Here is your afternoon snack. It's chocolate. Each chocolate bar had to be divided into small pieces, and it isn't easy to break into equal parts. So, guys, be patient, don't get angry if this time your piece looks smaller than someone else's. Next time, you will get a bigger one than somebody else. Is that clear?"

Stunned and delighted, we all kept silent. I saw chocolate in small uneven pieces, placed attractively on the plate. After four years of war with no chocolate around, finally, here it was! The teacher gave everyone a piece, took the last piece from the plate and put it in her mouth.

Instinctively, I wanted to do the same, but some mysterious force stopped me. Like my little sister Louisa, I had forgotten the taste of chocolate. So I looked and looked at the delicacy but didn't dare taste it. In a split second, I decided to keep it for a while and not eat it all at once. I carefully wrapped my square chocolate piece in a white handkerchief and put it in the side pocket of my skirt. Grandma was right when she told me that pockets in the skirts could be very handy. *"I'll let it sit for a while in my pocket. I'll decide what to do with the chocolate later,"* I thought to myself.

Other children reacted to the sweet snack in different ways. The boys, for example, immediately ate it, almost gulping the chocolate without even tasting it. Some girls sucked and savored the delicacy, keeping it in their mouths, taking pleasure in the almost forgotten taste. Several girls, however, acted exactly as I did: they wrapped their portions in handkerchiefs and put them in their pockets.

That evening, I couldn't fall asleep. I lay in bed with my eyes wide open, quiet as a mouse. The convolutions of my brain, meanwhile, turned faster than bicycle wheels as I tried to reach the right decision.

Finally, I made it: I will save all the chocolate that I'll get during twenty-six days in the camp as a present for Louisa, Zhanna, Grandma, Grandpa, Aunt Valentina and Mother. It was a tough decision to make because I myself still was twelve and a half years old girl who for four years of war had been deprived of any candy, not to mention chocolate. Once the decision was made, I breathed with relief. *"I'll stick to it, no matter what,"* I said to myself with conviction.

Now, I had to find a safe place to keep my treasure. In the camp building, we actually had no privacy. We had no lockers, and each of us had to share our small, two-drawer night stand with another person. I used the upper drawer, and the girl whose bed was across from mine, used the lower one. She looked like a nice person, but I had just met her for the first time in my life, and I didn't know if I could trust her enough to put my chocolate treasure in our shared night stand.

It was risky to hide the chocolate under the pillow of my bed, as the pioneers on duty in the bedroom sometimes had to readjust blankets and pillows if they didn't look neat enough to them. They could discover my hiding place and steal my chocolate. The opportunity and the temptation were strong enough.

After long deliberation, I came to the conclusion that the best place to keep my treasure was under the blanket, just under the pillow. Thus, if the pioneers on duty would have to remove the pillow or readjust the blanket, they wouldn't notice anything suspicious.

Since that first afternoon in the camp, I tried to make

my bed as neat as possible in order not to attract attention to it. In addition, several times a day, while visiting the restrooms across the hall from our bedrooms, I tried to sneak into our bedroom to check on my treasure and to readjust my blanket and my pillow the best way I could, just in case. Our teacher even commended me for my always neatly and properly made bed. It was my secret operation, and I conducted it on a regular basis, keeping in mind one of Grandma's favorite proverbs, "It's better to be safe than sorry."

As the number of chocolate pieces kept increasing, I doubled my effort to protect them from curious eyes. I watched my treasure like a hawk. During the morning formation, some cases of petty larceny in several detachments were reported to the chief pioneer leader: combs, pioneer ties, socks, coin-purses with small coins in them, small toys, pencils, safety pins (called English pins in Russia) and ribbons.

One day, a bar of soap in a green soap box disappeared from my drawer. I complained to the teacher. She checked all the nightstands in both girls' and boys' bedrooms and discovered my green soap box in somebody's drawer in the girls' bedroom. The girl in question confessed, on the spot, that she had "borrowed" my soap to wash her socks, but had forgotten to ask my permission and to put it back into my drawer. Instead, she had put it in hers. She explained that her mother didn't include soap when she packed her things for the camp. Obviously, she inherited her forgetfulness from her mother.

The teacher made her apologize to me and warned everybody in our detachment that in the future, they should ask permission from the owner before taking such things as combs, soaps, pencils, anything. Otherwise, it would be considered a theft. As a result, the pioneer

161

could be expelled from the camp, and the theft would be reported to his or her school administration. My case was discussed during the formation as a reminder to everybody that they couldn't borrow anything without the owner's permission.

To my credit, I saved all twenty-six pieces of chocolate and brought them home as I had planned to do. It cost me extra trips to the restroom, but I didn't mind doing that.

In spite of those small nuisances, I had a good time that first post-war summer in the Pioneer Camp. I wasn't a helper to the adults anymore; I was a child again, doing children's things. In the camp, we played, we rested, we relaxed, we learned new physical exercises, we read new books and children's magazines, we learned new children's songs and new dances, and we played games. We learned, with three years' delay, how to be children again, not the premature adults of children's ages. But, like they say, "Better late than never."

The camp opening ceremony was a great success. After the concert, we sat around the Pioneer campfire and with huge enthusiasm, sang cheerful, newly learned Pioneer songs to the accompaniment of the accordion. It was fun and a delight to sing all together. Even local residents from the town, both children and adults, came to listen to us singing and awarded us with loud clapping.

Sitting at the campfire and looking at the sparks glittering in the background of the dark, starry summer sky, I had a premonition that something wonderful would happen very soon in my life. What would it be? I had no answer to that question, but my heart was pounding with the sweet joy of anticipation.

At the closing first camp shift ceremony, the chief pioneer leader handed awards to the most active pioneers for their positive contribution to the Pioneer Camp work.

Among the prizes were soccer and volleyball balls—the dream of all the boys—new silk pioneer ties with shiny metallic clips, children's books, fairy tales, boxes of colored pencils, and note pads.

I was awarded a box of twelve colored pencils, and I was happy and proud of myself. Twelve colored pencils! It was one more treasure for me and my sisters. We never had so many colored pencils. I couldn't stop smiling; I considered myself a lucky girl.

I was proud of my achievements at the camp. First, I had learned to swim; second, I had a sweet present for my sisters and the entire family; third, I learned new songs and wrote down all the lyrics of the new songs in my special summer camp diary which I brought from home; fourth, I had won a prize—a box of twelve colored pencils; fifth, I made new girlfriends whose addresses were written down in my diary. We had decided to write to one another.

Finally, as I promised Mother, I hadn't lost a single piece of my clothing, as other children had. I had no injuries, while some other children managed to break their noses, arms, legs, fingers and toes. I was going back home in one piece, in good spirits and with twenty-six small pieces of chocolate!

Long live the summer Pioneer Camp and its happy campers!

28. Farewell Pioneer Camp!

*T*he morning after the camp closing ceremony, it was announced at the formation that the after-lunch nap for two senior detachments was canceled for that day. Instead, we would go to our favorite lake for a last swim. We greeted the news with the loud-voiced *Ura!*

After breakfast we were told to wash our clothes, underwear, socks, handkerchiefs and even pioneer ties and lay them out to dry. Later that afternoon, when we returned from the lake, we would have to iron everything so that we would arrive home with clean and pressed clothes.

We had to do the laundry by hand, as there were no washing machines nor dyers at that time. We had only two wash-boards and several wash-basins in our group, and we had to take turns using them. In order to speed up the process, we rinsed the laundry under the bathroom faucets. We decided that everyone would use the wash-board for five minutes only. As there was no clock in our bedroom and nobody had a wrist watch, the girl next in line was counting to three hundred: and one, and two, and three, and so on — not a bad way out of the situation.

We had to move fast in order to finish our laundry

by lunch. Nobody complained as we all were eager to go to the lake one more time. The spirit of cooperation and mutual support reigned in the bathroom facility. Pushed by the irrepressible desire to get rid of the laundry as soon as possible and jump into the lake, we helped one another. We shared the remnants of a bar of soap with those who were running out of it; there were several of those.

I myself offered the thin piece of my soap to the girl who several weeks ago "had borrowed" my soap from my nightstand without my permission and then "had forgotten" to put it back. After we finished our laundry, we dried it in our bedroom on the head and footboards of our metal beds, as there was not enough space in the bathroom to hang everything to dry.

After lunch we went to the lake. The weather was warm, the sky was deep blue and cloudless. We jumped into the lake and joyfully screamed and splashed in its refreshing waters. We were happy, and even the silty bottom of the lake couldn't spoil our good mood.

We walked back from the lake singing pioneer marching songs. As usual, we stopped our column not far from the camp at the railroad crossing, so that the other detachment could catch up. At the railroad crossing, we moved in the direction of the camp in an orderly manner, measuring out our pace and adjusting it to the beating of the drum and the sound of the bugle. Every detachment had its own drummer and a bugler who marched in front of the column, just after the standard-bearer, establishing the rhythm of the movement.

At the next turn, behind the trees, there was a commotion on the side of the road. It was a detachment of orphanage children from our camp, ages from seven to nine. We recognized them by their identical clothes and hats. That day, those children were not scheduled to go to the lake; instead, they were taken to the nearest forest plantation for a walk. We knew those girls. Many of them had braids, so once a week, we older girls helped them wash their hair.

The children stood in a circle on the side of the road. We couldn't see what was happening there, but something, for sure, had happened, as they all stood and looked at something or somebody in the middle of the circle.

Our group leader ordered us to stop. Then she said very strictly in a loud voice, "Don't move! Wait for me here. I'll go to find out what is happening." And she left.

We were burning with curiosity and impatience. We wanted to know what happened. We stretched our necks, we got on our tiptoes, but we still couldn't see what was happening in that tight circle of children, across from us. A boy's voice behind me said loudly, "Maybe somebody fell and broke a leg? Maybe somebody died?"

That assumption stirred us up. We got more and more impatient, wanting to know everything at once. The children at the back started to push forward, and then we were all moving forward toward the orphan girls who were crowded on the side of the road in a close, silent and motionless circle. We quickly reached them and stopped. It was like a scene from a silent movie: the children stood with their mouths wide open. Nobody talked or asked questions. Everybody was quiet.

All eyes were fastened on a little girl who sat on her knees on the side of the road sobbing uncontrollably while wiping the tears from her face with her crumpled summer hat.

A teacher squatted in front of the girl trying to console her, "Don't cry, Masha! Look, here is your father. He has returned from the front and has found you. He will take you home to see your aunt and your cousins. They all are waiting for you. Let me dry your tears with my handkerchief." The teacher awkwardly tried to wipe the tears from the girl's cheeks with her not very fresh white handkerchief, but she couldn't make her stop crying. Some other little girls about Masha's age, started to cry. We older children didn't know what to do.

I looked around and noticed a short, somewhat stout man in a military uniform without shoulder-straps, standing in silence not far from the teacher. The absence of insignia meant that he was out of active duty. There was a look of dismay and helplessness on his face, as if he didn't know what to do, how to react to Masha's behavior. *Masha's father*, I said to myself quietly.

Then somebody whispered in the crowd, behind my back, "Masha's mother and two older brothers were killed when the Germans bombed the train with Jewish evacuees from Kiev. Many people had died. Masha, who was only three years old, survived by a miracle. When the rescue team found her under the train wreckage, she was first sent to the hospital and later to the orphanage. She was lucky that she knew her first and last name. That's how her father had found where she was and had now come to visit her. He was walking from the railroad station to the camp when he saw the orphanage detachment and asked the teacher if his daughter was in it. That's how he met Masha. Unfortunately, the poor thing didn't recognize him, as she had been in the orphanage for almost four years. Now she is confused and scared."

Finally, the teacher managed to quiet Masha. She still was sighing and breathing heavily, but she didn't sob anymore. The teacher took her by one hand, her father by the other, and they led Masha to the camp. We followed them. There was no drum beating, no sound of the bugle. We were late for supper, and our teachers were alarmed

167

and were waiting for us at the gate as they didn't know the reason for our delay.

At supper, Masha's father, as a guest of honor, sat at Masha's table and ate with her and two other girls. Our teacher warned us, "Try not to look at Masha's table. Leave her and her father alone. Don't embarrass them by staring." All the children, including myself, were attracted to that table like by magnet, and, on the sly, from time to time, we all enviously glanced at them.

Thus, the war which four years ago had interrupted our normal lives, had taken our fathers away and had deprived us of our childhood, once again was breaking into our lives, reminding us that it wasn't finished yet, that there still would be terrible consequences of that war.

All the camp was under the effect of Masha's meeting with her father and the terrible fate of a little girl who had lost her mother and her two brothers at such a young age. Later that evening, in the bedroom, sharing the stories about our fathers and relatives, we couldn't fall asleep.

One of the girls told us while crying that her father was killed at the very start of the war, and they had already received his death certificate. Yet another girl said that her father was heavily wounded and was in the hospital in Kazakhstan, but her mother didn't have money for a train ticket to visit him. Some families had received notices that their fathers were missing in action. Some fathers were captured by the Germans, and nothing was known about their fates.

There was good news, as well. One girl boasted of a big postal package with nice clothes which her father had sent from Germany and his promise to send more. Several girls bragged that their fathers had received military awards, orders and medals, such as "Order of Lenin," "Order of the Red Banner," "Order of the Red Star." Some fathers were awarded with "Medals of Bravery," "Medals for Defense of Moscow, Leningrad, Stalingrad," and other cities of the Soviet Union.

In order to boost the patriotic spirit of the Soviet soldiers and the general population, new military rewards were established commemorating the names of the famous Russian military leaders of the eighteenth and nineteenth centuries, such as Field Marshals Suvorov, Kutuzov, and Admiral Nakhimov. "Order of the Great Patriotic War" was also a new one. The new awards were mentioned by some girls. Our family hadn't heard from our father yet, nor had Aunt Valentina heard from her husband, Mitya.

The next morning, after an early breakfast we said warm good-byes to our friends from other detachments and to our teachers. Then we received our snacks for the bus trip — several cookies and an apple — got onto the buses, waved to all camp teachers gathered around, and started on our way home.

The bus ride was about two and a half hours long. I was lucky to get a window seat. At first, we sang all our favorite pioneer songs. Then, tired of emotional partings from our friends and the camp teachers and lulled by the monotonous movements of the bus, we stopped singing and sat quietly for the rest of the trip. I looked out the window at the yellow fields of the late summer crop, at the green strips of acacia and the bright blue sky being crossed by the flocks of cranes flying to the south.

My thoughts were about my own father from whom we received only two letters during the first two months of the war. Was he alive? Was he wounded? Was he lying somewhere in a hospital? Was he lying on some battlefield? I remembered the site of the soldier's communal grave, and immediately I felt like crying. Reaching into my skirt pocket for my handkerchief, my fingers unexpectedly touched something besides my hankie.

What is that? I wondered. It was a small piece of paper folded in four sections. I slowly unfolded it and saw a short message written with a pencil in slipshod handwriting. It said, "I love you. Yura." I couldn't believe that it had been addressed to me. *It must have been some mistake,* I knew for sure that there was no boy with such a name in our detachment.

For several minutes, I racked my brains wondering who that could be. Then it struck me. I remembered an incident which took place several weeks ago. I was running down the stairs from the second floor when a boy from the other detachment, jumping over two steps, reached me, and passing by, painfully pulled my braid. I staggered and almost lost my balance. In order not to fall, I flung up my hands accidentally scratching the neck of the boy whose name, I knew, was Yura.

He screamed and covered the scratch with his hand. Without another word, Yura hurried down the stairs in front of me. *Idiot!* I called after him; he didn't even turn his head. I was nervous and scared. That incident could cost me dearly if he dared complain to the teacher. Fighting was considered a violation of camp discipline. I could be expelled from the camp, just like that.

At the next day's morning formation, I stood more dead than alive waiting for the pioneer leader to call my name and to admonish me for my inappropriate behavior. But nobody called my name that morning. For some reason, Yura didn't inform on me. For several days more, I waited for something bad to happen to me, and I tried to avoid encounters with that boy.

At twelve and a half years old, I had received my first love message. I sat in the bus quietly, looking at the open window and twirling the note in my hands without knowing what to think or what to do with it. The girl who sat next to me was dozing.

What should I do with the note? Should I keep it or should I tear it and throw it away? Maybe I should show it to Mother? Somehow, I knew that I wouldn't dare show it to her. I would rather share it with Grandmother and ask her for advice. How about my girlfriends? Should I show it to them?

On the one hand, I felt guilty for that accidental scratch. On the other hand, I felt flattered that somebody wrote me a love note, and I wanted to brag about it to my girlfriends who had already shown me their love notes.

That note was burning my hand. For some inexplicable reason, I didn't want to tear it up. Without realizing what I was doing, I extended my hand with the note in it through the opened bus window and whispered in a low voice, "Farewell, Pioneer Camp!" Then I slowly unclenched my fist and let the note fly away. A gust of wind picked up my love message and carried it away.

As I said a final farewell to my beloved Pioneer Camp, I suddenly realized that because of the war I had missed not only three school years, but trips to the Pioneer Camps which could have been located in different places: among the high snowy mountains, or on the shores of the Black or the Baltic Seas, or maybe on the banks of picturesque, swift-flowing rivers with willows and green meadows full of colorful, fragrant flowers. I could have practiced swimming in the transparent cool waters, instead of that murky small lake full of frogs where we swam during the hot summer days in the camp.

I might have received more love notes in those camps. Who knows? The terrible sense of irreplaceable loss saddened me, but only for a moment. In spite of everything, I felt happy and full of hope as if that love note was the first messenger of a new and promising stage of my life.

29. Surprise! Surprise!

*T*hree hours after leaving the Pioneer Camp, the bus approached the main entrance of our school building where a small group of parents and relatives were waiting for our arrival. From the bus window I saw Louisa, Zhanna and Aunt Valentina with baby Oleg. I waved to them. Louisa was the one who saw me first. Smiling joyfully, she jumped forward and waved her hand with a piece of paper in it. I recognized its triangular shape at once. *It's a letter from our father, from the front!* I gasped.

During the war, there was a shortage of everything, including postal envelopes. The letters from the front were sent on one piece of paper folded as a triangle. The address was written on the face side of the triangle; the return address was on the back. In the center, there was a black round stamp with the number of the military unit and next to it was a small, red square stamp which said "checked by military censor." The sender's name was written at the very bottom.

Louisa rushed to the bus window, brandishing the triangular letter as if it were a battlefield banner. "It's a letter from our father! He is alive! We received it last week!" she screamed, full of joy and impatience, jumping like a playful kid, eager to share with me the wonderful news.

My heart started to race. *Our father is alive! He is alive! He wrote us a letter!* I wanted to jump through the window and scream along with Louisa. She was so excited that she didn't give Valentina or Zhanna the chance to open their mouths.

"Uncle Mitya also sent a letter. He is in Eastern Prussia," she screamed. I didn't know if Eastern Prussia was a city or a country or where it was located, but the unknown foreign name struck my ear and imagination. It was so wonderful that Valentina got the letter from her husband, Mitya, too. I was happy for both Valentina and Zhanna.

When I finally got out of the bus, I kissed and hugged everybody, including the little smiling face of baby Oleg. He recognized me, smiling happily, extending his arms towards me and screamed, "Nina, Nina!" I was happy to see their faces. I had missed them a lot.

I wanted to read Father's letter right there, but Aunt Valentina took it from Louisa, put it in her pocket and said, "Let's go home first. The rest of the family will soon return from the vegetable field. They had been working hard the whole day, and they are hungry. We barely have time to heat the food before they come. Let's hurry, girls!"

When we reached Grandma's house, Valentina asked Zhanna to watch the baby and started to reheat the food, while Louisa and I helped her to set the table in the backyard, under the apple tree. We did everything quickly, and I still had enough time to read Father's letter. During the first two months of the war, we had received only two letters from our father. Then Germans occupied Grandma's town, and we couldn't send him letters anymore. He didn't know whether we had managed to evacuate from Ukraine or stayed with our grandparents in their town during the German occupation.

As soon as the postal services were reestablished after the liberation of our town from the Germans, Father wrote us a letter to Grandmother's address. He wrote that his unit was in Germany, but he didn't name its exact location because of the military censorship. He had been wounded twice and had been hospitalized. His unit passed through several countries such as Poland, Romania, Czechoslovakia, and Hungary. He had seen many destroyed cities, burned villages and dead people. When his unit drove through the numerous desolate towns and villages, they had seen few domestic ownerless animals wandering among the ruins. Somehow, those animals had managed to survive artillery shelling, bombing and hunger, but the majority of them had been killed or had starved to death.

Father wrote that there was a shortage of everything. People were suffering from hunger, diseases, lack of medical services and medications. All the medical supplies and drugs were sent to the front, to the field and military hospitals on the home front. The main war slogan was: "Everything for the front! Everything for victory!"

Father knew nothing about our fate. In his first letter, he asked Grandma to write him everything she knew about us. He had tried to find us and had written several inquiries to the Evacuation Center, but in their files they had no information about our family. He also asked our grandparents about their lives during the German occupation, about the situation with food supplies and other goods in their town, and how they managed to survive.

At supper, all the attention turned to me. Everybody asked me questions. I told them about our camp schedule, our menus, our singing at the campfire, my swimming success, about winning a prize—a box of twelve colored pencils. I even sang a new song I had learned in the camp which Louisa and Zhanna liked very much. When supper was almost over, I said quietly, "I brought you something from the camp, for all of you. Guess what it is?" I put the small bundle wrapped in my hanky on the table. Everybody stopped talking and looked surprised.

30. The Chocolate Treat

I slowly unwrapped my handkerchief and emptied its contents onto the flat ceramic candy tray which we used as a bread plate — all twenty-six pieces of chocolate which I had secretly collected and kept safe as a gift for my family from my summer camp trip.

"What is this?" Louisa, goggle-eyed, with her jaw dropping in surprise, looked at the tray as if she were spellbound.

"It's something I want you ..." I started but didn't even have the chance to finish the sentence when my adored aunt Valentina who sat between Louisa and Zhanna swiftly extended her hand, grabbed a handful of the dark brown pieces and hurriedly threw two of them into her mouth. For a moment, she savored them with her eyes closed, slowly smacked her lips and said, "How lovely! What a pleasure! I had already forgotten the taste of it." Then she turned to her daughter and gave her two pieces, "Go ahead, Zhanna, taste one! It's so good."

After that, without even looking at anyone, she held out her hand again and wanted to take more chocolate from the tray. However, it was not to be. Grandpa intercepted her arm, his brows knitted with reproach and said quietly but sternly, "That's enough, Valentina. Stop it! Nina hasn't eaten a single piece and brought all of it for her sister and her cousins. You are not a child anymore. Besides, you have grabbed a lot. So leave it for the children."

"Let's do it this way," Grandma said in a low conciliatory voice. "We all take one piece each of chocolate for our tea. The rest I will keep for the children and will give them one piece every day. It will last longer this way, and they will enjoy it more." Turning her head to Valentina, she continued, "You, Valya, have already taken twice as much. So, please, put it back."

Reluctantly, with her lips pouting, Valentina returned two pieces to the tray. Then, Grandma distributed the chocolate among us, with the exception of Valentina. Louisa, however, was not satisfied with such an arrangement. She curled her lips, angrily shook her tousled head, and said in a pathetic tone, "Aunt Valentina has gotten two pieces. I want one more!"

"Look what you have done, Valentina!" Grandpa said in irritation. He was puffing like a boiling samovar and didn't want to calm down without a battle. The atmosphere had become very tense. "It wasn't enough for you that you had robbed your own sister," Grandpa continued, "now you're after the children's candy. *Fu!* Ugh! Your behavior is disgusting. *Kak ne stydno!* Shame on you!"

Grandpa decisively banged on the table with his fist. The plates jumped. Everybody shuddered. Valentina's face was pale; her eyes were swollen with tears. Little Zhanna seized hold of Valentina's arm, while Louisa, scared as a rabbit, sought refuge under our mother's wing.

I sat motionless, trying to understand what was happening, what Grandpa was talking about. Who has stolen what and from whom? Suddenly, in the heat of the moment, something clicked in my head. I remembered a very suspicious conversation between the adults. It had taken place during the German occupation.

One evening, when I was already in bed, I accidentally overheard the angry words between my grandparents in the kitchen which was next to our small bedroom. It was difficult to understand as they talked in low voices, and I was half asleep. I heard only fragments of their talk and couldn't comprehend much. I remembered that Valentina's name had come up more than once and that Grandpa's voice was angry and annoyed. *What was all that about,* I wondered.

The next day early in the morning, Grandma and I collected eggs in the chicken coop. The hen nests were on the upper perch of the barn; only several of them were on the floor. "Some of the hens prefer floor nests," Grandma used to say. I had to climb up to take the freshly laid eggs from the upper nests and hand them to Grandma. She waited nearby on the barn floor, holding the wicker basket with a handle. She always reminded me to leave at least one egg in the nest because laying hens avoided empty nests. I was not sure if that was true or it was just Grandma's fantasy, but I followed her advice strictly.

I liked that morning routine; the empty barn smelled fresh of cow's milk and of some unknown dried herbs which Grandma picked up in the fields, tied up in small bunches and put to dry on the line in the barn. I didn't pay much attention to her explanation of the medicinal values of those herbs.

In the middle of that morning routine, I seized the moment and asked Grandma, "Is that true that Valentina has robbed my mother as Grandpa said? What did she take from her that made Grandpa so angry?"

Grandma carefully laid several eggs that she held in her cupped hands into the basket and said in a low conspiratorial voice, "Do you remember when Valentina came with Zhanna to visit us at Easter? They lived in the city at that time after Uncle Mitya had managed to escape from the German captivity."

"Yes, I do!" I nodded. "She wore her favorite blue crepe de chine dress, with clusters of lilacs on it. I liked that dress a lot. It was so beautiful!"

"I remember that silk dress," Grandma said with a dreamy smile on her lips. "What surprised me more was her pair of well-matched blue shoes with high heels. I noticed them immediately because it was impossible to get such shoes at that time. No way! No! Where did she get them? At the flea market? They looked new; she couldn't have bought those shoes there!"

I recalled the image of blue-eyed Valentina with her gorgeous dark wavy hair, in her blue dress and in the matching blue leather shoes. She made an unforgettable impression on all of us when she appeared like an angel from the sky in our front yard. We stood motionless, like statues — Louisa and I barefooted, the adults in worn down old sandals and slippers which were beyond repair.

Grandma's voice made me come down to earth, as if she overheard my thoughts, "Oh yes, our Valentina looked good in her blue silk dress and in blue shoes." Grandma stubbornly didn't want to use the fashionable word 'crepe de chin'. "But," she continued, "one question nagged me all the time. Where did she get those shoes? She told us that her neighbor who happened to be a shoemaker had managed to buy a piece of blue leather at the black market and made those shoes for her. She even took one shoe off and showed us a factory stamp inside. I didn't believe her. Besides, that blue color looked familiar to me, but I couldn't recall where I had seen it. Then your mother came up and, with trembling lips, whispered into my ear, 'I had two pieces of blue leather and one piece of black hidden under the mattress of my bed. You saw it, Mother!

Now one piece of blue has gone! I am sure that Valentina took it. The color is identical to the color of her shoes! How could she do it, Mother? *Besstyzhaya vorovka!* Shameless thief!"

I couldn't believe what I had heard. It couldn't be true! I refused to believe it. Valentina, my mother's baby sister, wasn't just my adored aunt, she was like my older sister. She was my closest friend, my mentor, and my confidante, although the last word was not at that time a part of my vocabulary.

I trusted her, and she trusted me. Sometimes she told me things that she didn't dare to tell Louisa and Zhanna. I was proud of her trust. I liked her, and I spent more time with her than I spent with my mother. Valentina had to take care of baby Oleg, and she, in the heat of the field work season, stayed at home a lot, while the adults — Grandma, Grandpa and Mother — had to go to work the fields. Sometimes, I went to the fields with them. But often, I stayed at home to help Valentina with the baby and to take care of both Louisa and Zhanna.

Valentina always was in a cheerful mood; she did everything quickly and enthusiastically. She smiled and laughed easily at our childish pranks and never admonished or punished us no matter what mischief we had committed. She also liked to mimic Grandpa's irrational behavior when he got angry at one of us children, and chased us along the yard, with his tongue between his teeth, his eyes sparkling menacingly, and a fresh twig in his hand. He never hit us, but he liked to scare us. And scared we were, running like frightened rabbits in different directions.

When we children misbehaved, Grandpa always accused Grandma and his daughters.

"You have lost control over the children. They have

gotten out of hand. They are spoiled and don't understand what discipline is."

"They are just children," Grandma used to defend us. "They can't understand everything at their age the way you want them to. When they are older, they will understand. Let them be children now! They will be adults for the rest of their lives!"

I trusted my Grandmother, and I relied on her judgment, but at that moment I couldn't accept the idea that Aunt Valentina was a thief. It was some kind of confusion and misunderstanding. Maybe that was just slander or envy? I was disappointed and offended for my aunt.

Submerged in my own world, saving every free minute to read books and to study, I didn't pay a lot of attention to the relationships among adults. That's why I couldn't admit that my aunt Valentina was able to commit such a hideous crime — to steal from her own sister, *Nyet! Nyet! Nyet!* No! No! No!

Now, more than seventy years later, I don't exclude such a possibility. Valentina was young and beautiful. She liked to dress up, to show off, and spent a lot of time in front of my mother's heart-shaped table mirror, in which, according to her own words, she looked extremely beautiful. She probably was tempted to enhance her gorgeous blue crepe de chine dress with the matching blue leather shoes at the expense of her sister and her children; both Louisa and I desperately needed school footwear.

I maintained a cordial relationship with Valentina till the day she died at the age of eighty-six. We never talked about that incident which took place during the German occupation. It did, however, put the first chink in the armor of my childish trust in adults' decency.

31. Boys and Girls Socializing

Our everyday life was taking its normal course. At first glance, everything was as usual. Autumn was approaching. The efforts of our family were concentrated on collecting the fruit of our labor from the field. We had to harvest potatoes, beetroots, carrots, pumpkins, corn, beans and sunflowers as soon as possible and to store everything in the cellar for the winter before the rainy season began.

School started on the first of September. Louisa, Zhanna, Mother and I spent the first half of the day at school. Back home, we children had to do our homework first. In addition to that, like every member of our family we had to participate in household chores. I swept and mopped all the rooms and did the dishes. Louisa did the dusting and watered the flowers. Little Zhanna helped her. Sometimes, they fed the chickens together.

Mother helped Grandma do the cooking and the laundry and did the ironing of the bed linen. Grandpa provided the drinking water from the community well, took care of the cow and the pig. He also fed our dog. The dog loved him and barked loudly when Grandpa opened the gate. Valentina took care of baby Oleg, and, to the best of her ability, helped Grandma and my mother with food preparation and laundry.

The German occupation was over, but we still had to work hard in order to survive, as there were no grocery stores and very little money. One had to get up at dawn and stay in a long line at the bakery to get a loaf of rye bread. We were happy that the post office was functioning. The mail was sent and delivered on a regular basis.

The improvement in our lives was hardly noticeable, and the changes happened slowly. We still didn't have radios or bus transportation. The local newspaper was worth its weight in gold because people used it not only as a source of information but as toilet paper. They also used newspapers to roll homemade cigarettes. One of my classmates complained, crying bitterly, that her father had smoked all the books they had on their bookshelf. However, there was no deficit of tobacco. All the smokers planted tobacco seedlings in their vegetable gardens and had their own fresh crop of tobacco leaves every year.

The most important thing for me was that the school was re-opened. I was one of the best students in my class. School was my life and my delight. It was always a great joy for me to learn new things in any subject. I studied easily and enthusiastically. I prepared my homework quickly and diligently as soon as I got home from school. I also participated in extra-curricular activities such as folk dancing and the school choir. To my great surprise, I succeeded in those areas, too.

Spring of 1945 came unusually early and was fast. The snow melted in just one week, and field work started earlier that year. At the farmers market, the talk was that the war was approaching its end. Newspapers and the radio at the school announced that the Russian troops had crossed the eastern borders of Germany. People couldn't believe that the end of the war was close.

Meanwhile, our sixth grade class was infected by some kind of a spring bug — we didn't know the word "virus" at that time. Without any obvious reason or necessity, students started to write one another notes during the classes. At first, I didn't notice anything suspicious. Later, during the big break after the second class, when I was walking in the school yard, one of the girls, Vera, whose desk was behind mine, gave me a push with her elbow and whispered in my ear, "Look, look! Have you seen? Lyudka is handing a note to Vovka. It's from her friend Mashka. Vovka is in love with Mashka! Look! He took it and hid it in his pocket," Vera whispered.

"What does Mashka write to him?"

"Love notes. They write each other every day," she sighed enviously.

"About what?" Now I was even more bewildered.

"Don't you know? About love, about their feelings, and how they like each other. They offer friendship to each other! He even wrote her a poem. She showed it to me, I swear! Cross my heart."

"Vovka? A poem?" I asked in disbelief. I couldn't imagine that.

Vovka (short for Vladimir) was a fifteen-year old lanky guy, a lazy-bones and loafer, with a face generously sprinkled with big ugly pimples. He adored math and hated literature. Every poem which the girls had recited with feelings at the blackboard he met with a wry, mocking smile, screwing up his face. He never prepared his literature homework assignment, and when our teacher called him to the blackboard to answer a question, he stood like a wooden idol mumbling something unintelligible or just came out with all sorts of rubbish. And now he was writing love poems? I was stunned, to say the least.

I immediately recalled the note which I had found in my skirt pocket the day before my departure from the summer camp, but it had contained only three words — *I love you.*

Then Vera continued, "Almost all the students are in love and write notes to one another. Haven't you noticed?"

"No, I haven't! Nobody had written a single note to me, I haven't written to anybody," I retorted in confusion.

In class, I always concentrated on my classwork, listened carefully to the teacher, and looked at the blackboard. I tried not to miss a word from the teacher's explanations. So, I didn't see or hear anything else. Now, I decided to watch and to observe what was happening during the lessons. The next class was geography. I, on the sly, looked back several times, as I sat at the first desk in the middle row. Then, without turning my head, I squinted my eyes to the right, then to the left as soon as the teacher, with the pointer in her hand, turned her head to the map with her back to the class.

To my big surprise, the notes were jumping out in the open like fleas using that split second when the teacher's eyes were on the map. The technique the students used to deliver their notes was a revelation to me. I saw that one student handing his note didn't even turn his head. He sat straight, motionless. He just extended his hand without taking his eyes from the map on the blackboard as if he were following the explanations of the teacher. I felt as if I were watching a silent movie.

Obviously, my mouth was wide open because one of the boys put his finger to his lips and warned, "Don't you turn back!" There was no sound, but I understood what he had said. I changed my position and fixed my gaze upon the map hanging on the blackboard. I was curious, but I had no time, and I didn't wish to be involved in that spring fever of love note.

Vera continued to keep me posted as to the new development of the note-writing. According to her, the girls who were two or three years older than Vera and me played a leading role in that feverish social communication. Those girls hadn't received home schooling during the three years of German occupation when the schools were closed, and, therefore, they had fallen behind in their studies. They should have been in the eighth grade, but now they were only in the sixth. One of them, Luydmila, with three other girls, including Vera, appeared uninvited one afternoon at the door of Grandma's house. I was more than surprised because they never had visited me before. They were not my friends, just my classmates. It turned out that Lyudmila had her eye on one of the twin brothers from the tenth grade who were my neighbors and lived across the street from our house. She wanted to invite them to her sixteenth birthday party.

The names of the twins were Boris and Elias. They had just recently returned with their parents from the Ural Mountains where they had spent more than three years in exile. The twins knew me from the day I was born as my mother had come to Grandma's place after she gave birth to me. Grandma had told me more than once that when I was a baby, both twins who were five years older than I asked her to let them hold me and to play with me.

Now I was a teenager, while they were tall, sporty young men and wore a soldier's uniform, except without badges of rank like many other young men at war time. Grandma mentioned that they were handsome, and she tried her hardest to shower praise on them. I didn't care.

187

To me, they looked like adults, maybe because they were very tall and looked serious.

Lyudmila and Vera asked me to go to the twins' place and to bring at least one of them to our house so that she could invite them to her birthday party. I felt too shy and didn't want to go. They talked me into it and invited me to Lyudmila's birthday party, as well. I crossed the street and knocked at the twins' door. Only Boris was at home. He was surprised when I asked him to come with me to our house. He smiled but didn't say anything and followed me in silence.

Lyudka, faltering, her face as red as a beetroot, mumbled her invitation to her birthday party. Boris thanked her, obviously flattered, then patted me on the head as if I were a child or a puppy. Then he left.

As for me, my efforts were in vain. Grandma didn't allow me to go to Lyudka's birthday party. She told me that I was too young to go to such gatherings alone, without adult supervision.

"It's not a good idea for you, at your age, to go to parties. All these girls and guys are much older than you are. Look at Lyudmila. She will be only sixteen and she is already chasing older guys. You'd better stay at home and do your homework. It will be safer and more useful for you. Your time hasn't come yet," Grandma said.

All week before the party, I tried to persuade Grandma to let me go. I played up to her, promising her that I would shower her favorite geraniums with the watering can every week. Grandma demanded that I wash every little leaf separately. It took much time and it was boring, so I always tried to avoid doing that. I preferred to wash the leaves of the ficus. They were big and dark green and shone brilliantly after being washed.

I also promised Grandma to help her fight the bed bugs which nested comfortably in the big Persian rug — Grandma's wedding present — hanging on the wall by her bed. From time to time, Grandma undertook bug chasing operations. She needed my help because her vision was weak, and I had to scout the bug nests, "with my young, sharp-sighted eyes," as she used to say. I tried hard to persuade Grandma to let me go, resorting to all the tricks I knew. I even cried in the hay loft, my favorite hiding place, but my tears were in vain. Grandma stood her ground.

A week later Vera, who was also invited to that ill-fated birthday party brought me two pieces of staggering news. First, at the party they played a popular game called "spin the bottle." The rules of the game were simple. All the participants sit on the floor, in a circle. They spin the bottle in turn. The person who spins the bottle has to kiss the person indicated by the bottle neck when it stops. If the spinner is a girl and the bottle neck indicated a girl, the spinner has to do it again until the bottle neck is pointed at the boy, and vice versa.

My eyes almost popped out in astonishment. Observing my reaction, Vera remembered just in time, "Watch out! Don't you blab out to your grandmother. She doesn't like me, I know," Vera said regretfully. "She thinks that I am a bad influence on you, that I spoil you." On the spot, I swore to be careful and not to tell anybody about the "spin the bottle" game at Luydmila's party.

The second piece of news made me feel as though someone had poured cold water over me. At the party, somebody told Vera that one of our classmates, a boy whose name was Vadim Dorminev liked me very much and wanted to write a love note to me! At first, I didn't believe her. I suspected that she invented that news out of pity for me and in order to console me because I had not been allowed to go to the party and missed all that "spin the bottle" and kissing excitement. She swore on her health that it was true.

I still had my doubts as to the sincerity of Vera's news about my classmate Vadim because I knew Vera very well. She was an inveterate gossip, and she liked to make things up. Very often, she got carried away, and in the process of creative gossiping, sometimes, she made a mountain out of a molehill. Even more, several times I had caught her telling lies.

After I had recovered from that shocking news, I decided to observe and to watch our male classmates' behavior, both in the classroom and in the school courtyard. Before, I never paid special attention to the boys of my class. They always tried to stick together and shunned the girls with the exception of organized, formal class activities in which they reluctantly had to socialize with us. So, now I concentrated on them.

The ages of the boys in our class ranged, as in the pre-revolutionary parish schools, from thirteen to sixteen years old. Some of them, even though thirteen years old, still looked like children; they were short and physically underdeveloped. Their behavior was also childish. They treated girls the way they treated boys: they pushed and elbowed girls, pulled their braids, tripped them up, and, in general, didn't show any respect for them. They called girls by their last names, never by their first names.

Another group consisted of teenagers who were more strapping than the "children." These teenagers tried to hide their interest in girls. They were shy and, very often, tried to disguise their shyness with rudeness. They didn't dare greet the girls when they met them outside of the school premises. They pretended that they didn't know them, nor did they dare call them by their first names.

The third group were teenagers of fifteen to sixteen years old who openly demonstrated their sincere interest in girls. They were tall and physically fit, not because they went to the gym to work out (we didn't know the words "gym" and "work out" then). They were tall and strong because they did a lot of a hard physical labor helping their parents in the fields and doing household chores. They were the ones who had started that feverish spring campaign of writing love notes to the girls with whom they had decided they were in love.

Vadim, who supposedly was in love with me, belonged to the second group. He was a typical thirteen-year-old teenager, tall and skinny, but extremely shy, maybe because he had no sisters, only two brothers. He sat at the last school desk across the classroom. Every time I turned my head back, I met his frightened, watching eyes. He never smiled at me, and he never wrote me a single love note. Not one single time did he dare talk to me. He just devoured me with his timid brown eyes, and that was it. Yura from the Pioneer Camp at least was brave enough to pull my braids and to slip a love note secretly into my pocket at the eve of my departure. I didn't know what to think or what to expect. The school year wouldn't be finished for another month. So I decided to just wait and see what would happen.

32. Hitler Kaputt!

*M*y exchange of glances with Vadim was in full swing, when, like a bolt from the blue, at the end of the school day the news which was beyond belief was broadcast by radio located in the principal's office — the war was finally over. After the classes, the school administration organized in the school courtyard a general meeting dedicated to Victory Day, the ninth of May 1945. It was hot, and both teachers and students were tired, hungry, but excited.

Thank God, the impromptu speeches were not long, as the great news about the victory over Fascist Germany took everybody unawares. The principal of the school, a middle-aged, baldish man in horn-rimmed spectacles, congratulated all of us on the occasion of the end of the war and said that we had to study more in order to get better grades and, in this way, help our country recover from war wounds. He added that now everything would be better and promised us that we would have volley balls and soccer balls for each class. We had only one of each for the whole school, and our Pioneer leader kept them for safety under lock and key in her office. In response, there was a burst of trice-repeated thunderous *Ura! Ura! Ura!* Then the meeting came to an end.

The gathering of students and teachers broke up. Everybody was tired, hungry but happy as never before. Everybody was in a hurry to get home to share that long-awaited wonderful news. We had no radios yet in private houses, and it was hard to get current newspapers.

I was worn out by the heat and nervousness. I hardly dragged myself along on my way home. Mother had to stay at school longer. In the main street, I saw a large group of tenth-graders from our school walking and loudly singing marching Soviet songs, exuberantly waving red flags. The big round loudspeakers installed in this case on the lamp posts of the main street with the voice of well-known Soviet radio announcer Levitan nonstop congratulated Soviet people and warriors on occasion of the great victory.

When I came home and opened the small entrance gate, I screamed in German, *"Hitler kaputt!* We won! The war is over! *Ura! Ura! Ura!"* There was no answer. There was nobody in the yard. I dropped my school bag on the porch and entered the house where I found only Aunt Valentina in the small bedroom having an afternoon nap with baby Oleg. I left the bedroom on tiptoe and went out to the backyard. Then I saw Grandma coming out of the barn. I rushed to her screaming, "Where is everybody? The war is over! They just told us at school, at a meeting. Mother is still at school. She will be home later. Our principal told us that Germany and Japan had signed the capitulation documents!" I felt proud that I remembered the unfamiliar word "capitulation" and was able to pronounce it correctly.

Grandma looked at me in disbelief. As ill luck would have it, on that day of all days, Grandma and Grandpa had decided to clean the cellar and to prepare it for the fall season. They had taken out all the empty barrels from the cellar, washed them with hot water and were letting them dry for a while in the yard.

Aunt Valentina cooked lunch, taking care of her baby at the same time. No one had ventured into the street, so no one had heard anything, because they were busy doing their chores. I was so happy that I brought home such wonderful news. Suddenly, I didn't feel tired or hungry. No, it was not true, I still was hungry, but it didn't matter that much anymore because the war was over! Finally, it was over!

33. American Gifts

*M*other was late for lunch that afternoon. We all waited for her for a while, but then Grandma said decisively, "Wash your hands, children, let's eat! We all are hungry, and you have to do your homework after lunch, and it's already late."

When we sat at the kitchen table Grandpa said, "Thank God the war is over, but we still have to make a stock of fresh and marinated vegetables for winter from our vegetable garden. It will take a long time before everything will be like it was before the war."

"That's good that we have cleaned the cellar and have prepared it for stocking vegetables and fruits," Grandma said, sighing heavily. She crossed herself and continued, "I am saying my prayers that your father and Uncle Mitya return safe and sound from the war." There was sadness in her voice that surprised me, but I was too tired and excited to ask her about it.

For lunch, we had my favorite cold spinach soup. Grandma always said that it was the easiest soup to cook. You had just to wash, peel and cut in small pieces several potatoes, two carrots and a bunch of spinach. Then cook the potatoes and carrots up to the boiling point; then at the last minute, you add the spinach and boil everything for five minutes more. Then put the pot aside, let it cool for another five minutes, and lastly pour into it two fresh beaten eggs while mixing the soup. As a rule, this soup is served cold, so Grandma always put it into the cellar to cool off. Before serving the spinach soup, Grandma used to put in every plate a tablespoon of cut fresh radish or cucumber, green onions, one hard-boiled egg cut in small pieces for every adult and a half egg for us children, and seasoned it with a tablespoon of sour cream and a dash of nicely chopped fresh dill. And, bon appétit! I still consider this spinach soup a delicacy during the hot summer.

For the second course, we had millet *kasha* seasoned with pork cracklings, the leftovers from the winter season. At the end of spring, we had no meat at all, as we had already eaten all the pork. The pig was traditionally butchered for Christmas. We couldn't afford to kill chickens, as they had started to lay eggs early in the spring, and eggs were an important part of our diet. "Eggs always come to the rescue," Grandma used to say.

For dessert, this time we had a glass of cool compote, a drink made of dried stewed fruits. We children liked it very much. We liked it sweet, but sometimes we had no sugar at all. If we had honey, Grandma sweetened the compote by adding a teaspoon of it in every glass.

Our late lunch was almost finished when Mother appeared in the backyard carrying a big bundle under her arm which was wrapped in some colorful fabric. "Guess what I have brought," she asked smiling. She looked pleased with herself.

"What, what is it?" Valentina jumped to her feet, but Grandma stopped her.

"These are American gifts," Mother continued, "which our school has received for the teachers' families.

The principal wanted to give them to the teachers at the end of the school year, but today he decided to distribute the gifts among the teachers in honor of Victory Day. That's why the teachers had to stay at school after the meeting."

Louisa, Zhanna and I sat quietly like mice. We waited impatiently. American gifts! We had heard a lot about them. The local leaders of the Communist party and the employees of the town administration were the first ones who had received American gifts. Their children had already shown off nice silk dresses and beautiful sweaters and pants; some even wore new leather shoes and boots.

As we had found out years later, those gifts were transported by American ships via the dangerous Northern Atlantic where more than once German submarines attacked them. But it didn't stop the brave Americans. They continued to deliver military equipment, supplies, and the gifts, donated by American people, to the Northern Soviet port of Murmansk, on the Kola Gulf of the Barents Sea. That port is ice free year-round, thanks to the Gulf Stream, which reaches all the way to that point. It was humanitarian aid (as they call it nowadays) to the suffering Soviet people who had worn out all their clothes. This was the first time that our school received "American Gifts" for the teachers' families. For some inexplicable reason, the Soviet press hadn't publicized the American military aid and the American Gifts programs.

Mother dropped her schoolbag on the floor, washed her hands, put the bundle on the stool in the middle of the kitchen and carefully untied it. We all looked at it as if we were hypnotized. We hadn't seen new clothes for four years! All our children's clothes were altered from adults' old clothes. They were worn out, faded and colorless. Their designs were as primitive as could be because we had no trimming materials.

197

Louisa's eyes were like saucers, her mouth wide open. She moved closer to me, grabbed my arm and whispered, "What is American?"

"It's from America," I explained. "It's a country located far away."

"Is it like Estonia?" she asked.

"Something like that, only bigger." I had already taken a course in Physical Geography, and I knew where America was located on the school globe and on the map. I felt proud of myself. At the same time I was sincerely surprised that my baby sister still remembered Estonia where we lived only half a year, on the eve of the war.

The bundle was unwrapped, and Mother polled out its contents. There was a dark-blue sweater for me, with short sleeves trimmed with yellow stripes and two strings at the neck. I nervously grabbed it and went to the small bedroom to try it on. The sweater was like new. Just my size! I never owned something so beautiful before. I jumped joyfully in front of the mirror and rushed back to the kitchen to show off my new outfit. On my sixth-grade class photo I was depicted wearing that short-sleeve American sweater. The photo had been taken at the end of the school year in June of 1945.

There were brown leather shoes Louisa's size and a green silk girl's dress which Mother gave to Zhanna. Both girls immediately put them on. There was a beige long-sleeved sweater with a brown skirt for Mother. The multi-colored piece of fabric with bright flowers in which the bundle was wrapped turned out to be a head shawl for Grandma. She put it on her shoulders, patted it with delight, and said, smiling, "I'll put it on when I go to church on Sunday." The shawl and the smile seemed to transform Grandma — she looked younger, and her eyes were radiant.

Mother gave the brown skirt to her sister, Valentina, whose face immediately became wreathed in smiles. Grandpa got a pair of long navy blue socks, and he didn't try to hide his satisfaction. I knew why, because I was the one who had to darn his socks again and again. Sometimes, I had no darning thread of the matching color for invisible darning. So I used any color I had. What else could I do?

Only baby Oleg received nothing, but he was too small to understand that. Caught up in the general rejoicing, he light-heartedly smiled showing us his front teeth.

That night, I couldn't fall asleep for a long time. I relived that long day of May 9, 1945 in my mind, from the general meeting in the school courtyard where the end of the war was announced up to the late afternoon in our kitchen where Mother handed us those much appreciated "American gifts." Maybe our principal was right when he had promised us that now that the war was over, everything would be better and easier.

Suddenly, I remembered that before the war every spring Mother took Louisa and me to a big footwear store. We went there by streetcar to buy each of us a pair of sandals, simple brown sandals which smelled of leather and reminded us that summer was around the corner. Our feet grew fast, and we needed a new pair of sandals every spring. I liked the light-brown ones. Louisa preferred dark-brown. We both liked to ride by streetcar which for us was an adventure in itself.

I desperately needed new sandals this year; I even felt envious that my sister had gotten a new pair of brown American shoes with a big metallic buckle. *If only they would bring 'American Gifts' again*, I thought to myself, *I would ask Mother to choose for me a pair of shoes or sandals.* I had had no new shoes for four years. We walked barefoot all summer. Before the war started, we never walked without shoes.

We always had new sandals and two new pairs of cotton socks for summer.

Then a strange thought struck me like lightning: the war just ended today, and the same day I had gotten a new American sweater, and all the family members had received American gifts, as well. Maybe everything will be getting better. I was delighted at that thought, and, finally, fell asleep.

I couldn't envision in my dreams that the ruthless echoes of war would break uninvited into our lives again and would open one of the hidden macabre pages in the war history of our town.

34. Reburial Ceremony in the Town Park

Soon after the liberation of our town by the Soviet army, the Soviet authorities discovered the burial place of fourteen tenth-graders from our local high school. During the occupation, the Germans had executed by firing squad a group of local high school seniors who were caught red-handed listening to a radio news broadcast by the Soviet Informbureau.

As soon as the German troops had entered the town, their military and civil authorities had issued a written ordinance that, under threat of death, demanded that all radio sets be delivered to certain collection points.

Unfortunately, a group of tenth-graders had not taken the ordinance seriously and decided to keep a radio. They wanted to listen to a news broadcast by the Soviet Informbureau. For that purpose, risking their lives, they gathered under cover of night in the house of the radio's owner, in the outskirts of the town. They tried to be cautious, but somebody must have seen them and informed the German authorities.

At night, the Germans, accompanied by the local police, descended unexpectedly on the group and caught them listening to the Soviet broadcast. All fourteen students, including several girls, were arrested and executed by firing squad, without investigation or trial. The same night, after the execution, the Germans secretly buried their bodies in the forest which stretched for many kilometers along the railroad tracks. They didn't tell the parents of the victims that their children had been buried. Instead, the Germans informed them that all the tenth-graders who had been arrested that night were found guilty of violating the official orders of the German authorities. For that crime, the Germans told the parents, they were sent to Germany, like many other young people from the occupied territories, as conscripts, to work at military factories.

The rumors had been secretly spread that those tenth-graders were executed the same night of their arrest, but nobody knew anything for sure. There was a lot of conjecture and speculation. There was no proof, no evidence, only the fact that the teenagers had been arrested and never came back. This complete ignorance was more painful and excruciating than the most cruel truth.

The high school seniors executed that night were seventeen years old. They hadn't even been drafted into the Soviet army because draftees had to be eighteen years old to be eligible for military service.

In February of 1944 the Soviet Army liberated our town. Boxes of archive materials which belonged to the local police were seized. Somehow, the Germans managed to load their own archives on the train, while the archives of the local police collaborators were left unattended on the tracks close to the railroad terminal. Both the Germans and their collaborators had to retreat in a hurry under the powerful pressure of the advancing Soviet troops.

It took some time for the Soviet authorities to check the local police archives. Finally, several days after the war was over, the terrible truth about the massacre was officially announced. If one of the locals had known the secret place of the burials, that person never dared to report it to the authorities, probably because of fear of being accused of collaboration with the Germans.

Once the bodies had been discovered and the terrifying truth came out, it was like a bomb explosion. The entire community was in shock. There was no hope anymore for the parents that their children, maybe, still were alive working like slaves somewhere in Germany.

The local Communist party and civil authorities made the decision to rebury the remains of the victims of the massacre in the Town Park and to raise a monument to immortalize the memory of those brave teenagers.

One Sunday afternoon, the senior students of our school took part in the memorial reburial ceremony. The pioneers were dressed in pioneer uniforms — white tops and dark bottoms, and red pioneer neckties. Older students, members of the Komsomol (Young Communist League) also wore white tops and dark bottoms, as well as small Komsomol badges on the left side of their chests.

We all held flowers in our hands. Every family planted flowers in their front gardens, no matter how small those gardens were. Mother carried a bouquet of fourteen white carnations, Grandma's favorite flowers. Grandma gave me a small metallic flower pot with beautiful pansies. She used to pick up all the metallic cans which the German soldiers stationed in our house had thrown away. She asked Grandpa to make several holes in the bottom and utilized them as flower pots to plant pansies which she liked very much. "They are so modest and undemanding. They can grow even in metallic cans."

There was a sea of flowers at the funeral service. I couldn't imagine that there was such a variety of flowers in our region. Strong-smelling red, yellow and white roses together with tulips, daffodils, regal orange lilies, gorgeous mauve mallows and irises dominated the funeral landscape. Bouquets and small bunches of modest but extremely delicate white and pink cyclamens and snapdragons completed the funeral floral mosaic. Some bouquets and bunches of flowers were wrapped in decorative silk grass. There were also dozens of wreaths made of branches of jasmine with black cotton ribbons.

All fourteen caskets, each covered with a piece of red fabric, were placed in a row, next to the deep and wide communal grave. A small photograph of each student was placed on every casket. The local leaders of the Communist party, town and railroad terminal management, as well as the representatives from provincial and regional party administrations, were present.

Many speeches were given praising the bravery of the fearless teenagers who had not been intimidated by the Germans and preferred "to die standing straight than to live on their knees," as Dolores Ibarruri, the then popular leader of the Communist party of Spain, used to say.

Bitter tears were shed. The unrestrained sobbing and despairing, hysterical weeping of parents and relatives of the victims, broke the silence of the memorial. Everybody cried; loud moans and sobs filled the air. I never thought that the fragrance of flowers could be so sickly sweet, yet suffocating.

A line of mourners passed by the caskets, placing flowers and crossing themselves, while the military brass band played funeral marches. There was something hopeless and tragic in the slow rhythm of that solemn music which touched and disturbed my young, unprotected heart.

I grew to hate funeral dirges which I had heard for the first time at that memorial reburial. Later, as an adult, when I still lived in the Soviet Union, I always turned the TV off when on every channel, for hours, the official funeral ceremonies of the Communist party leaders and other dignitaries were broadcast, profusely accompanied by requiems and dirges.

35. Surviving the Aftermath of the War

$\mathcal{F}$or several weeks after the teenagers' reburial ceremony people kept talking and gossiping about
it while standing in line at the bakery or doing business
at the farmers' market. Then, gradually, life had its way,
and everyday routine chores, worries and cares pushed
the tragic, untimely death of the tenth-graders into the
background.

The end of the war brought emotional relief to many
people, but not to every family. The men and women who
had been drafted at the beginning of the war hadn't yet
returned home. The Soviet troops still were stationed in
dangerous and hostile territories of Germany and its war
allies — Bulgaria, Hungary and Romania. The people of our
town still received from the Ministry of the Armed Forces
official "Killed in the Battle" notices listing the deaths of
their family members and relatives. The conditions of our
lives didn't undergo drastic improvements. All the families,
including ours, had to work hard in order to survive and
to meet the enormous challenges of the aftermath of the
war.

There had been some improvements, though. The
local bakeries were opened, and Grandpa or Grandma

had to get up at dawn in order to buy with ration cards two loaves of rye bread for our family. The manufactured goods stores were still closed. So clothes and, especially footwear were the most desirable but difficult items to purchase.

During the four years of the war and the three and a half years of German occupation, we children grew up and out of everything. All our clothes and footwear were old, worn out, mended and mended again, but there were no places to buy replacement clothes and footwear. The only source of getting them was the American Humanitarian Aid Program distributed by the Communist Party committees at the schools, hospitals, factories and industrial works.

Mother, like many others, went back to work. She received her teacher's salary and some benefits such as a free package to the summer Pioneer Camps for me and for my sister. Her school also received clothes and footwear from America, which were distributed among the teachers for their families.

The American Gifts were a huge help and the source of joy for many families in those hard times. (Now, seventy years later, I, having been one of the many lucky recipients of the American Gifts, want to thank the American people for their unprecedented generosity. *Bolshoye vam spasibo!* Thank you very much!

When the postal service was re-established, we suddenly realized how we had missed it during the German occupation and how wonderful it was to receive letters in triangular military envelopes, from Father and from Uncle Mitya. Without the postal service, we lost communications with our relatives who lived in other cities and republics of the Soviet Union. Now, gradually, Mother, Aunt Valentina and Grandma started to write letters to our relatives to find out how they had survived the war and how they were doing.

There was one more important reason why we children were fascinated by the postal services. During the German occupation, the retirees, including our grandparents, hadn't received pensions. Now, once a month, a mailman, as it was before the war, delivered their pension money straight to our house.

This always was a special day for us children. Our mailman was not a man, but a woman whose name was Lyusia. She worked as a mailman before the war, and our grandparents had known her for a long time. She had not worked at the post office during the German occupation, as there were no postal services. Now Lyusia returned to her former position. As long as I could remember, if there was any mail for us, it was personally delivered by Lyusia to the addressee's hands. I don't remember a mailbox hanging on our front gate.

The day when Grandparents had their pensions delivered, we children, sitting astride on the front fence, watched like hawks, for the moment when Lyusia, with the overloaded postal bag across her shoulder, appeared on our street. One of us immediately rushed to announce to Grandma, screaming like crazy, "Lyusia is coming! Lyusia is coming!"

Grandma met Lyusia on the veranda, where there was a dining table and offered her lunch. It was simple food: cooked potatoes with sour cream and a cup of milk or carrot tea with pancakes or a bowl of cabbage soup and ravioli stuffed with mashed potatoes and fried onions, sometimes even seasoned with pork cracklings. Lyusia never declined the food. She ate with great appetite and praised Grandma's cooking. "Oh, it's so devilishly good, so tasty!" she used to say approvingly shaking her head with tousled dirty hair while stuffing down ravioli with mashed potatoes and fried onions. Grandma also treated her with fresh seasonal fruits from our orchard — apples, apricots and pears.

Lyusia was a single mother and was raising her son alone. She lived in a subsidized apartment which had no orchard, so she always saved the fruit for her son, hiding them in her bottomless postal bag. In addition, every time when Lyusia delivered Grandparents' pensions, Grandma gave her a ruble as a tip.

Zhanna, Louisa and I received ten kopecks each for the Sunday matinee in the Town Park movie theatre which also reopened. Grandma gave me ten kopecks more so that I could buy a glass of seltzer water for the three of us. A glass of seltzer water with fruit or berry syrup cost three kopecks; without syrup — only one kopeck. There were pleasant rumors that very soon they would sell ice-cream cones in the Town Park as they did before the war. Life was getting sweeter and sweeter for us.

Every day, we impatiently looked forward for Lyusia's arrival because we waited for letters from Father and from Uncle Mitya. In his previous letter, Father had written that very soon he would send us a postal package. So we waited for that package to arrive each day.

Uncle Mitya also promised to send Valentina a package. He wrote that his unit had been stationed in Eastern Prussia near the city of Koningsberg, which before the war had belonged to Germany and was populated by native Germans. The German civilian population was afraid of the fast advancing Soviet army and ran away in panic, leaving everything behind in their houses and apartments, as they had neither time nor transportation to take their belongings with them. Soviet soldiers could take everything they wanted from the empty houses and apartments, from the closets, wardrobes and the chests of drawers and send those things to their families.

One summer day, Lyusia handed Valentina a long-awaited notice for the package from Uncle Mitya. It was pretty heavy, about twenty pounds. Valentina, in a hurry, folded and tucked the notice inside her bra, grabbed her baby's carriage and ran, gasping for breath, to get it at the post office on Main Street, not far away.

Half an hour later, all our family, with the exception of my mother, who was conducting summer school classes, gathered in our kitchen around the package. Valentina placed it on the wooden stool, in the middle of the room and with scissors cut the strings tied up around the plywood box. Then she opened it and began to unpack, carefully examining and demonstrating each item to us. With eyes wide open from excitement, we looked at Valentina and at the outfits she showed us.

In addition to the women's and girls' clothes, there were white sheets, pillowcases trimmed with lace and flounces, towels, and small white window curtains. There were no men's clothes in the package. There was no footwear at all, not a single pair.

Valentina gave to Grandma a wonderful checked kitchen apron in green and brown colors, with two large pockets. "It will suit you," she said. "Those are your favorite colors." Grandma immediately tried on the apron and even went to the small bedroom to look at the big mirror. The apron fit her nicely. It made Grandma look younger and grand.

"You look like a real *Frau*, Anastasia Konstantinovna," Grandpa said with satisfaction, and even giggled. My jaws dropped. It was the first time in all those years that I heard Grandpa telling a joke. Or was it a compliment? I wondered.

I had gotten a beautiful nightshirt made of pink cotton with lace trim. I was thrilled. I had never had such a wonderful nightgown. Before we went to bed, I admired myself in my new pink nightshirt standing in front of the mirror. "In this outfit, you look like an angel," Grandma said, straightening the lace flounces on my shoulders and sleeves. That night, I slept an angelic sleep dreaming about nightgowns of different colors — light blue, light green and light yellow trimmed with beautiful lace of the same color as the nightshirts.

Louisa was the lucky one. Valentina gave her a light blue dress, almost new, which was too big for Zhanna. Everyone received something from Uncle Mitya's package. Grandpa and baby Oleg, however, had to be content with new pillowcases and bedsheets, as there were no clothes for them in the package. Nevertheless, everybody was excited and happy.

The next day, when our rapture subsided, Valentina, being herself a skilled needlewoman, was the first one who noticed that many items from the package were used but skillfully darned, with almost invisible stitches. All the clothes and bed linen items were so thoroughly washed, starched and ironed that they looked like new. But they all were used. It was really an artistic darning. We admired such fine and elaborate skill. Aunt Valentina was the one who had taught me to darn. So we both appreciated and were delighted with such wonderful, skillful work of German women.

Several days later, new cheerful coquettish German curtains hung on all three windows of the rooms which faced the street, attracting the attention of passers-by. Even the flower pots with geraniums looked more fresh and colorful against such a wonderful background.

Yes, I mused, feasting my eyes on the curtains while standing on the street, *our life is definitely changing for the better. The day the war was over we received American gifts, Valentina had already received a package from Uncle Mitya, my father's package was due to arrive any day, and I have some new clothes. I hope Father will send me some new shoes or boots. I need new shoes so badly. God, let it be shoes, sandals or boots for me in the package.*

Then, suddenly I realized that so many good and pleasant things had happened lately. It couldn't be that only good things occurred all the time. Grandma used to say that happy and unhappy events alternate in our lives, according to God's will. So, what will happen next? I didn't want it to be a bad thing. Let it be a good and happy thing for all of us! Deep down in my heart, I knew that anything could happen. I felt really scared. I only prayed and hoped that Father and Uncle Mitya would be alive and well.

36. A Glimmer of Hope for a Better Future

*G*randma's remarks about the inevitable alternation of happy and unhappy events in people's lives were imprinted in my mind for two reasons. First, I myself had the opportunity to notice that it had been true. Second, by the age of thirteen, some girls in our class, for some unknown reason, had become very superstitious. Maybe this was because many girls in our class were older than we, thirteen-year old teenagers. They had had a longer contact with adults, and they were exposed to more life experiences. Regardless, old-fashioned superstitions suddenly became a popular topics among us, the seventh-graders.

For example, it was considered a sign of bad luck to meet a black cat crossing a street in front of us. To avoid it, we should spit three times over the left shoulder.

If by chance, in the street we met a person carrying empty buckets, good luck would avoid us that day, and vice versa: if we met a person with buckets full of water, we would definitely have a lucky day. As the closest communal well was located at one end of our street, I started to walk in the direction where I could only meet people with full buckets. Though I could easily take off the spell with three spits over my left shoulder, I tried to get around the dangerous directions where I could meet the people walking with empty buckets towards the well.

If we were leaving our house and had already crossed the threshold, then we suddenly realized that we had forgotten something very important for that day, such as our ink-pot or a notebook with our homework, or our school diaries as we called our report cards, we shouldn't turn back. If we turned back, we should not expect good luck to accompany us that day, unless we apply the rule of three spits over our left shoulders.

We religiously applied those superstitious rules to our everyday school routine.

If we had gotten an excellent grade on the first oral or written exam at the end of the school year (all our exams were orals, with the exception of math and Russian written composition), we had to come to the next exam exactly in the same outfit, without washing it or ourselves—our dresses, hair, hair ribbons and white collar. Otherwise, our exam grade would be lower. What was even worse, in order to reinforce our good luck, we shouldn't wash our hair for two weeks while the oral and written exams were being conducted. That was the most unpleasant demand which Mother didn't allow me to stick with when I told her why I didn't want to wash my hair on Saturday, as usual.

"What stupid ignorance to believe in such things!" Mother said full of indignation when I categorically refused to wash my hair.

"Do you want to breed lice? Do you remember how hard it was to get rid of nits and lice while the Germans were still here, and we didn't have soap to wash your thick hair? You have already forgotten how disgusting it was for all of us to stand the smell of kerosene which I had used to smear on your hair because of the lice and nits? You had to stayed at home for two weeks and had to sleep in the hay loft. Don't you remember that?"

I didn't know what to answer because it was true. Mother, meanwhile, was getting angrier.

"Are you afraid that I will wash away all the knowledge from your head? You are a pioneer, Nina. Pioneers don't believe in such obsolete things as superstition and sorcery."

"All the girls believe that it helps at the exams," I retorted, my eyes swimming in tears, and my chin trembling.

"If you have studied well during the whole school year, if you have been attentive in the class and have reviewed all the topics, you will be fine," Mother said with a strict voice. "Lice won't help you give correct answers if you don't know the topic. If you don't allow me to wash your hair, on Monday I'll tell the Pioneer leader of the school," she warned me.

I got a fright. I didn't want to become a laughing stock for the whole school, especially for boys. They were always giggling behind our backs calling us "evil sorceresses" and "witches," when we discussed during the breaks in a whisper the power of superstition among us girls.

On Monday, I went to take my oral exam in geography with clean hair, but without sorcery support, as I had violated its rules. I felt like a traitor, shaking like an aspen leaf although I had managed to review all the topics included in the exam question cards which we called "exam tickets." Besides, I had been an "A" student for the last three years.

Mother turned out to be right once again. I had gotten my usual "A," while my classmate and friend Vera, a true believer in the power of the superstition and its rules, who came to that exam with dirty, greasy hair and a dirty collar, had gotten a "C," although usually she was a "B" student. She was devastated and cried inconsolably, wiping her tears with her dirty, crumpled handkerchief.

The result of Vera's oral exam considerably lessened my belief in strict sorcery rules and their omnipotence. But, not completely. As they say, "Old habits die hard."

I do remember when as university students and members of the Young Communist League, my class-mates and I came to every exam in the same outfits. The explanation was always very simple: we were so busy studying and reviewing the exam topics that we became oblivious to the outfits and other small problems and inconveniences of life.

Although an unfavorable outcome of Vera's exam had weakened my faith in omnipotence of sorcery, I still continued to expect bad things to happen to me after a chain of good events had taken place in my life. I was anxious and full of fear.

That is why, every time that our mailwoman, Lyusia, a herald of the good and bad news, walked into our yard, I felt extremely nervous as if I were sure of the arrival of bad news. However, it was Lyusia again who one afternoon delivered us a notice for Father's package which finally reached its destination.

While Grandma, as usual, treated Lyusia with freshly fried green cabbage pancakes and fruit compote for lunch on the veranda, Mother and I hurriedly went to the post office to get the parcel. Lyusia said that it was not big but pretty heavy. My sister Louisa dogged our footsteps, jumping and smiling with joy, announcing loudly to all the neighbors and acquaintances we met on our way to the post office, "We have gotten a package from Father! Father sent us a package!"

Mother and I carried the parcel between the two of us, holding it by strings which painfully cut into our hands. We were so excited that we didn't pay attention to the pain and cheerfully strode, periodically changing hands. When I complained to Mother that the strings cut into my hand and it hurt, she commented smiling happily, "That's all right. We are almost there. We carry something good into the house, not out of it."

At home, Mother put the box on the stool in the kitchen, cut the strings and opened it. Although there were no clothes in the package, its contents left us with our mouths wide open. It was full of food we hadn't seen since the start of the war and which taste we had utterly and completely forgotten: canned meat and fish, several packs of cube sugar, small packs of cookies, two packs of buckwheat flour, two packs of tea and one pack of cocoa.

The biggest surprise for us children were two small paper bags of our favorite caramel candies. One of the bags contained bon-bons called — *podushechky* — "small pillows" because of their square shape. They were filled either with fruit jelly or with melted chocolate. The chocolate-filled ones were my favorite, while Louisa preferred the jelly-filled bon-bons.

Another kind of our favorite caramel was called *rakovye sheiky*, "crawfish necks," because of its red and white combination of colors. They were crunchy and tasted wonderful. I still like them a lot, I do. At that time, it was like a miracle for us to see our favorite caramel candy which we hadn't tasted since the start of the war.

That evening, we drank a real Georgian (*Gruzinskiy*) tea with one cookie, one caramel bon-bon and one cube of sugar each. The rest of it Grandma put aside to give us for school later. It was a real feast for us children because we really missed sweets in our ration maybe more than anything else during all the years of war and German occupation.

I drank my tea with a cube of sugar. I saved my cookie and my caramel for the next school day to share it with my friend Vera. I also saved for her several caramel wrappers to play with later. On the wrappers, the crawfish looked as if it were alive. Vera liked to copy different pictures, and those wrappers were a real treat for her.

It was another happy event, a sweet one! Luck was still holding. *Touch wood! Life is getting sweeter thanks to our father*, I told myself, smiling and knocking three times on a wooden kitchen stool. *Touch wood! Bozhe! Oh, God! Don't let something bad or tragic happen to us! Help Father and Uncle Mitya to return back home as soon as possible! We need them. They are our only hope.*

The packages we had received from Father and Uncle Mitya were the glimpse of that fragile hope for a better tomorrow.

37. Post-War Worries and Expectations

*T*he beginning of my first post-war summer was promising. On June 5 of 1945, I took my last exam. I had gotten all "A's" and had moved to the seventh grade, and was awarded with a certificate of good work and conduct. Thanks to my mother's home schooling, the German occupation hadn't affected my academic progress, and I hadn't missed a single year of school.

I was thirteen and a half years old, skinny, shy and serious. My motto was: "Study, study and study!" This slogan, written in bold print with big letters, hung above the blackboard in our classroom. That was the behest of the great Lenin, "the friend of the Soviet children" and founder of the Soviet Socialist state.

The next day after the last exam, the class group black-and-white photo of all the students of our 6A grade was taken by the photographer invited by the school administration. It was the first photo of me taken after the four years of war and German occupation. The last photo of my mother, Louisa and me was taken on May 1, in 1941, two months before the start of the war.

In my first post-war class photo, I am dressed in my favorite American short-sleeved sweater from American

Gifts, but I look sad, tired and crestfallen. I didn't feel like myself during the last several days before the exam: I lost my appetite, I was languid and drowsy like a sleepy autumnal fly. I felt exhausted, my throat was swollen, my ears were aching. I complained to Mother, and she took me to the clinic where the doctor diagnosed me with mumps. I was really sick.

I had to stay in bed for a week in a small bedroom. Louisa and Zhanna were not allowed to approach me because mumps is very contagious. Staying the whole day alone, I just listened to the fragments of conversations in the kitchen, adjacent to that bedroom, and talked to the girls through the open bedroom window. I slept and read a lot. Mother brought me books from our school library which had reopened again. All teachers and students had donated their own books to the library. Grandma had turned out to be right: one happy event, an excellent completion of the sixth grade, was immediately followed by an unhappy one, my belated mumps.

During the disease, my sleep was not deep. Sometimes, I just dozed. In the intervals between sleep and dozing, my thoughts swarmed like bees in a beehive. Again and again, my mind went back to the events of the last months of the school year: the end of the war, Uncle Mitya's and Father's letters and packages, and Father's promise to visit us at the end of the summer. His leave had been postponed several times. That postponement was another unhappy event, coming so close to my illness.

The spring, summer and early fall, as usual, were busy seasons for all of us, especially for the adults. We had to take care of our vegetable garden: we planted, harvested, processed, and stored vegetables in the cellar for winter. Canning of the vegetables took a lot of time and effort. September was an extremely hard and busy month because it was the harvest season.

On the first of September, the school year started everywhere in the country. Mother had to return to work after the summer recess.

By the beginning of the school year, Louisa, Zhanna and I had grown a little. Louisa was already a Pioneer, like me. Zhanna was ready to join the Pioneer organization by the October Revolution holidays. Louisa persuaded Mother to let her hair grow long. She looked very funny with her short blonde pigtails and her snub, peeling nose with freckles.

It was already autumn of 1945, but Father still wasn't allowed to take his leave. He wrote in his letter that all the leaves had been cancelled as his unit was going to be transferred back to the territory of the Soviet Union in the near future. It was good news. We hoped that he would be closer to our location. Impatiently, we waited for the next letter from Father and from Uncle Mitya. Lyusia, our mailwoman, also hoped to enjoy Grandma's hospitality and her lunches on our veranda.

My school activities were rolling smoothly. The class materials became more interesting as we had gotten new subjects such as geometry, physics, and anatomy. Russian literature became more exciting. We studied the poetry of Pushkin, Lermontov, and other Russian writers and poets.

More and more often, my classmates, especially those who were two or three years older than the regular seventh-graders like me, started to discuss their academic plans for the future. After the completion of seventh grade, one could be admitted to the three-year training technical schools or training colleges in order to learn a profession.

Unfortunately, at that time in the Soviet school system the position of school counselor did not exist. At that age, however, I understood that in order to be accepted to the four-year college, which in the USSR was called "institute" or to the five-year university, one should be successfully graduated from the ten-year high school. I didn't know then that in the Soviet Union the term "Academy" was applied only to the military, religious, and the highest scientific institutions.

Several girls and boys from our class who were left behind because the schools were closed during the German occupation decided to apply to different technical colleges and training schools after graduation from the seventh grade. They would have to move to other cities because our town didn't have a single training college or training technical school.

It seemed very tempting to them to move to another city. They dreamt about and looked forward to living in the dormitories and being independent adults. Those students were already sixteen or seventeen years old, while I would be only fourteen and a half years old upon completion of the seventh grade. I didn't perceive myself as an adult. I didn't look like one, either. The idea of moving to another city to study and to live without my family scared me to death.

Finally, we received a letter from Father in which he wrote that his unit had already been transferred to the Western Ukraine and was now located in the city of Lvov. *One more happy event!* I rejoiced.

The territories of Western Ukraine and Western Byelorussia previously belonged to Poland. In September of 1939, those territories had been annexed by the Soviet Union and joined to the Eastern Byelorussia and Eastern Ukraine, accordingly, on the pretext that they were populated mostly by Ukrainians and Byelorussians. By the way, both Western Ukraine and Western Byelorussia had a huge Polish population, as well.

Father wrote in his letter that the city of Lvov was big and reminded him of Tallinn where we had resided when WWII reached the Soviet Union on June 22, 1941. Miraculously, the city hadn't suffered much damage during the German advance and retreat. Only several dozens of buildings in Lvov had been destroyed by bombs and artillery shelling.

There were many old edifices and modern buildings in the city, a lot of Roman Catholic and other churches, beautiful parks, and even an Opera House in the main square of downtown. Numerous movie theatres, high schools, different types of technical schools, eleven four-year colleges, the university and the conservatory were located downtown and in the area adjacent to it. The high schools operated in three languages — Russian, Ukrainian and Polish. The majority of the schools were Russian and Ukrainian, and only two high schools were Polish, as ethnic Poles were permitted to emigrate back to Poland.

Father also mentioned that the city had a well-developed public transportation system with many routes of streetcars, buses and taxis. I didn't know what the word "taxi" meant. Mother explained that it meant passenger cars which could be rented individually.

Father wrote that the shelves of numerous big department stores were almost empty, as consumer manufactured goods were scarce. The grocery stores were empty, as well. People got their groceries at several big farmers' markets located in different areas of the city. They were full of all kinds of fresh produce, meat, and poultry which farmers delivered to the city. A huge flea-market where one could buy and sell different merchandise, used and new items, including imported ones, was located in the outskirts of the city. The Soviet-Polish border was only twenty-five miles away.

Father's letters were for us like a window into another world, into a different life which we had experienced before the war, a life with streetcars and sidewalks. That is why Mother read and reread them relishing every small detail of that interesting, exciting news. From time to time, one of us asked her to read again separate fragments of Father's letters. We couldn't believe that Father was already not far from us, in Western Ukraine. Again and again, we listened to Mother read Father's letters, cherishing a hope for the future and remembering the happy pre-war times when we lived in Minsk, Shiauliai and in Tallinn. Those were the cities which both Louisa and I remembered best; I was nine years old, and Louisa was seven at that time.

We recalled the New Year's Eve celebration in the kindergarten in Minsk. Louisa was dressed in a rabbit costume, and I was a snowflake in a white starchy tutu and short white socks, dancing around a Christmas tree which in the Soviet era of unbridled atheism was simply called *yolka,* "spruce tree."

We always had at home a fluffy spruce decorated with glistering ornaments and a red star at the top—a combination of the religious past and the present Soviet lifestyle. We hung on the spruce small red apples, chocolate candies in silver wrappers and small mandarins. We children considered mandarins hanging on the New Year's spruce a real treat. Since my childhood, I've always associated the fresh smell of spruce branches and mandarins with my birthday which is on the first of January.

During the German occupation, we never had a real Christmas tree. Spruces and fir trees didn't grow in that area. So, instead, we decorated a tall, leafy ficus plant with ornaments, small red apples and homemade cookies.

38. My Pre-War Childhood Memories
in Minsk, Byelorussia

Somehow, in a very mysterious way, Father's letters in which he had talked about our future life, forced us to look back and to relive again carefree, serene and irrevocable moments of our pre-war existence. Our life in Minsk was one of them. My sister Louisa reminded me of one particular incident involving our radio.

Recently, I was having some kind of memory block. No matter how hard I tried, I couldn't visualize scenes from my early childhood depicting me or any member of our family listening to the radio. I wasn't sure whether we had one or not. But then again, my first encounter with the radio had probably happened more than seventy years ago.

I did what I always had done when I needed more information about our family history: I called my baby sister Louisa in the Ukraine to ask, "Did we have a radio in our apartment when we lived in Minsk?" I knew that it was one of the last two places we both remembered well. I was seven and a half years old and Louisa was five. The year was 1939.

My unexpected question must have surprised my sister. She remained quiet for a while, then joyfully shouted, "Yes, we had a radio! Don't you remember, Nina? It looked like a black round plate that hung on the wall above the kitchen table. One Sunday, our parents went shopping, and we stayed at home. Mother asked us to behave and not to fight and definitely not to scratch each other. Before leaving, she promised to give us ten kopecks each for fruit ice cream which we liked so much. Father said, switching on the radio, 'Listen to your favorite fairy-tale, girls. They will broadcast the story of Little Red Riding Hood.'"

"I remember as if it happened yesterday," Louisa continued sighing heavily, and I could clearly hear a trace of nostalgia in her voice. "We sat in the kitchen and listened to the radio. All the characters of the fairy-tale performed wonderfully. Grandmother's voice was soothing and sad. The roar of the wolf was menacing. I sobbed hysterically when the Big Bad Wolf swallowed the kind, trustful grandmother. After that, he gobbled up Little Red Riding Hood. You also cried, Nina, but at the same time, you tried to console me and calm me down. How naïve and trustful we were then. We don't believe in fairy-tales, anymore, dear sister, do we?"

"I remember now," I said, recalling that scene. Both of us were crying over the tragic death of Little Red Riding Hood and her grandmother." I remember stroking Louisa's hair and wiping my tears with the sleeve of my cotton dress. Suddenly, Louisa stopped crying and looked at me. I didn't like the way she looked.

"Why didn't the radio kill that terrible, hungry wolf? Why did it kill the kind, poor grandmother?" Louisa cried.

I didn't know what to say or how to explain it to her. Unexpectedly, she jumped to her feet and screamed, "Let's smash the radio! It shouldn't kill the poor grandmother and her granddaughter."

I was shocked and scared. Since a very early age, Louisa always was the troublemaker between the two of us. I tried to talk her out of it and said in a calming voice, "If we break the radio, we will be punished. Mother won't give us money for ice cream."

"So what?" Louisa screamed. She quickly climbed onto the table, somehow she managed to reach the radio and drag it down. I didn't have time to say or do anything. But when the radio was on the table, I grabbed and pressed it against my chest, covering it with both arms for protection. Louisa, with a bellicose expression on her freckled face, tried to attack me like a small tiger cub.

"Give it back to me! Bad radio! It killed Grandmother and Little Red Riding Hood!" She pushed me and tried to pull the radio out of my arms. In the heat of the battle, our parents walked into the kitchen.

"What is going on? What are you doing, girls? Stop it!" Mother shouted at us. "Nina! Give the radio to your father!"

"Whose idea was it to take the radio off the wall? You could have damaged it!" Father said angrily, snatching the long-suffering radio from my hands.

"Louisa's. She wanted to destroy it because the Big Bad Wolf ate Grandmother and Little Red Riding Hood," I said tearfully.

"You, Nina, are older than Louisa. You should have stopped her. She could have fallen from the table. She could have broken her leg, her arm or her nose. You are the older one, Nina, you should have known better," Father said reproachfully.

I started to cry again. I felt miserable and angry at Louisa. We always seemed to get into trouble because of her. Being the older one, I, as a rule, was accused of being the guilty party. This time, our parents punished both of us. For two weeks, we had to forget the sweet taste of our favorite fruit ice cream which we both liked so much.

The black, round radio that looked like a plate *did* survive Louisa's ferocious attack, and later was successfully rehung on the wall by Father. However, this time he placed it much higher.

39. My Pre-War Childhood Memories
in Shauliai, Lithuania

Our life in Shauliai, Lithuania, was another childhood memory. In the late autumn of 1940, Father's unit had been transferred from Minsk, Byelorussia, to the Lithuanian city of Shauliai. We traveled there by train. When we arrived, all the city was covered with deep snow which was falling nonstop. Shauliai was a small and cozy city which had only a few streetcar routes, none of which reached the area where we lived. Although we had been there for only three months, both Louisa and I remembered well our stay there. I lived through several unforgettable physical and emotional experiences during that short span of time.

For the first time, at the age of nine, I crossed the state border of the USSR, between Byelorussia and Lithuania.

It was in Shauliai, where I made the one and only unsuccessful attempt to smoke. For that attempt, I had been smacked in my face by Mother.

Never before had I seen such small charming private shops with doorbells, and I thoroughly enjoyed my own shopping experiences.

In Shauliai, I discovered a new product — saccharine —

which some people used instead of sugar. I even tasted candies made with saccharine.

There, I had heard the word *America,* and I had learned that some Lithuanians could move and live there if they wanted.

To my big surprise, I paid attention to the fact that some adult men could be very handsome. Never before had I been aware of men's beauty.

In Shauliai, I also had a chance to ride alone, as a passenger, behind the coachman, in a sleigh drawn by horses.

Finally, and luckily for me, it happened in that city that my young developing brain had registered such marvelous treasures of the Russian language as proverbial figurative comparisons which later became an integral part of my spoken and written vocabulary.

As it always had been before, we lived in Shauliai in one room of a two-room communal apartment which we shared with a Lithuanian family that had two daughters. The younger girl, Anna, was two years older than I was; her sister, Martha, was fifteen. She smoked cigarettes on the sly, stealing them from her mother. Both girls spoke a little Russian, so we could socialize and spend some time together, playing and talking.

The winter in Shauliai was very cold, and we often stayed inside reading books, mostly fairy tales for Louisa, playing dominoes and lotto, or playing with the girls.

Once, when all our parents were absent, Martha invited me and Louisa to try to smoke a cigarette. Louisa categorically declined the offer, but I, as if the devil tripped me up, decided to take a risk and warned Louisa, "Don't you dare tell Mother about it."

I took a cigarette with trembling fingers, inhaled slowly, and, at the same moment, I started to choke. I couldn't breathe, my eyes leaped out of their sockets. I coughed and coughed and couldn't catch my breath. I thought that I was dying. Louisa got scared and started to cry and scream, "Don't die, Nina, don't die!" Both Martha and Anna were laughing at me.

At that moment, Mother returned home from the store. When she saw me, she dropped her bags and started to shake me like a pear tree, screaming, "What has happened? What did you do to yourself?" When she sniffed the cigarette smoke, she looked at me, then smacked me in my face. I uttered a scream and began to cry. "Where did you got the cigarettes?" Mother continued in confusion. "Who gave you the cigarette?" she insisted. I looked at her with tearful eyes, took a deep breath, and nodded in the direction of our neighbor's room.

Like an arrow, Mother rushed into their room and confronted Martha. "Why did you give a cigarette to Nina? She is just a child!" Mother yelled full of indignation.

"She asked me for it," answered Martha, defensively, lifting her shoulders in dismay .

"She is lying! She is lying!" I screamed in despair. "She steals cigarettes from her mother." I easily gave away my girlfriend Martha because she had betrayed me.

My punishment was discussed that evening when Father came home. It was cruel. My parents decided that I wouldn't go to the New Year's spruce children's party at the Officers' Club. I was disappointed and miserable. I knew that those children's parties were always full of fun and joy. There always was a concert in which many children participated, singing holiday songs, reciting poems and dancing around a nicely decorated spruce tree.

Besides, every child always received a New Year's gift — a bag full of candies, mandarins, apples, and cookies.

I was devastated, but what could I do? I was guilty because I had violated the rules and had set a bad example for Louisa, as Father stated it. So, I cried quietly into my pillow, covering my head with my blanket. I shared the bed with Louisa. For some reason, all our belongings were not unpacked yet. Louisa felt sorry for me and promised to share her New Year's gift with me.

So, on the day of the children's party, Mother stayed at home with me while Father and Louisa went to the party. Mother and I prepared supper: we fried small pies stuffed with ground meat, fried onions, and fresh cabbage.

Father and Louisa returned home in a good mood and brought a New Year's gift for me, as well. They had invitations for two children, so they had gotten two gifts. I was happy for the gift, but I was still sad because I had missed the opportunity to participate in the concert for which I had learned a song about the New Year's fir tree—*A Little Spruce was Born in the Forest.*

Since then, Mother never left us alone at home; we always accompanied her wherever she went. If she needed to go out for a short period of time, she used to lock us up in our room. Although after the smoking scandal our relationship with Anna and Martha was tense, we still continued to exchange words with them through the closed doors.

One day, Anna, the younger sister, pretended that she was alone in the room and asked me, "What do you think about Martha?" I couldn't see them through the locked door, but I was sure that Martha was hiding close by and could hear me. I answered honestly, "Your sister is a bad girl because she smokes, and she is only fifteen. Martha is also a liar and a thief. Do you know that she steals cigarettes from your mother? She lied about me. I didn't ask her to give me a cigarette; Martha offered it to me, and then she lied to my mother. I was smacked and punished because of her, and I missed the children's New Year's party."

As soon as I finished my speech full of anger and resentment, I heard Martha's voice admonishing me as if I really were the guilty party, "You are a bad girl yourself, Nina, because in front of my eyes you are smooth as silk, but behind my back, you are like a wolf. In Russian that proverb rhymes: the word "silk" (*shyolk*) is rhymed with the word "wolf" (*wolk*), – *Pered glazamy kak shyolk, a za spinoyu kak wolk.*

"You are not my friend anymore, Martha," I said firmly. "It is you who were like silk in front of me and behind my back, you turned out to be a wolf and lied to my mother. You forced Anna to tell me that you were not in the room. You lied again. You are not honest; you stole cigarettes from your own mother," I retorted.

I didn't want to continue arguing with Martha. Since then, I became keenly aware of such phrases, and I was able to distinguish them in the flow of words of other people. Later, as a high school student, I copied in a special notebook, the expressions from the books which I had read and used them in my oral speech and in my written compositions.

That smoking episode left a deep dent in our relationship with Anna and Martha, but with time, as always happens with children, we continued to play and to talk with both girls and with Antonas, a bold and nasty boy, age thirteen, who lived upstairs, on the second floor in our apartment building.

When I first saw Antonas in the hall, he asked me, "Are you the Russian girl who lives in Martha's apartment?"

"Yes, I am. My name is Nina, and I am in the second grade. Which grade are you in?"

"I don't go to school anymore. I don't have to," he answered. I was surprised, but I didn't have time to ask why, because he continued, "In two weeks, we will leave for America. They don't speak Lithuanian or Russian there; they speak English. I will study English. My uncle lives there. My father will work with him. It's better to live in America than here. When we leave, Martha's family will move to our apartment, and you will occupy Martha's room."

That was when I had heard the word "America" for the first time. As to Antonas, he also smoked on the sly, like Martha. In front of us girls, he pretended to be an adult. He swaggered and looked at me as if I were a nonentity. He liked to brag about his skating and skiing skills, as well.

One evening, Antonas' father dropped by our neighbors to borrow some cigarettes from Martha's mother. I saw him for only a few minutes, but I was surprised at how good looking he was. That was the first time that I distinguished between handsome and ugly men. Up to then, all adult men looked alike to me.

Antonas' father was tall, with short brown hair and dark-blue joyful eyes. He smiled a lot, and was nicely dressed in a fancy, checked light-beige sweater.

Antonas resembled his father, but I didn't consider him handsome, maybe because he was arrogant, boastful, and always laughed at Louisa and me when we fell down on the ice on the nearby frozen pond. He never helped us up like other Lithuanian boys, who immediately rushed to our rescue, making intricate circles around us, showing off their skating skills as soon as they noticed younger girls sliding face down or sitting helplessly on the ice. They lifted us as if we were weightless and put us back on our feet, while laughing and horsing around.

Antonas hung out with Martha, Anna and me, probably, because we all lived in the same apartment building. He was the one who introduced me to saccharine. It had happened one Sunday afternoon, when Anna and I went to a small nearby shop to buy some school supplies. Antonas, who was walking his dog in the street, followed us just to keep us company.

In the shop, with an air of importance, he greeted the shopkeeper lady and asked in Lithuanian, "*Saccharina ira?*"

She responded, "*Saccharina nera.*" Then he bought a small pack of candy, I selected two pencils, and Anna acquired a school notebook. When we were out of the shop, in the street, I asked Antonas, "What is saccharine?" I already knew the meaning of the Lithuanian words "*ira*" and "*nera*" ("yes" and "no"), and I understood that he asked if there was saccharine in the shop, and the shopkeeper answered that they were out of it.

"It's like sugar, only cheaper," he said. "These candies are made with saccharine," he explained. "They are twice as cheap as the candy made with sugar." Then he opened the small cone paper bag and treated us to saccharine-made candy. I took two: I put one into my mouth, and I saved another for Louisa. The candy had a strange, sweet taste, but not sweet enough for me. I said *spasibo*, thank you, to Antonas but said nothing about the taste of the candy.

40. Leaving Lithuania for Estonia

*I*n the middle of January 1941, Father had told us to pack our things and be ready to leave. His military unit was being transferred from Lithuania to Tallinn — the capital of Estonia. We had to travel there by train. I carefully jotted down Martha's and Anna's address in my new address book, my birthday present from Mother, said good-bye to my classmates and was ready to leave. It snowed heavily the day before our departure, and all the streets were covered with thick layers of fresh snow.

The next day, the car that had to take us to the railroad terminal was not able to get to our house as the streets were impassable for autos and even for streetcars. We could reach the terminal only by a sleigh driven by horses with a cabman. As we had no telephone, Father asked me, the oldest, to walk to the main square, to the parking lot for cabmen with horses and sleighs to get a sleigh and bring it back to the house to pick up the rest of the family.

"Hurry up!" Father said nervously. "We can't be late. The train won't wait for us."

I grabbed my mittens and rushed into the street. Thank God, by late morning janitors had already cleaned narrow paths on the sidewalks. I managed to get quickly to the sleigh parking lot which was located several blocks away. I was sweaty, nervous and scared because we had little time to get to the terminal; we could miss our train.

I showed the note with our street address written in Lithuanian by Martha's mother to the first cabman I saw. He was a big man, dressed in a long sheepskin coat, tall conical sheepskin hat and long felt boots—*walenky*. He helped me to get onto the sleigh, covered my legs up to my waist with some kind of a curtain or special blanket, got up to his seat, whipped the horses, and the sleigh rushed forward through the deep snow.

I rode alone in the passenger seat of the horse sleigh behind the cabman. The scenery was amazing: the roofs, the smoking chimneys of the houses, and the churches were covered with fresh snow. Snow was everywhere— on the fences, on the trees, on the bushes, on the street gas lamp poles, and, of course, on the streets and on the sidewalks—piles of it.

Passers-by looked in amazement at that unusual picture early in the morning—a little girl riding alone on a horse-drawn sleigh, in the middle of the street, covered with deep snow.

I felt as if I were the Snow Queen from the fairy-tale play "Snowy Kingdom" which my sister Louisa and I had seen at the children's theater in Minsk. I felt strange, as if I were performing on stage: the horse-drawn sleigh moved quickly, with snow flying away from under the horses' hooves. I was the Snow Queen, standing in the sleigh, holding the reins tight, in a snow-white, shining regal robe streaming in the wind, with the Snow Queen's crown on my head.

Thanks to the sleigh-driver services, we didn't miss our train. The same evening, we arrived at Riga, the capital of Latvia, where we had to change trains and board the Riga-Tallinn Express.

"It's called an express train because it moves faster than a passenger train," Father explained to us. "You will see it yourselves. Everything will be new to you . . . Please don't open your mouths and stare at it dumbly as a ram at a new gate," Father instructed us.

When we got to the platform, the train was already there. It was dark outside, but all its windows were lit like a decorated spruce at the New Year's party. First, Father with the help of the porter, brought all our luggage into the coach. Then we boarded the train and followed the conductor who took us to our compartments. We occupied two compartments, each with two soft sleeping sofas.

The interior was gorgeous: nice curtains on the window, a lamp on the table and several more on the walls. A decanter with drinking water and glasses were on the tray, next to the table lamp. A big mirror was hanging on the door which led to the individual bathroom with a lavatory pan and a washing sink. Several terry cloth towels hung on the hooks. The bed-linens were clean, starched and ironed. The blankets were soft and warm. Louisa and I had to sleep on the lower sofas. Father and Mother each occupied the upper bunks.

After we washed our hands and faces, and combed our hair, Father took us to the dining car for a late supper. Before we went there, he warned us again, "You girls, behave yourselves. Don't open your mouths too wide. Don't talk too loud! Don't forget to say "please" and "thank you" when the waitress brings you food. Don't fidget, and don't whisper to one another."

Then Mother continued to instruct us in a low voice, "Try not to put your elbows on the table and eat neatly so that you don't drop crumbs of food on the table, and keep your hands with food over the plate."

The dining car was beautiful. It had colorful curtains on the windows, white tablecloths, and bunches of artificial flowers in vases on each table. Those flowers immediately attracted Louisa's attention, and she unobtrusively tried to touch them.

"They are dried! They are not fresh," she said to me.

"No, they are not. They are made of something, and they are not dried like those roses and chamomiles which we used to dry between the pages of a book," I insisted. Only a few people were in the dining car. The radio played quietly, and the atmosphere was cozy and festive.

When a waiter but not a waitress served us tea and sandwiches, Louisa's eyes started to widen, as she never before had seen waiters at the officers' dining hall where we sometimes had Sunday lunch with our parents. Only waitresses dressed in cute uniforms with white short aprons worked there. I liked their uniforms very much. I secretly decided to become a waitress when I grew up. Louisa made an attempt to open her mouth, but I managed to pull her by the sleeve under the table and whispered almost without a sound, "Don't!" She froze, her mouth half-open.

All in all, the evening tea was finished without a major blunder. We returned to our compartments, washed up and got ready for bed. Before we went to sleep, Louisa said to me, "I like it here. This train looks like a king's palace, like in the picture in the fairy-tale book."

"This is not a palace, *glupyshka*, silly," I said. "It's just a train, only it's an express one."

That was the one and only time our family ever traveled in the sleeping car of an express train. In the morning, Mother woke us up when the train was approaching Tallinn, where we lived until World War II reached the Soviet Union in June of that same year.

[The next time I had the chance and luxury of traveling by sleeping car in an express train happened forty years later, in May if 1981. Leaving Russia for good, I, as a member of a large group of the Soviet Jewish refugees, arrived in Vienna by Soviet Aeroflot from Moscow. Three days later, we had to take the Vienna-Rome express train. While we walked, surrounded by Israeli soldiers, dressed in civilian clothes and armed with their invariable short-barreled Uzis, from the train terminal plaza to the platform, two young Austrian guys started to walk next to us and then asked in broken English, "Where you are going to? To Israel?"

"No, we are going to Rome, and from there to America," I said.

"Have you seen Vienna, our city?"

"No," we answered. We were not allowed to go to the city because of the recent terrorists' attacks on refugees.

"Why don't you stay here, and we show you our beautiful city," said another guy, mixing English words with German while smiling and giving us despairing looks.

"We can't, we have to stay with the group," I said "So, good-bye! *Auf Wiedersehen!*"

"*Auf Wiedersehen*, girls!" they said in unison, but didn't stop and followed us to the coach.

My twenty-year-old daughter, Elena, was filled with indignation by their address—"girls."

"Don't they see that you are my mother?" she reacted angrily.

I smiled, shrugged my shoulders and said indifferently, "It's already dark, and maybe they are nearsighted.

241

They're both wearing glasses. They were nice and friendly with us—complete strangers. It's a pity that because of those damn terrorists we were deprived of the pleasure of seeing this *wunderbar* historic city. Now, thank God, we are in the free world behind the Soviet border, and we can come later at our own convenience any time we want."

We put our hand luggage into our compartment and approached the window across the passage. And there they were—standing on the platform under the window, both smiling and blowing us kisses and waving their friendly *Auf Wiedersehen!* Farewell!]

41. Tallinn — Trip Down Memory Lane

I recalled when we lived in Tallinn, being only nine years old, I managed to ride a streetcar to school and back home alone. For the first few days, Mother accompanied me during my ride to school and back. She showed me the way and made me memorize the streetcar stops. After that, I rode alone, and I always was on time at school and back home.

I was still an inexperienced child, and once I spent more money at the school cafeteria than I should have. On my way back home, I took a streetcar and started to fumble in my school bag searching for my fare, but I couldn't find three kopecks for a ticket. A female conductor, an Estonian woman who collected the fare, patiently watched me while I nervously rummaged in my school bag. Finally, I realized that I had no fare money. The conductor looked at me without smiling and said firmly, "You have to get out of the car at the next stop."

The streetcar was almost empty. There was one other Russian girl who took the streetcar at my stop where I did. She wasn't in my class, but I had seen her at school and in the streetcar. I turned my head to her searching for support. She looked down, then fixed her gaze out the window.

None of the passengers, all Estonians, showed any reaction. My situation was hopeless. I felt embarrassed; my face was burning with shame. Awkwardly, I said, "Sorry!" As soon as the streetcar stopped, I hurriedly jumped out. I had to walk the next ten long blocks, feeling unhappy and angry with myself.

Piles of snow accumulated on the street, but the sidewalks were clean. I walked slowly; the heavy school bag was pulling down my hand and beating on my leg. I changed hands and continued to walk. The walking and the fresh winter sea breeze cooled off my flushed cheeks and dried my tears. I started to breathe freely and enjoyed looking at the nicely decorated shop windows.

When I got home, Mother asked me, "Why are you so late? I was worried about you."

"I didn't have money for the ticket. I probably lost it or spent it in the cafeteria, and the conductor told me to get off the streetcar. So I walked most of the way home." I felt guilty and frustrated.

Mother gave me a sad smile, patted my head and said as usual, "Take your coat off, go wash your hands, and sit down at the table. Both Louisa and I are hungry. We waited for you to have lunch. For the second course today, we have your favorite grated potato pancakes with sour cream. We'll talk later about your streetcar incident."

After lunch, Mother washed the dishes, and I dried them. Then she sat me on the sofa, next to her and said, reproachfully but mildly, "You have to learn, Nina, how to handle your money. Before you go to the cafeteria, always put aside three kopecks for your fare. By the way, I have an idea how to help you."

Several days later, she gave me a small brocade coin purse so that I could keep my loose coins in it. She also gave me a small booklet of ten streetcar tickets which she had bought from the conductor. I had to keep that booklet in my purse. Every time I rode the streetcar, I had to tear off one ticket and give it to the conductor. Since then, Mother kept several booklets in stock for me. Each day, she reminded me to check if I had tickets for both rides — to school and back home.

It was my first coin purse with real money. The coins were small, but I was happy and proud to have that coin purse in my school bag or in my pocket when I went to the school cafeteria. Having a coin purse made me feel as if I were a responsible adult. Besides, none of my classmates had a coin purse. Boys kept their coins in their pockets, and girls kept theirs in a special compartment of their pencil boxes.

My embarrassing streetcar adventure in Tallinn didn't overshadow other happy moments and episodes of everyday life which we had experienced while we lived there before the start of the War.

We lived in Tallinn through the winter, spring and June of 1941, longer than we had lived in Shiauliai, Lithuania. So, we had the opportunity to see more places and to do more as a family in Tallinn than we had in Shiauliai where we had stayed only two or three months in the fall and winter of 1940 before we moved to Tallinn.

On Sundays, if Father was free of duty in his unit, he would take us all to the movie theatre located in a beautiful old building downtown. In late spring and in summer, we went to the beach at the Gulf of Finland. Like many other people there, we walked barefoot on the very edge of the water, which still was too cold to bathe and to swim in.

While strolling along the sandy beach, we used to pick up small cockle-shells and collect the most beautiful of them into a toy wicker basket. Louisa and I jumped in the water, splashed and raced each other. We enjoyed the view, listened to the screaming of the gulls, and watched them diving into the waves and catching fish with incredible agility.

After the long walk, we had a picnic on the grass under the pine trees which were growing not far from the water. The word "picnic" wasn't a part of our vocabulary then. At that time, on the beach, Mother just said, "Girls, go wash your hands in the water, and we'll have a snack."

Sitting on the blanket, we enjoyed eating cheese and sausage *buterbrody* as we called sandwiches and drinking homemade cranberry drink from a big three-litre jar which Father brought in a string bag. Cheeky gulls carefully approached us trying to get crumbs, and, with great pleasure, we shared our snack with them.

If Father was busy on Sunday, Mother took us to the Kadriorg forest-park, across the street from our house. The big beautiful trees of the park were populated by hordes of squirrels. We always were happy to meet them, and visiting the park and those friendly animals was our favorite entertainment.

People treated them nicely, and, in response, the squirrels were trustful and brave with adults and children. All our family adored squirrels; we always looked forward to meeting them and never forgot to bring them their favorite treats: nuts, candies, cookies and even dried fruits. People took photos with the squirrels sitting on their shoulders and eating treats from their hands.

Father promised that some day he would borrow a camera from his colleagues and would take a photo of Louisa and me together with the squirrels. I even wrote about that promised photo with the squirrels to my grandmother. Every time, when my mother wrote a letter to my grandparents, I always added a line or two about my news. That time I wrote, "Very soon I will send you the photo of Luisa and me feeding squirrels from our hands in Kadriorg Park.

Regrettably, Father, being very busy, never managed to do that. So those scenes – Louisa and I with the squirrels enjoying their favorite treats from the palms of our hands – are depicted in our memory only.

42. The Long-Awaited Apartment

*L*istening to stories and recalling different episodes from our pre-war life made me realize how much we had missed that life — the cities we had lived in, the places we had visited, and the friends we had.

Since the start of the war, we had lived without Father for five years, and we missed him very much. His letters were our main source of information and our only hope for a better future. Very often, at the end of the day when all the household chores were over, Mother read us Father's letter again and again..

His last letter was about the apartment he expected to get. That joyful news gave us another grain of hope that maybe, just maybe, we would see our father soon, and we would have a chance to enjoy that wonderful apartment which Father had described in his letter.

The apartment was located on the top floor of a three-story building, and it had two balconies: one faced the street planted with chestnut trees; the other — the kitchen balcony — faced the backyard of the building. There was a special room for storage for each of the seven apartments located in the basement which could be used as a cellar, as well.

The apartment itself consisted of three rooms, a kitchen with a small pantry, a bathroom with a natural gas heater, and a small separate toilet room. The kitchen was equipped with a gas stove with four burners and an oven. There was running water, but only cold. The heating system was also powered by natural gas.

Never before had we a whole apartment the size of fifty square meters (around 538 square feet) for ourselves. Our family of four, like other officers' families, always lived in one room in the communal apartments. Two, three or even more families, about twelve or more people, had to share all the amenities, if there were any: one kitchen, one bathroom and, if they were lucky, a toilet separate from the bathroom. Every family consisted of at least three members, if not more.

It was a real communal hell, without exaggeration: long lines to get into the bathroom at every time of the day, lines to get into the toilet, several toddlers sitting in a row on their potties in the entrance hall next to the bathroom, regular squabbles and heated quarrels, even cat fights in the kitchen among the women, sometimes with a bloody outcome.

Kitchens were not equipped with electric or gas stoves, not to mention a hot water system. So, residents had to use different primitive cooking appliances such as kerosene Primus stoves *(primus)*, and oil and paraffin stoves *(kerosinka)*. Those devices were noisy and emanated toxic fumes. They were dangerous because they were not properly installed, and they often broke.

I still remember a piercing shriek of our neighbors' little son, Vasya, whose ball accidentally hit and overturned the paraffin stove with the boiling soup on it. The boy's hand and arm were scalded. There was no telephone in the building. His parents had to take him to the military clinic by foot, as there was no public transportation, no taxis in the residential area of that military town.

It was not easy to do household chores using those simple kitchen appliances: to cook three meals for the family, to do the laundry in a zinc washtub or in a basin, to heat water and to give a bath to the children in a washtub, to do the dishes and many other routine domestic chores. They all demanded hard labor and iron nerves from the dwellers of the communal apartments who were exposed to the presence of one another and one another's children each and every day of the year.

So, to get a three-room apartment with all modern amenities was like a dream come true for our family, like paradise on earth. Before we came to Tallinn, I had never seen such apartments, not in Byelorussia, nor in Lithuania, where we had lived before.

Father wrote us that our future dwelling was still occupied by a Polish family who had applied and was waiting for an exit visa in order to emigrate to Poland. As soon as the Soviet authorities processed their documents, they would be allowed to leave. The approximate time of their departure was the summer of 1946, almost a year after Victory Day — May 9, 1945. After that, Father would come to Grandma's place to visit our extended family for a short time. Then, Louisa, Mother, Father and I would travel to Lvov by train. That was the plan.

Father also mentioned that he had bought from that Polish family several pieces of used furniture so that we could have the most necessary things, such as beds, tables and chairs.

During the war, all industry was occupied with the production of goods and supplies for the front to satisfy the military needs. So, the main slogan for the Soviet industry was — "All for the front, all for the victory!" The needs of the civilian population were not taken into account. Therefore, a huge deficit of all kinds of manufactured goods, including furniture, existed in the Soviet Union for many years after the end of World War II.

The head of the Soviet State and the commander in chief, Stalin, categorically rejected the Marshall Plan (The European Recovery Program) offered by the United States which gave economic aid to Europe for rebuilding its economy. Therefore, the post-war economic recovery of the Soviet country turned out to be a hard and slow process. The furniture stores, like the grocery ones, were completely empty.

The news about the apartment, with its detailed plan and the description made by Father, excited our family. The apartment itself and the furniture in it were something tangible to think and to talk about.

Grandparents, Mother and Valentina talked among themselves, admiring such amenities as a bathroom with a gas heater and a gas stove with an oven in the kitchen. Grandpa who, as a rule, didn't talk much and preferred to keep his silence, loudly approved the apartment, saying, "The bathroom with a gas heater? I have never heard about such a thing. A toilet and running water. That's something! Now you will live *kak burzuyi,* like bourgeois!"

"Like who?" Louisa asked, her eyes wide open, her thin neck stretched out. She looked at Mother in bewilderment. Mother smiled and said, "Like rich people."

Grandpa's comment puzzled me. I turned my head to Louisa, regarding her with suspicion. She wore a simple cotton dress which had been altered from one of Mother's old dresses. She was barefoot, revealing her filthy heels. Her elbows and knees were covered with old and fresh scratches. Her untidy pigtails stuck out unevenly in different directions, one lower than the other. To me, she definitely didn't look like a bourgeois kid. Neither did I, although I had neatly braided my own hair. But did that make me a bourgeois? I didn't understand Grandpa's reaction, nor his words, but I didn't dare ask him or somebody else. My thoughts were wandering. *Why did Grandpa say that?*

43. Plucking Feathers for a New Life

*M*other and Aunt Valentina often talked about things we had to do first in order to be ready for our departure. Grandma, however, was the most practical and experienced person to deal with such issues. She sighed heavily, her head nodded pensively, then she said, "It's a pity that you can't take with you new bed-linen. We had no fabric, and there is no place to buy it. What we can do, at least, is to make new down pillows for all of you, as we have a lot of chicken and goose feathers to pluck. As soon as the fall harvest work is over, we'll start doing it in the evenings. If everybody helps, we can do it quickly."

Nobody said a word, because we all hated to pluck feathers. I secretly hoped that Grandma would forget about that plucking venture, but it turned out to be a vain hope, as the making of down pillows became Grandma's biggest project for the near future.

Listening to all those conversations of the adults and to their plans, I gradually realized that soon some changes would come into our life, maybe sooner than we had expected. Were we ready to meet and to embrace those changes? I asked myself. Yes, we all were ready for some changes for the better. We needed them. We were thirsty for change. Only let it be for the better.

I had a premonition that Mother, Louisa and I would soon leave Grandma's house and would travel to the city of Lvov, in Western Ukraine, to join our father in the new apartment. How soon, we didn't know yet. That was a good premonition. *Stuchu po derevu!* Knock on wood! I still was afraid of scaring away my good luck.

The one thing we knew for sure was that all possible changes in our lives depended on letters from Father and from Uncle Mitya, Valentina's husband. Only they could bring us good news, which would support our hopes. We, however, couldn't just sit on our hands, placidly waiting for our mailwoman, Lyusia, to deliver their letters to us. We all had to work hard, including us children. We spent the first half of the day at school, and after that, we had to do our homework and to help around the house.

The curriculum of the seventh grade was tough, so I had to spend more time doing my homework. I also had to help Grandma and Mother in the house. I cleaned rooms, dusted furniture, mopped the floors and peeled vegetables in the kitchen. I also patched and mended my own and Louisa's clothes.

In the evenings, after supper, we all sat in the kitchen and plucked chicken and goose feathers. It wasn't hard work, but monotonous and annoying. The small kitchen was full of down floating in the air, tickling our nostrils and causing repeated sneezing. We didn't know back then that down provoked allergies. We hadn't even heard the term "allergies."

"The time will fly like a bullet," Grandma used to say while plucking feathers together with us children. "You won't even notice it; you won't even have a minute to look around before you will leave for Lvov with your father," she continued with a heavy sigh. "At least, you will have new, soft down pillows to sleep on. When you move to a new place, it's better to bring everything new: new furniture, new bed-linen, kitchen utensils, plates and dishes. But where can we get new things now? There is no place to buy them even if we had the money — which we don't. Maybe your mother will buy new pots and pans at that big flea market, *barakholka*, your father had written about. In the meantime, I will give you my favorite blue enamel soup pot. It is still in good condition, without a single chip. You need a frying pan, cups for everyone, spoons, forks, maybe two knives, and some plates. I will give you eight soup-plates from my Kuznetsov's dinner set. We never used them, so they look like new."

I was shocked. Grandma's Kuznetsov's dinner set, her wedding gift, was her most valuable possession. Miraculously it had survived the October Revolution, the Civil War and the starvation years, when Grandma had to sell all her gold jewelry in order to live on. It sat on the lower shelves of the sideboard in the living room for ages. Grandma didn't allow anybody to touch it during the cleaning. She herself always wiped the dust from every item with a soft moist cloth. No one was allowed to use it or to remove it from the sideboard without Grandma's permission.

During the German occupation, the dinner set was carefully wrapped in used bedsheets and newspapers, packed in a wooden box and secretly hidden under the wooden floor of the small bedroom along with another of Grandma's valuable items — her small, cardboard suitcase containing all the clothes she would like to be dressed in when she dies. She called it "*A suitcase for death.*"

It was Grandma's decision to hide our most valuable possessions under the floor of our small bedroom. She learned the idea from the farmers' market where the people openly and heatedly discussed the danger which the hastily retreating German troops presented to the civilian population of our town.

There were rumors that German soldiers, on various pretexts, including the official document checking, had invaded private houses, marauded and robbed citizens, as there was nobody to protect defenseless and helpless women, children and elderly people.

Those who lived in the outskirts of the town and had large orchards and vegetable gardens decided to hide their "treasures" outside of their houses. Under the cover of night, they dug pits in the orchards as far away as possible from the houses and put whatever they wanted to hide from the envious and greedy eyes of the retreating German soldiers in those secret pits: clothes, shoes, bottles of homemade vodka, even pork fat packed in the big vats made of fire-clay, and many other things They conducted those digging operations in pitch darkness of night to avoid curiosity of their neighbors.

Our house was located not far from downtown, and our vegetable garden was small and closely surrounded by the houses of our neighbors. So, the only solution for us, according to Grandma, was to hide our most valuable possessions inside the house, under the painted wooden floor.

It was a real underground operation in which almost all the members of our family participated. It was conducted late in the evening in order to avoid unexpected visits of friends or neighbors. Grandpa had to perform the most difficult job — to remove several painted boards of the floor so that we could put our valuable possessions there.

As luck would have it, Grandpa was that evening in

a bad mood, angry and irritated, and more than once he snapped at Grandma for no reason at all.

"What do we have to hide, and what for? That junk dinner set which we never used? Or that suitcase of yours with the clothes which you never put on? If a bomb hits the house, we won't need that stuff for sure, especially the dinner set," Grandpa raged.

Grandma's eyes were full of tears, but she remained cool. "Don't get angry, Vanechka," she said imploringly. "That dinner set was our wedding present, and it is very dear to me. As to my new clothes in my suitcase, you know it's a tradition to have all new clothes for a funeral. Just think, if I didn't have my suitcase and something happens to me tomorrow, where would you get new clothes for me for the funeral? Just think about it, Vanechka, *moy dorogoy,* my darling."

"I am tired as a dog. I have been on my feet since early morning. The children should be in bed, and they are not, and you always come out with some silly, crazy idea," Grandpa retorted.

"Vanechka, Vanechka, calm down, please, take it easy, we'll do it fast, and as soon as we finish—" At that moment, Grandma looked at her Vanechka and saw his angrily distorted, flushed face. Suddenly, she got silent, screwed up her eyes, and slowly passed out, falling on the floor.

I got scared and screamed, "Mama, Mama, Grandma died! She just died!"

"She is not dead," Grandpa said angrily. It's her best acting part. She always plays this trick if she wants to have her own way," Grandpa said with satisfaction.

"What is her own way?" I asked.

"Fainting on time and calling me Vanechka," Grandpa retorted sarcastically.

At that moment, Mother rushed into the bedroom with a glass of water and generously sprinkled Grandma's face. She quivered and opened her eyes, then slowly pulled herself into sitting position.

"Let's go to my room, Mother, you need to rest, to lie down," my mother said to Grandma. "I'll give you your favorite Valerian drops. They always help you calm down. We will finish the rest without you. Nina will help me," Mother said, giving me a wink.

"Yes, Mother, I will." I said hurriedly "Don't worry. I know where Grandma wanted to put every item."

My mother took Grandma to the living room and put her to bed. Meanwhile, Grandpa took away the third board from the floor, and we had the chance to see what was under the floor. It was an empty space covered with locomotive slag.

"Why is the slag there?" I asked Grandpa.

"It's very dry and clean. Worms and insects don't live in the slag. They can't feed on it. They don't like it." Grandpa explained.

When Mother came back we carefully put the boxes with the Kuznetsov dinner set, Grandma's *Singer* sewing machine, several homemade doormats and floor coverings, some calf hide, and other small items into the opening under the floor.

Grandpa still was on edge, and his remarks were brief and sarcastic. "We should not destroy the floor to hide this trash. This sewing machine is older than I am." Grandpa then installed the boards in their place and said, "I am tired as hell. I'm going to bed. Tomorrow I will close up the boards and paint them in order to conceal the damage."

That night Mother slept next to me in Grandma's bed. Grandma slept in Mother's bed. She had fallen asleep as soon as she took the Valerian drops, and Mother didn't want to disturb her.

That day I made several discoveries for myself. For the first time I heard Grandma calling Grandpa "Vanechka," which is a term of endearment for Vanya — the diminutive form of Ivan, Grandpa's full first name. It was the first time I saw how a completely healthy person like Grandma could lose her consciousness in a blink of an eye and miraculously regain it with the help of natural cold water.

That night I dreamt about Grandma's suitcase for death. That suitcase was a mystery for us children. We were always interested in it. During the spring cleaning, we more than once asked Grandma to open it and to show us its contents. I couldn't understand why Grandma, being still so young, healthy and beautiful, had already prepared her "clothes for death."

44. Grandma's Suitcase

*I*n was late spring of 1946. The first round of field work was finished. The weather was warm and dry. As we had a small break before the next round — weeding, Grandma decided to clean our small bedroom. I, as usual, helped her.

Only one wide bed in which we both slept occupied the right part of the room. Grandpa slept on a narrow, backless couch, which stood on the opposite side of the room, across our bed. As the room was tiny, a little space was left for a small rectangular table and for a chair. The table was in front of the only window, between the bed and the couch. Grandma's *Singer* sewing machine was on the table when it was in operation, and under the table when it was not being used.

As usual during the spring cleaning, Grandma turned to Grandpa for help.

"Please, Ivan Danilovich, do me a favor, take the rug from the wall to the yard and beat the dust out of it," she used to say in a mellow voice. She knew that Grandpa hated to do that kind of work. I, meanwhile, under Grandma's supervision, dusted the furniture, swept and mopped the floor with a wet cloth.

"Don't miss those far corners under the bed and the couch," she reminded me. She had some kind of obsession about the corners and always mentioned them. That irritated me a lot because I was very thorough in my cleaning and never neglected those spots.

At the same time, Grandma rechecked and rearranged the content of her suitcase which always was hidden under her bed, her favorite hiding place. She decided to organize all the clothes differently. First, she took all the items from the suitcase to the backyard. Grandpa had already beaten out the rug and sat on the bench, smoking.

"You, Nina, take care of my underwear, my stockings, my headscarf, and my jacket. Those things are not heavy for you. I'll take care of the heavy stuff — my rabbit fur coat and my wool dress," Grandma said. I didn't think that her wool dress was heavy. I just had a feeling that Grandma didn't trust me to deal with her favorite item.

We took everything outside and hung all the clothes on the line in the backyard to dry and to air the smell of mothballs. I shook out Grandma's underwear — her white cambric slip with narrow shoulder straps, and white knee-long cotton drawers, trimmed with lace at the knee.

On the clothes line I hung up Grandma's grey silk stockings and a pale grey silk headscarf, with hardly noticeable pink stripes. At both ends, the headscarf was trimmed with long grey tassels. Following Grandma's advice, I, with special care, shook out her wool-knitted, long-sleeved jacket with vertical brown and yellow stripes. The jacket was waist long with an elastic hem.

After that, I helped Grandma shake out her dyed rabbit fur coat and her dress. We hung those two things to dry and to air for a while.

I liked that dress very much. It was made according to a design which came into fashion at the very beginning of

the twentieth century. It was long-sleeved and had a long
bodice, half-fitting at the waist which ended lower than a
waist line. The long pleated skirt of the dress went down
to the ankle. The sleeves had cuffs. A long turn-down lace
collar was a nice addition to the dress design.

Several hours later, we brought the clothes back to
the clean bedroom. Grandma started to pack them neatly
into the suitcase. I pressed her grey dress against my chest,
and enjoyed looking at myself in the mirror.

"It is too big and too long for you," Grandma
commented, looking at me. "You'd better try the jacket;
it's short but warm, made of pure wool." I followed her
advice and put on the striped brown jacket. It fit me, but it
was loose. Suddenly, I felt a strange sensation.

"Oh, it stings!" I screamed, scratching myself and
taking it off in a hurry.

"You should put it on over a long-sleeved blouse, not
on the naked body—that's why it stings," Grandma said.
"The pure wool always stings. But it will keep you warm
in winter."

I immediately disliked that jacket. I took it off and
handed it to Grandma who folded and packed it back into
the suitcase.

"Maybe later, before you leave, you'll change your
mind and take the jacket with you," Grandma said with
a smile. She continued to pack the things. Then, suddenly
she stopped and, without looking at me, with her eyes
down, said quietly, "If you don't want to go with your
parents, you can stay here with me, while they get settled
in their new place. You can join them later if you wish.
All your girlfriends are here, and I would like to have you
here with me."

I froze with my mouth half-open, as Louisa did when
she was shocked by something or someone. Grandma

kept her silence; she didn't dare look at me or to talk to me again.

I didn't realize how long we both sat on the bedroom floor without saying a word. Grandma was aimlessly rearranging things in her suitcase in which she kept prepared her favorite outfit in which she wanted to be buried when she dies. I was silent as a fish and motionless as a wooden statue without knowing what to say or what to do. Finally, with my breath only, I whispered, "No, Grandma, I can't. I want to go with Mom, Dad and Louisa to our new apartment. I want to live in a city like we had lived before the war," I mumbled pitifully. My lips trembled, and my eyes swam in tears.

Grandma didn't say a word. She didn't repeat her offer. She didn't even try to make me change my mind. Her eyes were sad and empty, and there was such helplessness in their expression that I felt sick. She finished her packing and put the suitcase back under the bed. I carefully mopped the painted wooden floor of the bedroom. That day, we didn't say a word to each other. We didn't look at each other either.

I was heartbroken. All my feelings were in turmoil; all my thoughts were in disarray. I felt pity for myself, for Grandma, and for everybody else in our family. I was miserable and inconsolable. I wanted to talk to somebody, but, on the other hand, I was scared of facing my mother. I didn't know what to do or whom to turn to. So, I kept it to myself.

I suffered because I thought that I had betrayed my grandmother, that I didn't justify her hopes. She relied on me, but my first reaction to her offer was a decisive "*Nyet!*" By saying no, I was sure that I had been rude, and I shouldn't have. Grandma didn't deserve that. She was always honest with me and nice to me. I knew she loved me, trusted me and treated me as if I were an adult. I liked that. She never punished me even when I was guilty. Her love to me wasn't demonstrative, but I knew I was loved and protected by her.

I never discussed Grandma's offer to stay with her with anybody else—not even with Mother. Intuitively, I felt that I shouldn't.

That night I couldn't sleep. Lying down next to Grandma in her wide and comfortable bed, I played the conversation with her over and over in my head. Scenes from my pre-war happy, carefree life in big cities came back to me, dancing kaleidoscopically in front of my eyes, enticing me, seducing my imagination, and trying to silence that aggravating, terrible sense of guilt and desperation which pressed on my heart.

Many years later, I understood that saying "No" to Grandma's offer, without hesitation, I, being only fourteen years of age, for the first time, had made a very important decision on my own.

45. In Anticipation of Father's Arrival

*I*n June of 1946, I graduated from the seventh grade and received a *Pohvalnaya Gramota* (Certificate of Good Conduct and Progress). I took all my seventh grade textbooks to the school library. In exchange, I received a set of used textbooks for the eighth grade. I thoroughly examined them and erased all the pencil marks and notes written by a previous owner. The shortage of school textbooks was huge, so schools had to recycle them in order to satisfy the students' needs. The textbook recycling operation continued for several more years after the end of the war.

I packed my textbooks in my pre-war, old and shabby school bag. I definitely needed a new school bag, but there was no place to get one. *Maybe later, my parents will get me a new school bag, or, hopefully, Father will bring both Louisa and me new ones.*

During spring and summer, our family continued its laborious farming routine. It took great effort to work the land; it's a long time from planting vegetables in springtime to processing and storing the harvest in the cellar and in the pantry. We had to do all that without using any machinery or transportation. Shovels and hoes were our only working tools. Our feet were our only means of transportation. All of us, with the exception of baby Oleg, kept busy as bees, and worked hard.

In addition, Mother, Louisa and I had to prepare all our belongings for our departure. We needed to mend, to wash and to iron our clothes. Our sandals, shoes and boots also needed a trip to the shoe repair shop at the farmers' market. Grandma decided that we had to take with us homemade strawberry and cherry jam. So we needed time to make the jam.

At the height of all those activities, one afternoon in July, our mailwoman Lyusia, the messenger of all good and bad news, rushed into our front yard waving a small piece of paper in her hand. It didn't look like a letter because it was smaller.

"A telegram for Raisa! A telegram for Raisa!" she screamed, smiling widely.

Raisa was my mother's first name. She rushed to Lyusia, snatched the telegram out of her hand, nervously opened and read it aloud: "ARRIVING JULY 15 TRAIN 34 COACH 7 MEET ME ANDREI."

"This letter is so strange," I said looking inquisitively at Mother.

"Why?" Mother asked, surprised at my comment.

"It's so short—" I hesitated.

"It's not a letter *glupyshka*, silly. It's a telegram. They are always short because every word, every comma, every period costs money, but they travel fast. Look, it was sent today in the morning, and we already know that Father will be here on July 15. We know which train we have to meet and even the number of his coach. Tomorrow, on my way to school, I'll stop at the railroad terminal to find out the time of arrival of his train. We'll go there to meet Father," Mother said, smiling happily.

We all were full of anticipation and excitement. Grandma, slightly nervous, looked at everybody with happy, sparkling eyes. As usual, she treated Lyusia with lunch and shared our plans with the mailwoman. "I will bake small pies stuffed with fresh cabbage, and a big sour cherry pie. This year's cherries are so sweet and juicy; the pie won't require a lot of sugar."

Then she asked Grandpa, "You, Ivan Danilovich, will cut a chicken, and we'll make a meat jelly. I do remember that Andryusha, your father, liked my meat jelly and praised it," she said to me, "when he visited us the last time before the war." Then she turned to my mother, "You should take Louisa to the hairdresser's shop to cut her hair properly. She looks like a little scarecrow with her tousled, uneven pigtails."

Louisa pursed her lips, wrinkled her nose, and was ready to cry. "I don't want to cut my hair. I want to let it grow and have braids like Nina," she whined, but Grandma, insisted.

"Your father won't recognize you when he sees your shabby hair and won't give you a present."

Reluctantly, my sister said good-bye to her dream of growing her hair long and having braids like mine. She had agreed to sacrifice her short pigtails in order not to disappoint our father on the first day of his arrival.

46. Father's Visit

On the day of Father's arrival, we all went to the railroad terminal to meet him. Only Valentina stayed in the house with little Oleg. She had to watch the samovar, prepare the green salad, and to peel and cook young fresh potatoes as a side dish for Grandma's chicken meat jelly.

When the train slowly approached the platform, I immediately recognized Father's face in the coach window. Five years had passed, but he hadn't changed much. His face looked thinner and tired, but his eyes were smiling. I couldn't believe our luck. Our father was finally here!

Grandpa rushed into the coach to help my father with his luggage—two suitcases and a big soldier's knapsack which looked very heavy. When they came down to the platform, greetings started: handshakes, hugs, embraces and kisses accompanied by smiles and tears of joy. Everybody talked at the same time and in loud voices.

Louisa and Zhanna jumped around the adults, smiling and laughing, shamelessly trying to attract attention to themselves. I stood aside watching them. I was excited but I couldn't jump like a small kid. I was fourteen and a half years old with noticeably growing breasts.

Father hugged us both, Louisa and me, and kissed our heads, saying, "Oh, you grew up a lot, my little girls!"

My cousin Zhanna who watched that happy moment suddenly started to cry, smearing the tears on her cheeks with both hands. "Don't cry little one. Calm down," my mother said, patting her on the back, "your father will be home soon, in no time. You'll see."

We all headed to the square adjacent to the railroad terminal where Grandpa had left his two-wheeled handcart which we used to transport vegetables. Father and Grandpa loaded the luggage onto the cart, and our small group moved in the direction of our house.

Grandpa walked in front pulling the cart. Father followed him, holding Louisa and Zhanna by their hands. Louisa, all smiles, was chirping happily, without stopping. Every time we met acquaintances in the street, she screamed, unable to hide her excitement and joy. "Our father has come! Our father has come to take us to the new city!"

In response, people smiled sympathetically, turning their heads in our direction and waving, watching for a while the movement of our small, happy group following Grandpa and his cart. I walked next to Louisa and tried not to miss a single word pronounced by Father. Grandma and Mother brought up the rear.

Soon we entered our yard where Valentina and little Oleg met us. Our dog, Sharyk, greeted us with loud joyful barking. When my father approached Valentina and kissed her on the cheek, little Oleg who never saw his father, extended his hands to him and said, "Papa!"

Valentina laughed and said to him, "No, *malysh*, little one, he is not your papa, he is Nina's and Louisa's papa. He is your uncle Andrey, *dyadya*. Your papa will come later, very soon. He wrote us a letter which I have read to you and Zhanna," and she lovingly tousled his short hair.

The table was set up under the old, spreading apple tree. "Everybody go wash your hands," Grandma said, "then we'll have lunch." That lunch lasted longer than usual because adults wanted to talk to Father and listen to the news from different parts of the country. I didn't listen much to those conversations, but one topic stuck in my head—the money reform. There were persistent rumors that money reform was expected in the near future. People were scared because they didn't know in which way the reform could affect and change their lives.

When lunch was almost over, Father said, looking at Grandma, "A lot of changes took place in our country, but one thing, thank God, has not changed, Anastasia Konstantinovna. Your meat jelly is delicious and tasty, even better than it was before the war. Thank you very much!" Then he got up, approached Grandma, and kissed her hand like a real hussar.

Grandma blushed, with downcast eyes, and replied firmly, "No, Andryusha, thank you for your service. You helped liberate our country, and now my grandchildren can go to school again, and you can build a new life, in a new place. I wish you luck, and thank you again!"

Everybody applauded Grandma's impromptu speech.

Father's arrival definitely changed our routine. We still had to do the same chores as before. Besides, we had to spend some time visiting relatives and friends who wanted to see our father and to talk to him. It was the harvest season for apples, pears, plums, apricots and cherries. Those relatives and friends who lived in the outskirts of the town had large orchards. When we visited them, they treated us with fresh fruits and freshly baked fruit pies. Besides, we always returned home with a gift—a bucket or two of seasonal fruits so that we could make jam.

One Saturday, Grandma told us that tomorrow, on Sunday, we all would go to the cemetery to visit the graves of our relatives.

"It's a good time to remember them and to pray for their souls," she said. "All our family is here together, with the exception of Mitya. We never know when we'll have such opportunity again, if ever," she sighed heavily.

Never before had Grandma taken us children to the cemetery when she went there. We always stayed at home. This time it was different. I even helped Grandma and Mother prepare traditional Russian food for funeral repast: a bowl of boiled rice with raisins and honey, called *kutya*, a Russian salad consisting of chopped cooked beetroots, carrots, white beans, pickles, and white onion, seasoned with sunflower oil, called in Russian *vinegret*. Several metallic plates with marinated herrings, and an oval metallic plate with piles of browned pancakes concluded the menu. Grandma explained to me that the most important dishes for the memorial repast were boiled rice and the pancakes.

On Sunday, after breakfast, we packed the food in small bundles made of clean cotton square headscarves and headed to the cemetery located far away from the town. It was a vast open space. Every grave was fenced in, with a small wooden bench inside. There was a tree or a bush next to every graveside: poplars, acacias, rose bushes, jasmine or lilacs. Gravestones were unpretentious, decorated with Orthodox crosses with Crucifixes.

Under Grandma's guidance, we visited several graves located at different parts of the cemetery. I never knew those relatives and didn't know their names. We put flowers on their graves. Then Grandma said, "Now, let's go to the grave of your great-grandfather, Daniel, and have lunch there."

By the main path, we headed to the oldest part of the cemetery where the grave of our great-grandfather Daniel, Grandfather Ivan's father, was located under the shade of the old leafy acacia tree. Grandpa unlocked the small gate of the fence, and swept dried leaves and small twigs from the grave. Grandma put the white, oilskin tablecloth on it. Then she placed tin plates for everyone, forks for adults and spoons for children. She also put cut glasses for adults and small tin mugs for children. All plates with food were also put on that makeshift table. When everything was ready, Grandma turned to Grandpa, "Ivan Danilovich, I hope you didn't forget that bottle of vodka you secretly kept in the cellar."

Grandpa took out the bottle of *samogon* from a bucket he carried and a bottle of fruit compote for us children. He poured vodka for the adults, and Mother poured compote for the children. Grandma said that before eating everything else, we all had to take a spoon of *kutya,* and she put a spoonful on everybody's plate. Grandpa raised his full glass and said, "For the peace of my father's soul!" Then, he crossed himself and drank his vodka without clinking glasses with anybody else, according to the tradition. Everybody did the same, and then we started to eat.

I took one pancake and put a spoonful of beetroot salad on it. It tasted good. So I ate only pancakes and drank fruit compote. I didn't like herrings or boiled rice at that time. While we ate, Grandma said in a low voice, "Your great-grandfather, Daniel, was a good, kind person. I liked and respected him, and he liked me. He loved his granddaughters — you, Raisa, and you, Valentina. He had left us the house in which we all lived during the difficult times of war and occupation, and we survived. Thank you, Daniel, for your kindness and care. God bless your soul!"

The adults drank vodka again; we children, including Oleg, drank compote.

The day was warm, but breezy. The sun was slowly setting, the steppe smelled of wormwood, and the pancakes with compote were wonderful. Sitting on the grass, like everybody else, I thought to myself. *Why hadn't Grandma taken us here before? The cemetery is not a scary place, after all.*

The next several days after our visit to the cemetery, we spent cooking apricot, plum and cherry jam, using the sugar brought by Father. Over time, he had accumulated the sugar rations that he received so that we could make fruit jam. All the country was still using ration cards for produce, including sugar and other consumer goods.

Father had brought presents for all of us. The gift for Grandpa was my father's used black leather high officer boots which needed only small repair. For us, girls and women, he brought a big roll of printed pink cotton fabric with small blue flowers which he managed to buy on the black market. It was decided to make new nightshirts for all of us. So Grandma and my mother spent several days at Grandma's *Singer* sewing machine. As a result, we all, including baby Oleg, received new beautiful sleeping gowns.

When the sewing was finished and the jam was cooked and packed into three big three-liter glass jars, we started to pack all our belongings. The clothes were put into suitcases. Bed linen, blankets and new down pillows went into two big Hessian bags. Pots and pans were packed into small wooden boxes. Those big bags and boxes had to be checked in a luggage van the day of our departure. Suitcases, knapsacks and small bags with food and jam had to travel with us, in the passenger coach, along with our school bags.

The last several days before our departure, we all worked hard. Father told us that we had to leave two days earlier because upon our arrival in Lvov, he was going to take Louisa and me to the Pioneer Camp for the children of military personnel, located in the Carpathian mountains, on the bank of the river Prut. We had to travel there by train and spend three weeks at the camp. So we were on a very tight schedule. Both Louisa and I were happy and delighted to get such a wonderful opportunity — to go to a real Pioneer Camp in the mountains and close to the river. We couldn't believe our luck. The events unwound pretty fast, and they were pleasant and promising. Knock on wood!

47. Departure

*T*he day of our departure from Dolguintsevo, Grandma's place, was July 25, 1946. We had spent there three long and difficult years of German occupation and two years of post-occupation revival. Now we had to leave for the new location of our father's unit, to the city of Lvov, in Western Ukraine.

Early in the morning, Grandpa and Father transported by handcart the heavy items of our luggage to the railroad terminal and checked them in. They went back home, loaded the rest of the things on the cart and returned to the terminal. All the family went there to see us off. Grandma asked our next-door neighbor, her close friend, to watch the house.

Finally, the moment of saying good-bye to Grand-parents, to Valentina, Zhanna and little Oleg became a frightening reality. I kissed Oleg several times on his little nose, like I used to do. He contorted his face, curled his lips, sneezed in a funny way, and then laughed joyfully. I laughed in response, gave him loud kisses on both cheeks, then hugged and kissed my favorite Aunt, Valentina, and little Zhanna.

Grandpa awkwardly kissed me on the crown of my head and quietly said, "Don't forget to write us, Grandmother and me. Help your parents with the chores. Study hard. You are a smart girl, Nina."

Saying good-bye to Grandma turned out to be the most difficult and emotionally charged moment of the parting. She cried quietly, drying her kind, sad eyes with the corner of her cotton shawl. There was a helpless anguish in her voice when she said pleadingly, "Don't forget to write me, at least once a month. Your mother will be busy, I know. You can do it. Write me about your new life. *Khorosho? Ladno?* Okay?

"I will," I whispered, trying to contain tears and not sob. I felt sorry and ashamed that I had to go, to deprive her of my company, my love, and my every day support. I hugged Grandma, kissed her on both cheeks, wet with tears, picked up my school bag and climbed into the coach.

I went into our compartment and stood next to Louisa at the open window. I waved and looked at a small group of my relatives on the suddenly deserted platform. The train started to move slowly. I looked again at the tear-stained, dear faces of my grandparents, of Valentina, Zhanna and little Oleg on the moving away platform. Unexpected, uneasy feelings squeezed my heart. When will I see them again? At the time, I didn't know I would not see Grandma for six long years.

I stood at the window and waved until the platform disappeared from view. Bitter-sweet tears streamed uncontrollably from my eyes. I didn't dry them.

48. The Return Trip to a Promising Future

On the train we occupied four hard sleeping seats. They were not as luxurious as the seats in the international sleeping car in which we had traveled before the war from Riga to Tallinn. The express sleeping train was decorated with soft couches, mirrors, and every compartment had an individual bathroom with shower. However, it wasn't a goods van either, in which we had evacuated, like cattle, from Tallinn when the war started on June 22 in 1941.

It was comfortable enough. Everybody had a place to sit and a place to sleep. There was sufficient room for all our luggage. However, the inconvenience was that it wasn't a closed compartment, but rather an open space. The tickets for the closed compartment cars were more expensive, and we couldn't afford them.

The soft mattresses were rolled up and stored together with pillows and flannel blankets on the third, upper luggage shelf of the compartment. Father took them down and put a mattress and a pillow on each bunk.

Then, the conductor brought us four sets of bed-linen. Each consisted of two flat bedsheets, a pillowcase and a towel, and cost one ruble each, which Father paid to the conductor. Soon, the conductor announced that in an hour, he would serve tea with two pieces of sugar, and the price would be thirty kopecks a glass. Father ordered two glasses of tea with sugar for each of us. Sugar still remained rationed and in short supply.

We made our beds. Louisa and Mother occupied the lower bunks, Father and I—the upper. I loved to lie on the upper bunk and watch through the window the scenery flying by while listening to the rhythmic rumble of the car wheels, and to the loud warning whistle of the locomotive. At that time, locomotive steam engines in the Soviet Union were fueled by coal.

After we settled down, we took turns going to wash up in the bathroom located at both ends of the car. Then, we had lunch. "First, we have to eat the fried chicken, as it can get spoiled in such heat," Mother said. So, she gave everyone a piece of chicken, a peeled fresh cucumber and a piece of bread. She also took salt out of her food bag and put it on the table. After that, we drank tea with sugar and with small pies stuffed with fresh cabbage, boiled eggs and green onions which Grandma baked for the road. It was a delicious meal which dried our good-bye tears, helped us forget the sadness of leaving, and improved our mood. Both Louisa and I drank two glasses of tea, maybe because it was served in metallic glass-holders which we liked very much. Drinking tea from glasses in glass-holders made us feel like adults.

After lunch, Mother cleaned the table, and I took the trash to the trashcan located near the bathroom of the carriage. Louisa and I were ready to climb to the upper bunks and to enjoy watching the scenery through the window when the conductor announced that in half an hour there would be a fifteen-minute stop. He reminded the passengers not to leave their luggage unattended, and warned parents that they should accompany their children if they wanted to stretch their legs during the stop.

Our parents decided that at the first stop Father, Louisa and I would go out for a stroll, and Mother would stay inside and watch the luggage. I hurriedly made my braids and combed Louisa's hair. Then I adjusted my dress and Louisa's collar.

As soon as the train stopped, Father jumped out from the car and helped us to disembark. It was hot inside the carriage, so a lot of people wanted to get out, at least for a moment. The platform of the station was crowded.

The locals sold fresh seasonal fruits, vegetables and simple cooked foods. The passengers of the train were buying fresh apples, pears, plums, melons and watermelons. Boiled potatoes seasoned with fresh dill, cucumbers, tomatoes, boiled eggs and lightly salted pickles were sold by the piece. Father bought for Louisa and me a small glass of fried sunflower seeds. We put them into our dress pockets and nibbled the delicacy with pleasure while walking up and down along the platform.

There were a lot of young soldiers among the passengers. Some of them were on leave and headed to their homes. Another group of soldiers had just been discharged from the military service. They talked and laughed loudly, and celebrated their newly acquired freedom by buying *samogon* by the glass and drinking it on the platform of the station, while snatching hasty bites of pork fat sandwiches with lightly salted cucumbers. To my big surprise, I noticed that the vendors poured out *samogon* from aluminum tea kettles. I had never seen that before.

"All aboard!" shouted the conductor. We rushed back to the carriage and treated Mother to tasty sunflower seeds while sharing with her our impressions of the food market and its customers.

49. Soviet Veterans of World War II

*U*nexpectedly, we heard the sounds of music. Minutes later, we saw a one-legged young man on wooden crutches in a military shirt without insignias moving slowly along the aisle of our carriage. The piece of cardboard hanging on his chest said, "I am a disabled veteran of war. I have no relatives. Please, help me with whatever you can. Thank you and God bless you."

The young man who accompanied him was dressed in civilian clothes. He played the accordion while the veteran sang a compassionate folk song called *Only the Steppe is Around Me*. They stopped at every train compartment, sang just one stanza and moved to the next. They went from one car to the other through the whole train. The passengers gave them what they had, mostly food. Mother treated them with two small pies stuffed with fresh cabbage from our food reserve.

Half an hour later, another disabled veteran appeared in our car. According to the cardboard inscription on his chest, he was a young man who had lost both legs in the war. He sat on a low homemade handcart which he moved forward by pushing off from the floor with the help of two wooden handholders. He had blond hair and a handsome face, and his arms were strong and muscular. The expression in his eyes was sad and indifferent. He was accompanied by an older man and a boy about seven or eight years old who held a cap in his extended hand, begging for alms.

Father put a ruble into the boy's cap, Mother handed them three big plums and added, "You can eat them; they are washed, sweet and juicy." I gave the boy a square lump of sugar which I saved from our breakfast tea and kept in the pocket of my dress.

The rest of that day and the first half of the next, one disabled veteran after another came asking for help. There were blind soldiers, one-eyed soldiers, one-armed veterans, one-legged veterans, and veterans who lacked one or more fingers. Some smelled of *samogon*.

When it became dark and the conductors started to prepare evening tea, we heard the radio announcement made by the chief officer of the train. He asked the disabled veterans of war to leave the train at the nearest stop which was expected to be in half an hour. "We are responsible for the safety of the passengers," the senior conductor explained. "Every car has only two conductors. There are different people among the veterans and those who accompany them. You never know what can happen. Those veterans are very nervous, and often get angry and irritated, especially if they are slightly drunk." The younger conductor continued, "We already had several unpleasant incidents when a disabled drunk veteran attacked one of the passengers in a drunken quarrel. So, we have to be careful in order to avoid such trouble."

During that train trip we listened to many popular folk songs performed by disabled veterans. Some of those songs, such as *Marusya Has Gotten herself Poisoned, The Three Pine Trees Were Standing along the Murom's Road, and Khan*

Bulat Being Bold were quite old, almost forgotten. I knew those three songs. The song about the Khan Bulat was my grandfather's favorite, and he would sing it to himself.

The most often performed song, however, was the hit of wartime — *Katyusha*. It's a diminutive of the Russian name *Katerina* used also as a term of endearment. At the same time, it is a nickname of the famous Soviet artillery rocket with which the Soviet military was armed during WWII, and which played a decisive role in the defeat of the German Army.

During the evening tea, the passengers discussed the terrible fates of the disabled soldiers. The war again reminded us of its irreparable consequences, forcing us to face the human tragedies that were so vivid in the broken bodies of the disabled defenders of our motherland.

Lying down on my upper bed, I turned my pillow in the opposite direction from the window, towards the aisle so that I could overhear fragments of conversations in the next compartments, or just pick up one or two phrases from the passing-by passengers. I was all ears, quiet as a mouse.

The majority of the people felt sorry for the disabled veterans. "My God! Such a young, handsome man without legs. What a tragedy! Who will marry him? He needs to be cared for like a little baby," said an elderly woman.

All the passengers were unanimous about one thing — the government should take better care of disabled veterans. It should provide necessary services for them and create appropriate living conditions for them, their families and relatives.

An older man, helplessly lifting his hands in dismay, added, "There are special facilities for disabled veterans called, The House for the Invalids of War. However, not all of the veterans want to stay there. They run away from those institutions and prefer to live by begging rather than being locked away. I have heard that the living conditions in those premises are horrible. They are like military barracks; the people are crowded together—thirty to forty in one room. What kind of life is that?"

Yet another man interjected, "Can you imagine! At such a young age, they fought for our country, for all of us. Now, they have to live in an asylum, in one big room. It's difficult for young men who only yesterday were strong warriors, and now they have to live like prisoners, deprived of freedom and comfort, in inhuman conditions. It's a shame!"

Another passenger interrupted the conversation with a muffled voice, cautiously looking around. "There are rumors that one day all disabled veterans without relatives will be removed from the cities and relocated to special settlements in one of the secluded islands in the Pacific Ocean to live out their days."

I couldn't believe what I just heard. The news stunned me. I shook with fright and felt pity for the unprotected and crippled veterans. I buried my face into the pillow and sobbed quietly. I was afraid of waking up my parents and Louisa.

All night, periodically wiping tears with a corner of the bedsheet which I had under the blanket, I thought about the tragic fate of war veterans.

I couldn't say that I hadn't seen disabled veterans before. One of our close neighbors, the father of three children, my playmates, had lost one of his legs in the war. Another neighbor returned from the war without an arm, with one empty jacket sleeve fastened with a safety pin. I had seen crippled veterans at the farmers' market, too. One couldn't escape them.

The endless line of young men maimed by the war, which we saw in our two-day train trip, stirred my feelings and graphically showed me the price of victory and our liberation. I forgot all our hardships and sufferings during the years of the German occupation, and all our fears and trembling which we children had experienced as soon as we heard the sinister roar of German bombers approaching our town.

I could see only disabled veterans passing by, one after another along the aisle of our train car, singing doleful popular songs and asking for help. My heart was filled with compassion and pity.

50. Another Trip Down Memory Lane

*A*s I was riding on the train, a tidal wave of remembrance overcame me. Another picture appeared before my eyes — a beautiful May day in 1945. The war had ended victoriously. The three of us — my friend, Vera, our classmate, Lydia Khomulina, and I were sitting on an old blanket spread over the grass, under an apple tree in Lydia's orchard, reviewing exam topics on Russian history. We had already passed all our written and oral exams. History was the only hurdle we had to clear in order to pass to the seventh grade.

Inhaling the intoxicating fragrances of the spring orchard and hearing the pesky buzz of May bugs, we worked hard. Our history teacher was obsessed with chronology and he made us memorize a long, boring list of historical names, events and their dates.

Our study routine was simple: one of us read the text aloud. Then, taking turns, we retold it and carefully recorded briefly with indelible ink pencils all chronological dates, names and events on our thighs.

Vera was the lucky one, as her handwriting was small and clear. She had no trouble fitting in everything on her thighs. Lydia's handwriting was larger, but she had wide and fatty thighs — the object of envy for us younger girls, who were physically underdeveloped, famished and emaciated from wartime malnutrition. Lydia, however, quickly adjusted to the smaller size of the letters, and successfully coped with the task. I was in big trouble. No matter how hard I tried to reduce the size of my letters, they still were too large. In addition, my thighs were small and narrow, no meat on them, just skin and bones. It took me a long time to fill in the chronological table with tiny letters and numbers. After I finished, I glanced at the other girls with a sigh of relief and satisfaction. For several minutes, we compared our decorated legs and enjoyed looking at the fruits of our labor.

At that very moment, Lydia's older sister, Galina, soundlessly approached us carrying a two-liter glass jar with a cold fruit drink and three tin mugs. "Take a break, *zubrilki*, bookworms, and have some fruit drink with freshly baked buns." She placed the jar on the blanket and gave each of us a mug and a sweet bun.

Galina's visit had taken us unawares. "What are you doing?" she asked in bewilderment. We didn't know what to say. We kept our silence, our legs shamelessly exposed so that the indelible ink could dry out.

I hardly knew Galina. I had seen her only once before. Lydia's family had moved to our town half a year ago. As Lydia and Vera were neighbors, Vera was closer to Lydia and her family than I was. When Vera and I decided to study together for the history exam, Lydia joined us and offered her spacious family's orchard to study.

Lydia's reaction to Galina's question was fast. "Please, sister, don't tell Mother about it, I beg you. I promise you that we will wash it out before the exam. We wrote it just in case so that it would be easier for us to review and memorize it." Lydia looked pleadingly at her sister.

Galina, still hesitant, said slowly, "If you swear that you will erase it before the exam, I won't tell anybody. Don't forget to get rid of it. Otherwise, if your teacher catches you, you will be in big trouble. You could be expelled from school, or your history exam could be postponed until the end of the summer. Do you really need that to happen, huh?"

"We will! We will," we cried vying with one another. "We promise, we will wash it off before the exam," we repeated in unison.

Galina looked at us reproachfully, said nothing and left, shaking her head in disbelief.

Panic seized us. We were confused and didn't know what to do. When we joined the Young Pioneers League, we had solemnly sworn to always be truthful and honest. I was scared to death. Vera, however, was not as fearful as I was. Her approach to our situation was more practical. She gave Lydia an inquiring look and asked, "What do you think? Will your sister keep her word or will she blab?"

Lydia remained silent for a moment, then said, "I don't know, girls. She is very honest. She always keeps her word. Anyway, she's not in the mood for creating trouble for anyone at this time. Something terrible has happened to our family." She looked around as if she were checking if anyone could overhear us. Then, lowering her voice to a whisper, she continued. "Galina's husband, Nickolai, was heavily wounded several months ago, in the lower part of his abdomen. The doctors saved his life, but his most important man's organ was damaged and couldn't be saved. So, now he and Galina can't live like man and wife because they can't make love and have babies."

Vera and I sat silently, not uttering a sound. After a short pause and a deep sigh, Lydia said, "It's a tragedy for our entire family. Nickolai loves Galina very much, and he

287

would like to stay in the marriage. My mother has baked sweet buns because his parents arrived yesterday. They want to help him save his marriage. Our parents think that Galina should divorce him. Mother says that Galina is still young and shouldn't sacrifice her life and her future," Lydia continued.

"Were they high school sweethearts?" Vera asked.

"Yes, they were. They have loved each other since the seventh grade. They got married after graduation. Several weeks later, the war started, and he was drafted. Now Galina's heart is torn apart. She is between several fires: her and his parents, her love for him and his inability to continue the marriage. So girls, don't worry. Galina won't tell anybody about us, about our walking chronological table. I am sure about it," concluded Lydia.

Vera finally managed to come out of shock and pressured Lydia to give us more details about Nickolai's injuries, but Lydia didn't want to elaborate. I didn't dare ask anything, although I didn't have the faintest idea of the nature of the wounds of Galina's husband. I felt pity for Galina. I noticed that her eyes were tear-stained, red and swollen, and she didn't smile much. She was so pretty, about twenty-three years old, and had to go through such a terrible ordeal at the very beginning of her married life.

What a tragedy! What a merciless fate! I thought, wiping my tears with the bed sheet. Grandma was right when she said that the war had left incurable wounds and indelible scars on almost every family, even if one can't see them with the naked eye.

Our group study for the history exam in Lydia's orchard produced good results. Maybe the recording of the chronological table on our young flesh which helped to refresh our memories wasn't such a bad idea, after all. The three of us received good exam marks and successfully passed to the seventh grade. As usual, I was awarded the Certificate of Progress and Good Conduct for being an A student during the entire school year.

In September, we returned to school after the summer break. Lydia seized the moment to whisper that Galina had gotten a divorce, and Nicholai's parents had taken him home. "It wasn't an easy decision for Galina, *bednyazhka*, poor girl," Lydia said. "We all cried like children when they left."

Lydia told us that Galina was inconsolable. She was in such bad emotional shape that her mother decided to take her on a trip to visit her sister, Claudia, Galina's aunt, who lived in the small city of Mariupol located on the shore of the Sea of Azov, two days' train ride from our town.

After two weeks, Galina's mother had to return home. The aunt persuaded Galina to stay with her family till the end of the summer.

When Galina's mother came home, Vera and I went to visit Lydia and to listen to her mother's stories about their vacation in Mariupol. Happily smiling, she told us that both Galina and she liked it there so much that Galina decided to spend the rest of the summer there. They both liked the appealing atmosphere of the small sea resort city, where the white private houses were surrounded by orchards and enveloped in a sea of flowers. The weather was nice and warm, and the abundant, tasty goby fish were biting well.

In the summer, the lifestyle was typical of a small resort city — slow, lazy and gratifying.

Galina's mother told us that they had helped Claudia

process fruits and berries into jams and dried fruits and into a delicious homemade fruit liqueur called *nalivka*. They also picked and sold gooseberries, red and black currants, mulberries, and different seasonal fruits at the local farmers' market. Galina's cousins, two teenaged boys, took her on several fishing trips in their small boat. After fishing, they cleaned and strung small fishes and hung them to dry on a line. Galina's aunt often prepared delicious fried goby for supper.

In the late afternoon, when all the domestic chores were done, they spent some time on the beach enjoying swimming, sunbathing and chatting with the neighbors and beachgoers. Galina and her cousins played volleyball with the boys and girls of their age and took long walks along the beach.

In the evenings, the local brass band played popular dance music in the city park. The tanned young people were spinning round in the whirlwind of waltzes, their faces smiling as the girls' short flared skirts flapped in the breeze. The wooden dance floor was surrounded by park benches where people of all ages sat chatting, swapping news and gossip, fiercely spitting out the local delicacy — a special sort of fried and salted sunflower seed.

In September, Galina returned home, tanned, rested and calm. Her parents prepared a big surprise for her. They had decided to sell their house and move to Mariupol. The removal was planned by Christmas because they had to collect, process, and sell all the harvest from their vegetable garden.

"It's a pity that I have to part with you and Vera," Lydia said. "I'll miss you, guys. You are my real friends. You helped me a lot. But we'll write each other, won't we? Right?" Then Lydia lowered her voice and continued, "Please, don't tell anybody about our departure. Let it be our secret. I promised my mother that I wouldn't tell anybody, but I just couldn't help telling you."

I didn't understand why their departure should be a secret, and said, "I won't tell a single soul. *Wot tebe krest!* Cross my heart!" It was a strange sensation: Lydia was still here, but I was already missing her.

Distracted by my recollection, I stayed awake for a long time, and then I suddenly realized that I was on the train, and it was pitch dark in the car. I wasn't asleep; I was awake and thinking about the events that had taken place just a year before.

Only by dawn did I manage to fall asleep when the first rays of gray light started to penetrate through the curtains of the carriage window. I thought how lucky we were that our father had come home with only two scars from light wounds, not disfigured or disabled, or like many others, buried in their white cotton underwear, without a casket, in a communal grave. I remembered so vividly those young soldiers whose burials Aunt Valentina and I had witnessed one cold winter day during our road trip, several days after the front line had passed, like a furious hurricane, through our town. Thank God Father was safe and sound, and, maybe, just maybe, there was hope for a better future for all of us.

51. Good Morning, Lvov!

*T*he day of our arrival in the city of Lvov the conductors woke all the passengers very early. They had to serve the morning tea, to pick up the dirty bed linen, and to clean the car before the train reached its final destination — the city of Lvov.

We hurriedly washed up and drank our tea with small, stale pies stuffed with dried apricots. Then Mother repacked our food bag, and I took the garbage to the garbage can. After that, Louisa and I went again to the restroom to wash our hands. We combed our hair, and I plaited my braids.

Mother collected our bed linen and made a neat pile of it on the lower bunk. Then she took out of the suitcase clean cotton dresses and socks for Louisa and me, and we changed clothes in the bathroom. After that, Mother went to the restroom to wash up, to comb her hair and to change her dress. Father rolled up all the mattresses and put them into the luggage trunk of the lower bunks.

The senior conductor collected money for the tea. Then he started to recount carefully all the bed linen from the pile. Louisa tried to explain to him that Mother had already put all the bed linen together. He interrupted her and said, "I have to check if all the items are here.

Sometimes the passengers steal small thing such as towels and pillowcases. Once or twice, we missed even blankets and pillows. Then we had to pay from our pockets and have it subtracted from our salaries. So, I have to check and recheck it myself and be sure that nothing is missing." After that, his assistant swept the floor, mopped it, and dusted with a wet cloth all the surfaces in our compartment.

The last hour we sat silently on the wooden bunks next to the window and watched the approaching green and woody landscape of Western Ukraine. I had slept very little that night, but I didn't feel tired or sleepy. I felt excited and full of anticipation of something new, unknown, and, hopefully, wonderful. *My God, Bozhe, let it be wonderful*, I prayed silently.

Louisa and I, glued to the window, were all eyes. Finally, the train slowly approached the Lvov's railroad terminal. "Look, girls, look!" Father pointed at the high hill covered with trees and bushes. "This is the oldest park of the city, called *Wysokiy Zamok*, "The Tall Castle." Someday, on Sunday, we'll go there and climb up to the top. One can see the entire city from there."

When the train stopped at the platform of the terminal, we slowly disembarked. With the help of a porter, we followed the crowd through the underground passage to the streetcar stop. The square was filled with bustling people scurrying around, talking loudly and paying no attention to us.

The porter unloaded our luggage from the cart at the wooden bench on the streetcar stop. Father told us that streetcar #9 would take us home with one connection only. We sat on the bench waiting for the streetcar. Father, who stood behind us, bent over the back of the bench and quietly, almost whispering, told Louisa and me, "Listen, girls, you will meet new people here, and you will make new friends in the neighborhood and at school. Don't tell anybody that during the war you had lived in the occupied territory. If you are asked, just say that you had lived in the city of Sverdlovsk, behind the Ural Mountains. After the war was over, you went to your grandmother's place and waited for me there. Do you understand?"

We didn't understand anything, but we both nodded obediently in response. I asked, "Sverdlovsk? Is that right?" As I had studied geography of the USSR, I knew where the Ural Mountains were located on the map, and that the city of Sverdlovsk was the largest city of that province.

Louisa, however, experienced difficulty in pronouncing the name of the city. Somehow, she was not able to speak out the combination of the beginning and ending consonants — *sv* and — *vsk*. In both cases she omitted the letter *v*. As a result, she uttered something like "*Sedlosk.*"

Father asked me to practice the word with Louisa so that she would be able to articulate it properly. Louisa promised him to try harder and to master the name of the city in which we allegedly had spent almost four years of our lives. Father, alarmed by such an unexpected obstacle, reminded me again to help my sister.

It was strange, but neither one of us dared ask Father why we had to do that, why we had to lie. Maybe we were just eager to see the new city and our new apartment. Maybe we were too tired and emotionally stressed after the two-day train trip and the endless parade of disabled veterans in our train car. Anyhow, I promised Father not to forget the new version of our biography and vowed to help Louisa memorize and to pronounce everything correctly.

Finally, our streetcar arrived. Father loaded our luggage on the rear open platform and stayed there. Mother, Louisa and I got inside and occupied window seats behind one another so that we could enjoy the view of the city, its streets, buildings and the people during the ride.

Well, hello my new city, my new home. I embrace you, my new life and my new future!

My heart was overwhelmed with emotion: confusion, apprehension and a glimpse of joy. Yes, it was the jubilation of finally having the opportunity for a new and better life. It took my breath away.

Gradually, I recalled Grandma's words on the eve of our departure. "You're leaving, Nina, to start a new life. Don't be afraid, *detka*, my child, of new places, new things and new people. People mostly are good and kind. They will help you with your new life, at your new school. Just be nice and honest with them. You aren't that timid, little girl anymore who five years ago came to my house with a school bag full of third grade textbooks. You are smart and strong now. You've grown up, you've survived the war and the German occupation, you've worked with adults in the vegetable garden, and just recently you've finished the seventh grade with excellent marks. Now you have a chance for a different life. Don't be afraid of your future, work for it: study hard, help your parents and your sister, be nice to your friends, and don't forget that while we're still alive, no matter how hard the life is, there's always hope."

Grandma, as usual, was right. And, as if by magic, all my worries began to dissipate like a bad dream or a morning fog. Liberated from my fears, I felt full of life and ready to meet new challenges — new hurdles and new joys. I smiled at my mother, gently squeezed Louisa's arm, and waved at my father. The streetcar was arriving at our destination, and the stop I called *Nadezhda* (Hope).

52. The Streetcar Ride to a New Home

*F*ather was right when he had written that Lvov resembled Tallinn, the capital of Estonia, where we had lived when the war started. The paved streets were wide and clean. The trucks, streetcars, buses, a few passenger cars, mostly the German Opel, sped along the streets. Father explained to us that those cars had been confiscated by the Soviet Army and retained as spoils of war. I saw wagons pulled by horses, their hooves clattering loudly along the paving stones.

The brick houses of three, four and even six stories had architectural designs different from the houses we had seen before. While we rode along the streets, I noticed small assorted shops, barber shops, and a pharmacy at the corner. A large farmers' market was located several blocks away from the railroad terminal. Farmers, loaded with sacks, baskets and bales on their backs like mules, rode the streetcars or just walked with their loads to the market.

At the intersection of two big streets, we saw a huge church building with tall pointed steeples. Father told us that it was a Roman Catholic cathedral. It was closed and was being used as a warehouse.

We passed small public gardens with lush trees, bushes and flower-beds. People sat on park benches, resting, reading newspapers, talking, watching small children playing or babies sleeping in fashionable baby carriages with large wheels and awnings. Never before had I seen such beautiful carriages.

Old chestnut trees stood like sentinels along both sides of some streets. The pavements were wide, clean and made of flagstones, with garbage cans placed at the corner of the blocks. The city looked clean, fresh and festive as if the war had never touched it. I hadn't seen a single destroyed building during our streetcar ride in that part of the city.

It was the end of July. The weather was pleasantly warm, and the people were dressed in summer clothes. I noticed that many men wore short-sleeved cotton shirts with pants or light summer suits. Some young men were wearing dark-colored knee-high boots military style; others wore short boots or shoes.

I was more interested in the women's clothes and footwear. Women and young girls strutted around in light, bright cotton dresses and short-sleeved blouses with skirts. Some young girls wore sundresses and charming straw hats decorated with colorful ribbons. They reminded me of the white fabric hats in which Louisa and I had been depicted in our last pre-war photo taking in Tallinn by a professional photographer in the park, two months before the start of the war.

For the last five years, we hadn't worn hats, nor had we seen anyone wearing hats in Grandma's town. As a matter of fact, I had never seen hats there. Instead, we wore simple, square head scarves, made of cotton in summer, and wool in winter. The old women tied the ends of their head scarves under their chins, *babushka* style; the young ones—on the back of their necks. During the German occupation, some young women started to copy German women, tying their head scarves in the center of their foreheads as we had seen in the movies.

For us, children, Grandma had made hoods from old woolen scarves. She just folded a long woolen scarf in half and sewed it from the center making a space for the head. We children adored those hoods. We called them *bushlyk*. They were comfortable and protected us from the cold winter winds. In summer, rain or shine, we preferred to run around with uncovered heads.

Mother, Louisa and I immediately noticed the unusual shape of men's and women's jackets which had wide, straight, square shoulders, military style. Mother explained to us that wearing shoulder pads was the latest rage of the post-war style. We also noticed that some women and young girls wore belts with their dresses and skirts. They also carried purses and simple shopping bags made of dark fabric with two fabric handles, and simple wicker straw bags, *kashyolky*.

Women's footwear was more diverse than men's. Some women wore flat open shoes; others wore shoes with straight arches, or shoes with small wide heels or flat colored sandals. We even saw several young women in high heels. It had been a long time since we had seen women in high heels.

At one of the stops, two teenaged girls about fourteen or fifteen years old—just my age—got into the streetcar, joyfully chirping and giggling. They sat across from us. They were pretty with wide smiles and merry eyes. They were well groomed and wore bright, colorful cotton dresses and cute straw hats with ribbons around the crown. They looked like two dolls which we had seen only in pictures.

Both Louisa and I just sat and stared silently, devouring them with our eyes.

When the conductor approached the girls and handed them tickets, they opened their purses and paid the fare. *"Oh, my God! How about that? They don't use their purses only for handkerchiefs and combs; they carry real money in them!"* I said to myself in surprise. Long ago, before the war, Mother had given me a small coin-purse for my streetcar fare. Since then, I never had a purse, even a coin purse.

At that moment, Louisa, her eyes opened wide like two saucers, nudged me and whispered, "Look at their sandals, Nina, look!" Concentrating on the girls' hats and their behavior, I wasn't paying attention to their footwear, but impelled by Louisa, I lowered my eyes, and my jaw dropped.

They were wearing real leather sandals. One of the girls wore red leather sandals which matched the red ribbon on her hat. What a beautiful combination! Her girlfriend wore green leather open shoes, and a green ribbon on the crown of her straw hat. I was mesmerized by their outfits and couldn't take my eyes away. Louisa also couldn't take her eyes off the girls. Then, with a deep sigh, she wrinkled her pug nose generously sprinkled with freckles, and grumbled, "I want red sandals, too. I do. I like them so much."

I said nothing. I had no words of consolation for my normally undemanding little sister who always was happy to wear my old dresses which, in turn, had been altered from Mother's old ones. I couldn't openly admit that I, too, was envious of the girls. I was stunned and flabbergasted because every item of the girls' outfits was new. I hadn't seen new clothes and shoes since the beginning of the war, five years ago.

At that moment, the girls seemed to realize that we were staring at them. They turned their heads away and continued their conversation quietly, from time to time looking at us, as if they were talking about us and judging our appearances.

I felt awkward. I looked at Louisa and said angrily, "Close your mouth and stop staring at them! It's embarrassing!"

"Why?" Louisa asked. "I'm just looking at their sandals. I've never seen red sandals before."

"So what?" I raised my voice. "Just don't look at them so openly. Do it on the sly!" I hissed.

"How is that?" Louisa wondered, looking at me inquisitively.

"Don't talk about them anymore. Just don't look at them, please," I whispered annoyed.

I myself tried, at all costs, to avoid looking at the girls. Instead, I looked down and saw, as if it were for the first time, our too-often repaired dark brown sandals. Then I stared at our simple, unstylish summer dresses, which had been altered from Mother's homemade outfits. From multiple alterations and washes, they were discolored and faded.

In comparison to the two girls in their ribboned straw hats, in colorful dresses and sandals and with purses, Louisa and I, with our thin, pale and underfed faces, looked like two motherless Cinderellas, riding the streetcar to the final stop named "Hopelessness."

A sudden thought struck me: how will I feel if all the girls in my new class are dressed like these two girls? Will they be friendly to me? Will they treat me nicely if I'm not dressed as well as they are? I was eager to meet my new classmates and to make new friends. But, what'll I do if

I'm rejected by my peers just because I don't have red or green sandals, a straw hat, or a purse?

I had never thought about such things before at my grandmother's home. We children were happy to have any dress, coat, or shoes. Everybody, adults and children, wore old clothes and old footwear, because there was no money and no place for buying new things, even when the war was finally over.

When the girls of my age, beautifully dressed in new outfits, neatly groomed and in a joyful mood appeared in the streetcar, I became aware of an all-consuming fear which settled into the deepest corner of my mind. Terror seized me with its iron teeth and didn't let go. I was scared of everything: my new school, my new classmates and my new as yet unknown teachers, my future neighbors, even of this beautiful new city, which, at first glance, I fell in love with. Ironically, I hoped that we would never have to move again to any new place as had happened many times before the war.

Epilogue

$\mathcal{W}$hen we first arrived in Lvov, I was scared because I didn't know then that my prayers would be answered and my father would be stationed in Lvov until the end of his military service. After his retirement, years later, we would continue to reside in Lvov. I would fall in love with that old and comfortable city. No matter where I traveled, I would always, with great excitement and eagerness, return to its beautiful, shady streets, its gorgeous parks, to my hearth and home — to my family, to my beloved friends, schoolmates and neighbors.

I didn't know then that after our arrival, I would attend, and three years later successfully graduate from the Lvov all-girls high school, #46. When I started school before the war, in 1939, we didn't have a dress code. But now, for the first time in my life, I had a brand new school uniform: a navy blue, long-sleeved woolen dress with attached white collar and white cuffs, and two aprons — a black one for week days and a white one with ruffles for holidays and solemn occasions. No more would I be obsessed with red and green sandals, colorful dresses, straw hats and purses. My main concern would be my new school uniform and my classes. I would still remember those oppressive, joyless years of the German occupation without school, without teachers, without schoolmates, without summer Pioneer Camps, and without the simple pleasures of childhood.

I didn't know then that in the tenth grade, at a school dance party, I would meet a boy, also a tenth grader, Vladimir Markovich, whom I called Volodya, whom I liked very much, with whom I danced the evening away to the popular melody of the post-war era — "Cherry and Apple Blossom Time." He would become my high school sweetheart, and eventually, the love of my life, my husband.

I didn't know then that the same year, 1949, after high school graduation, I would be admitted to Lvov State University, and six years later, I would graduate from the Department of Foreign Languages, magna cum laude, equipped with the knowledge of two modern foreign languages—English and Spanish—and the questionable acquisition of one dead language—Latin, with a cornucopia of whimsical dreams and the complete absence of any practical skills.

I didn't know then that during my high school and university years, I would make life-long friendships with some of my classmates.

I didn't know then that when I became twenty years old, a large photo portrait of me in a fashionable straw hat and in a bright yellow crepe de Chine dress would be displayed, for several years, in the central photo studio, located on the main street that crossed downtown Lvov. The photographer put my photo on display in the shop window without asking my permission. However, I wouldn't be angry. I'd be pleased and flattered. People would recognize me in the streets and give me friendly smiles, whispering to one another, "That's the girl from the portrait! That's her!"

—Nina Markos
Palm Springs, California

Photo Gallery

My Maternal Grandmother
Anastasia Konstantinovna ~
1885-1952

My Maternal Grandfather
Ivan DanilovichSladkovsky ~
1886-1946

My Mother Raisa, Age Three, and her sister Valentina,
age one and a half ~ 1912

My Maternal Grandparents' House in Dolguintsevo, Ukraine

Grandmother Anastasia seated on the chair; her younger sister
Barbara, standing. My aunt Valentina stands between them;
my mother Raisa is seated in front. Dolguintsevo, Ukraine ~ 1913

Grandmother Anastasia, seated in the chair;
her sister Maria, seated on the floor ~ July 1915

Mother's Classmates from the Pedagogical Institute,
Dnepropetrovsk, Ukraine; Mother is in the second row,
first on the left; Valentina is the third in the same row ~ 1929

Mother at the age of 20, Dnepropetrovsk, Ukraine ~ 1929

Mother's passport photo ~ 1929

My first photo at age six months; a group of military wives
with their children from the communal appartment.
Polotsk, Byelorussia ~ June 1932

Louisa and I. Photo taken at the farmers' market,
Dolguintsevo, Ukraine ~ Summer 1933

My junior kindergarten group, Polotsk, Byelorussia,
I am in the middle of the first row ~ May 1935

Aunt Valentina, I, and her friend   *Louisa and I, Dolguintsevo,*
~ Summer 1935   *Ukraine ~ Summer 1937*

*Father, Mother, Louisa and I
Gorky Park, Minsk, Byelorussia ~ May 1939*

*Mother, Louisa and I. Photo was taken to get a visa and passport
to cross the borders of Lithuania, Latvia and Estonia
where Father had been transferred ~ Winter 1940*

311

My favorite family photo. Father is dressed in his
pre-war military uniform. Minsk, Byelorussia ~ Winter 1940

Mother, Louisa and I
Kadriorg City Park, Tallinn, Estonia ~ March 1940

*In Finnish Bay Park, Tallinn, Estonia. Mother is in the light-colored
coat; I am standing in front of her; Louisa, the only blonde girl
in the photo, is next to me; our neighbor, Mother's friend,
is behind Louisa; her two daughters are in the front row.
The three of us girls are wearing white panama hats popular
at the time; we hold bouquets of spring wild flowers ~ May 1941*

Louisa and I, with the same two girlfriends as in the preceding photo on the balcony of our apartment building across Kadriorg Park, Tallinn, Estonia ~ May 1941

Father, Louisa, mother and I
City Park, Lvov, Ukraine ~ Winter 1947

Aunt Valentina and Uncle Mitya and their two children, Zhanna and Oleg, City Park, Riga, Latvia ~ Fall 1947

Uncle Mitya and his daughter, Zhanna, Riga, Latvia ~ Fall 1947

My sixth grade group photo, Dolguintsevo, Ukraine ~ June 1945
I am in the second row, third from the left

My seventh grade group photo, Dolguintsevo, Ukraine ~ October 1945
I am in the fourth row, fifth from the left

*My seventh grade group photo, Dolguintsevo, Ukraine ~ April 1946
I am in the second row, first from the right;
the teacher's son is standing to my left in the white beret*

*My tenth grade group photo, Lvov, Ukraine ~ June 1949
I am in the first row, second from the right*

317

My High School Graduation, Lvov;
All-Girls High School #46 ~ June 1949

Uncle Mitya's embroidered pillowcase
with his wife's name Valya in the center.
Made while Uncle Mitya was imprisoned ~ 1937–1939

Made in the USA
San Bernardino, CA
02 June 2016